Pond Birds

UNIVERSITY PRESS OF FLORIDA

Florida A&M University, Tallahassee
Florida Atlantic University, Boca Raton
Florida Gulf Coast University, Ft. Myers
Florida International University, Miami
Florida State University, Tallahassee
New College of Florida, Sarasota
University of Central Florida, Orlando
University of Florida, Gainesville
University of North Florida, Jacksonville
University of South Florida, Tampa
University of West Florida, Pensacola

POND BIRDS

GATOR BASKETBALL—THE WHOLE STORY FROM THE INSIDE

BY BILL KOSS

UNIVERSITY PRESS OF FLORIDA

Gainesville/Tallahassee/Tampa/Boca Raton
Pensacola/Orlando/Miami/Jacksonville/Ft. Myers/Sarasota

Copyright 1996 by Bill Koss
All rights reserved
Published in the United States of America

The photographs in this volume are reprinted courtesy of the University of Florida Archives and the University Athletic Association, Inc.

First cloth printing 1996
First paperback printing 2026

31 30 29 28 27 26   6 5 4 3 2 1

Library of Congress Cataloging-in-Publication Data
Koss, Bill, 1942–
Pond birds: Gator basketball — the whole story from the inside / Bill Koss.
p. cm.
ISBN 978-0-8130-1523-1 (cloth) | ISBN 978-0-8130-8156-4 (pbk.)
1. Florida Gators (Basketball team) — History. 2. University of Florida — Basketball — History. I. Title
GV885.43.U48K62   1996
796.332'63'0975979—dc21   96-44067
CIP

The University Press of Florida is the scholarly publishing agency for the State University System of Florida, comprising Florida A&M University, Florida Atlantic University, Florida Gulf Coast University, Florida International University, Florida State University, New College of Florida, University of Central Florida, University of Florida, University of North Florida, University of South Florida, and University of West Florida.

University Press of Florida
2046 NE Waldo Road
Suite 2100
Gainesville, FL 32609
http://upress.ufl.edu

GPSR EU Authorized Representative: Mare Nostrum Group B.V., Mauritskade 21D, 1091 GC Amsterdam, The Netherlands, gpsr@mare-nostrum.co.uk

To the Florida players – past, present and future.

Contents

Preface — xi

Acknowledgments — xiii

In the Beginning... 1916-1960

1 A Man for All Seasons — 3

2 The Early Years — 7

3 Setting the Stage — 11

Norm Sloan — A Basketball Man at Last: 1961-1966

4 The Turning Point — 17

5 Battle Scars — 21

6 Developing a Foundation — 25

7 A Complicated Coach — 29

8 Life and Death Experiences — 34

9 Achieving a Milestone — 38

10 Never Say Never — 44

Tommy Bartlett — An All-American Experience: 1967-1973

11 A Breath of Fresh Air — 49

12 The Best Season Ever — 53

13 WALKing to the Big Apple — 58

14 The Science of Success — 63

15 Taking a Final Shot — 69

John Lotz — Basketball Blue Bloodlines: 1974-1980

16 The Carolina Connection — 77
17 Having Fun Again — 83
18 LOTZ to Overcome — 87
19 Breaking Through Barriers — 90
20 A Fatal Blow — 94
21 Blindsided by Faith — 99

Norm Sloan — A Painful Taste of Glory: 1981-1989

22 Norman Stormin' Again — 107
23 Building a Base — 114
24 Trying Times — 119
25 A Five-Year Assessment — 123
26 Fighting for Respect — 128
27 The Art of Survival — 134
28 Winning is Everything — 138
29 Maxwell Lights Up Broadway — 142
30 Costly Mistakes — 146
31 Talent Personified — 152
32 Little Yellow Balls — 157
33 A Red LETTer Run — 163
34 Championship Rings — 168
35 From Penthouse to Outhouse — 173
36 Agony and Ecstasy — 176

Lon Kruger — Family Time: 1991-1996

37 The Healing Touch 183
38 Everyone Contributes 190
39 Finding a Way 195
40 Final Four Fever 202
41 Sailing Uncharted Seas 210
42 A Family at Last 216

Epilogue 223

A Collection of Memories 227

Preface

John Feinstein, in his book *A Season Inside*, quoted Ed Tapscott, the basketball coach at American University: "Basketball is a culture. If you don't grow up with it or come to understand it completely, you can never really appreciate it, but if you do, no one can ever say anything that will change the way you feel about it."

I've grown up with basketball and believe I have come to understand and appreciate it. My relationship with the sport began with the childhood experience of shoveling snow off frozen ground and then shooting baskets until the dirt had turned to mud. I remember the feeling of bitter cold December weekends in Ohio when Saturday morning high school practices in an unheated gym made the term "warmups" all too literal. I can still sense the excitement of sitting in our Bridgeport High School gymnasium in the early fifties as fans rhythmically chanted, "Let's go, Bulldogs! Let's go, Bulldogs!" And of course there were summer afternoons and evenings when shooting jump shots and hook shots made the long, lazy hours pass by in a heartbeat; when summer league games brought the community together as hundreds of fans flocked to outdoor basketball courts in Wheeling, West Virginia, to watch the action. I have learned that it is possible to experience a kinship with an activity that transcends any rational explanation of its influence on your life.

Like all sports, basketball is an opportunity for life-changing experiences. Years ago I was privileged to hear Dave Downey, a former All-American basketball player at the University of Illinois, speak about how athletics can inspire us to live by what we have seen: "You cannot stay on the summit forever. You have to come down again. So why bother in the first place? Just this. What is above knows what is below. What is below does not know what is above. One climbs, one sees, one descends. One sees no longer, but one has seen. And there is an art of conducting oneself in the lower regions by the memory of what you saw higher up. When one can no longer see, one can at least still know. We live by what we have seen."

Downey's words capture a fundamental concept of how sports truly can inspire us all to live our lives in a more accountable fashion. Additionally, his words motivated me in writing this book.

It would be presumptuous of me to imply in these pages that my perceptions of events which I observed and issues of which I was made personally aware are recorded here with their only meaningful interpretation. They do, however, present accurately and with conviction events which portray the history of Florida basketball.

It has been and continues to be a profound privilege for me to experience the competition of intercollegiate athletics. Representing the University of Florida as both a player and a commentator for its college basketball program has enhanced my life, and I'm grateful for having had such an opportunity.

This book is my best effort to relate the story and give a meaningful perspective to the

PREFACE

early history of the University of Florida's basketball program and to objectively report the events I've witnessed. It is, however, deeply influenced by my passion for the game and a sincere wish to promote the sport's success in Gainesville.

In 1961 I turned my back on Ohio State and West Virginia University to accept Norm Sloan's invitation to help construct a basketball championship program in the Sunshine State. With my high ideals and unbridled enthusiasm, I believed the University of Florida could become legendary, the Ohio State of the early sixties. Later I was certain it was destined to be the seventies UCLA of the South, and still later fantasized that it might be like the North Carolina Tar Heel religion.

I've traded in those fantasies for an accounting of the facts, and what I discovered from that early association to the present is offered in this chronological reflection of the Gators' basketball past. I sincerely hope it provides a meaningful bridge to the university's basketball future.

Some have suggested that the book be written as a first-person account of my experiences with the program. Others felt the work should be written as a third-party analysis of the sport's Gator history. Finally, some thought a reconstruction of historical anecdotes would make the book entertaining and inspire a storyline to capture the University of Florida's basketball personality.

In a journalistic sense, I have probably broken all the rules because I attempted to accomplish all three approaches at one time. Extensive research has assured the accuracy and integrity of the historical accounts. My Gator basketball love affair appears between the lines of almost every sentence, and in some places seems to stand out in bold print. And finally, a number of stories have been carefully selected to invite the reader to put on a Gator uniform and be transported to a view from the court.

Enjoy the game!

Bill Koss
Gainesville, Florida
December 1996

Author's Note: Throughout the text, a season is always referenced by the ending year, i.e. a basketball season always spans two calendar years, so the 1960 season actually began in 1959. The 1960-61 season would be the '61 season.

Acknowledgments

Several years ago, former University of Florida Athletic Director Ray Graves said, "Bill, why don't you write a book on Florida basketball?" Since that seed was planted, it has grown to become a passion. While this book has been my personal labor of love, there are others who have labored over these many months to develop what appears in these pages.

Mary Koss is beyond description for her inspiration and devotion to everything that I seem to find important. She became proficient at editing my punctuation and grammar more than 30 years ago when she would correct my love letters between Gainesville and Pittsburgh. Her patience and attention to detail are attributes that uniquely characterize her life.

Suzanne Smith is the most caring, devoted, and hard-working administrative assistant with whom I have ever shared a business day. She has the fastest fingers in the South on a word processor, and her positive attitude has made the journey even more enjoyable.

I am especially appreciative that Judy Moore provided her talented writing skills and personal encouragement to keep working when she and I thought it might be time for me to return to my real job. Judy's objectivity about the manuscript kept me in the center of the road and focused on the subject.

Gina Smith did a marvelous job of laying out the book. Her talent is reflected in the design of each page, and she painstakingly selected photographs to reflect all aspects of the basketball program. Nick DeCarlis executed his usual creative masterpiece on the book's jacket. UF sports information director Steve McClain, who seems to have memorized every Florida basketball fact, was extremely accessible through the project. He is devoted to Gator basketball.

Special thanks to Mike Bianchi, Dr. Augustus M. Burns, III, John Fitzwater, Joel Glass, David Steele, and Dr. Leonard P. Tipton, who read and critiqued the original manuscript, and to Anne Gilroy who polished the final draft with expert finishing touches.

John Fitzwater told me the anecdote in Chapter 1 about the boy who walked up behind Kruger during the Ole Miss game. The publisher of the *Gainesville Sun,* Fitzwater more than earned a place in Gator history with his resolve to reshape the newspaper's attitude toward reporting college basketball. His Kentucky Wildcat roots make him an especially credible commentator on the sport.

Years ago my Mom and Dad would drive up to the highest hilltop in eastern Ohio to pick up a faint WRUF radio broadcast of our Florida basketball games. Their faith in me and support of my interests is the foundation of my life.

For the encouragement of my business partner, Bill Olinger, and the inspiration of my 32-year marriage to Mary, the greatest person I know, I am grateful.

My thanks go, most of all, to the many former Gator players who openly shared personal feelings with me about their careers. Florida basketball players have had much in

ACKNOWLEDGMENTS

common through the years. The friendships they experienced with their teammates could easily be transposed into another era. It has been interesting to observe and discover just how much we all have in common.

None of us who have been awarded an athletic scholarship to the University of Florida can ever fully repay our debt to those many fans and alumni throughout the state who believe in the school's athletic integrity. The monetary value of an athletic scholarship is only a small part of the reward that an athlete receives through the intercollegiate athletic experience. This book is my personal effort to attempt a partial repayment.

To the friends, the fans, and the family of Florida basketball through these many years go my heartfelt thanks for the many contributions you have made to the Florida program. May the next 81 years be even more fun than the last.

Photograph at right: 1951 Gator team celebrates 59-55 win over Alabama. Left to right: Harold Schulman, Curt Cunkle (12), Coach Sam McAllister, Harold Haskins (24), George Hitchins, Harry Hamilton (35), and Sidney Richard (manager).

In The Beginning...

1916-1960

92-81 Gator win

Florida Downs Vandy in Spectacular Tilt, 24-23

Enter Tourney Finals

Gators-Miami Split Cage Series Here On Weekend

Cagers

Kentucky In Tourney

Gator Cagers Triumph In Tar Tilt 44 To

MIXED QUINTET GAINS VICTORY

Of David Players Forget To Whiskers With Them And Before Gators 50-2

Gators play brilliant

A Man for All Seasons

The 10-year-old boy slowly worked his way down the steps of the O'Connell Center bleachers.

He timidly stopped at floor level directly behind Coach Lon Kruger on the Gator bench. Kruger was intent on the tight, second-half action of his team's game against in-state rival Miami.

After about 30 seconds, the Gator coach sensed that someone was standing just off his left shoulder.

The boy smiled. "Hi, Coach Kruger."

Kruger recognized the youngster from his basketball camp the previous summer.

"Hi, Johnny," Kruger responded and returned his attention to the action on the floor.

A few seconds later, the coach leaned back in his chair so that his head was next to Johnny's and asked, "Got any suggestions?"

Shrugging, the boy's face lit into a beaming smile.

Regardless of the place, the time, or the circumstances, this Gator coach always took time for people.

• • •

Four years later in December 1995, Florida was in Oklahoma City for the All-College Holiday Tournament. At 3 a.m. Kruger was still awake in his hotel room watching a game tape in preparation for the next night's contest with Oklahoma.

There was a knock on the door. A young mother from the room across the hall needed some help, heard his television, and came to his door.

Her son was a diabetic, she explained, and she had forgotten his medication. She needed cash to buy medicine at an all-night drugstore some distance from the hotel, and she needed someone to stay with the sleeping boy while she made the trip. Could Kruger help?

Kruger handed her the cash and sat with the boy until 4 a.m. when the mother returned. Then he went back to work.

The next night Florida upset Oklahoma, handing the Sooners their first defeat in a championship game in eight years.

IN THE BEGINNING... 1916-1960

• • •

Florida's basketball coach wasn't only a good coach, he was a good man. Certainly, in Florida's 80-year history, there had been good coaches and there had been good men. But never had there been a coach who embodied such a strong combination of the two qualities.

The impact of Lon Kruger's coaching style took this battered and bruised program to heights not seriously dreamed of, let alone achieved. After decades of disappointment, he established an environment that invited success.

When Lon Kruger accepted the Florida job in April of 1990, the university acquired more than a basketball coach – it acquired a one-way ticket to the restoration of its collegiate honor. The university that so desperately sought forgiveness for its athletic indiscretions received a moral, ethical, and athletic transfusion from this coach.

And no one benefited more than the players. They had become lost souls among the NCAA investigations, the grand jury testimony, the unfulfilled seasons, the resignation of one hard-line coach and the hiring of another one.

But with the arrival of Lon Kruger, the players found a coach who sincerely cared about them. He cared about their schoolwork, their families and what they wanted to do with their lives.

The players first realized something special was happening in Kruger's first team meeting.

Veteran player Brian Hogan had been recruited by Norm Sloan and also played for Don DeVoe. Now, he pulled up his chair to listen to the third coach in as many years tell him how things would be done.

A bright, sensitive, and extremely competitive player, Hogan had come to believe that adults ruled the world very differently than his idealistic expectations had led him to believe.

"When Coach Kruger walked in, we could all sense something special in his presence," Hogan said. "His composure projected warmth, and yet he still presented a seriousness about our well-being. He talked that day about our goals for the program's future. We felt he really wanted to know who we were and where our lives were headed."

The players were elated with the anticipation of a fresh beginning. "Someone had to pinch me because I thought this might be some kind of a dream and I might wake up," said Tim Turner.

Gainesville Sun columnist Mike Bianchi later said that the most telling, touching response he ever received from a college athlete came when he asked Turner to compare Coach Kruger to his two predecessors.

"Sloan was like a stepfather. DeVoe was like one of those uncles who visited on the holidays," Turner said. "And Kruger, he's daddy."

● ● ●

Perhaps one of the most fortunate recipients of Kruger's fatherly approach was crowd favorite Dametri Hill.

When Hill first came to Florida in 1991, he had just lost his best friend and surrogate father to an untimely death. Dametri's weight had ballooned to 350 pounds.

Kruger took the boy aside. "You can play at this level; you can have a successful career," he said. "I'll do all I can to help you. But the weight has to go."

During the next four years, Hill did everything Kruger asked. Unlike other coaches who made promises to players they did not keep, Kruger was determined to reward Hill for his hard work. By his senior year, Hill weighed 275 pounds, and Kruger would give "Da Meat Hook" his due.

The freshman recruiting class that year was an agile group best suited to play in an up-tempo style of game. Hill was definitely not equipped to be a run-and-gun player, but he was a senior and had earned this final chance to shine. So Kruger established a half-court game that allowed Hill to capitalize on his strengths.

Hill's senior year became one he will always remember. In the final game of the 1996 regular season against Tennessee in Knoxville, he had a career-high 30 points and, with time running out, made an 18-foot jumper for Florida's 73-71 win. Hollywood couldn't have written a better script.

Hill also played a major role in Florida's greatest accomplishment ever – victory after victory in that 1994 NCAA Tournament that took the Gators to a place they never imagined they could be – the Final Four.

When Florida beat Boston College, earning an unprecedented and totally unexpected berth in the Final Four, fans witnessed a gutsy group of Florida players who had just refused to give up.

About 45 minutes after the game ended and most of the crowd had left the Miami Arena, ESPN's Andrea Kremer asked Coach Kruger for an interview to be used on Sportscenter. Kremer introduced Kruger and asked, "Lon, what were you thinking as you watched your team cut down the nets?"

Kruger, looking straight at the camera, was momentarily speechless. Then, with a little smile, he started to cry.

That emotion spoke volumes for legions of Florida fans and former players who had stopped daring to hope that a moment like this was possible for University of Florida basketball.

Florida athletic director Jeremy Foley called Florida's first-ever trip to the Final Four "the greatest sporting achievement in the history of the University of Florida."

IN THE BEGINNING... 1916-1960

The fact that basketball had become the source of such pride was overwhelming. Basketball had lived in the shadow of football at Florida for so long.

What Lon Kruger did for Florida basketball as much as anything else was to make everyone associated with Florida basketball feel like part of the family. At a football-dominated university where basketball had always seemed like an unwanted stepchild, that sense of caring and unity was essential for success. Perhaps that's why it was seldom achieved before Kruger arrived.

The magnitude of Florida's accomplishments under Lon Kruger can only truly be appreciated by understanding the struggles, the embarrassments, the disappointments, and the few shining moments of the many seasons that came before.

The Early Years

Maybe it was the beach. Or the nice warm winters. Or the preference for outdoor sports. Whatever the reason, the University of Florida was about a decade behind most of its future Southeastern Conference brethren in beginning a collegiate basketball program.

Oh, there were club games with the teams from Gainesville businesses like Ralph's Cleaners or Seminole Canoe or maybe even a team from a military base located in the north central Florida area. But it wasn't until 1916 that a group of basketball players who could officially be called a college basketball "team" began representing the University of Florida.

Florida actually had teams as early as 1913, but there are no records of any scores. In 1914 the lettermen's club officially recognized basketball players for the first time, and Bill Henderson, J. Miller, Wakefield Ramsdell, Jim Sikes, F.M. Swanson, Tom Swanson, and Roy Van Camp were the first-ever basketball players to be inducted.

Florida's official opening season in 1916, according to early records, consisted of only six games – against YMCAs in Jacksonville and St. Augustine and one lone college program, little Columbia College in Lake City. By that time, Kentucky was playing teams like Georgetown, Louisville, Tennessee, and Vanderbilt. Alabama was competing against Auburn, Georgia Tech, Mississippi, and other future southern powers. They, and most other SEC schools, have records dating back to just after the turn of the century.

The fledgling Gators had a long way to go, but they were on the court. And they had a coach. C.J. McCoy was the coach that first official year, and Roy Van Camp was the captain. There were seven team members: Warren Hayford, Bill Henderson, Wakefield Ramsdell, Jim Sikes, Tom Swanson, Roy Van Camp and Spessard L. Holland, known to his teammates as "Spes."

Spes Holland went on to become a noted United States senator. The Holland Law Center at the University of Florida was named to recognize his distinguished political career. Holland, Sikes, and Swanson were all in law school at the time they were playing on the team. The team record that year was 5-1.

But soon after it began, the new Florida basketball program came to a resounding halt. Under the shadow of World War I, basketball was suspended for three years.

In 1920 a team was organized again. There was no official coach, and all of

IN THE BEGINNING... 1916-1960

Florida's seven games were played away from home. C.A. Cone was the captain, and the Gators went 2-5. It was the first year the team had ever traveled outside the state of Florida to play, and the results weren't good. Florida lost all three games – to Mercer College, Macon YMCA, and Savannah YMCA.

Beginning in 1921, Florida would have a coach and a team every year until 1944 when play was once again interrupted by a World War.

From the program's infancy until 1933 when Florida joined the Southeastern Conference, the Gators had only three winning seasons. During that period from 1916 to 1933, Florida teams won 79 games and lost 120. The wins and losses of those inexperienced teams are included in Florida's overall win-loss record up to the present time.

The year 1933 marked a major milestone for University of Florida athletics as the Gators helped inaugurate the Southeastern Conference. Thirteen southern schools banded together to form a league that has substantially retained its original composition to this day. That inaugural group included: Alabama, Auburn, Florida, Georgia, Georgia Tech, Kentucky, Louisiana State, Mississippi, Mississippi State, Sewanee, Tennessee, Tulane, and Vanderbilt.

In the early years of the SEC, the conference champion was determined by a tournament. The conference tournament was a cost-effective way to determine a champion and made it unnecessary for the teams to compete in a round-robin schedule. Beginning in 1951, the round-robin schedule produced a regular-season champion, and the conference tournament was discontinued in 1953. It wasn't until 1979 that the conference decided once again to host a tournament.

In its first conference season (1933), Florida played only eight SEC games and finished sixth. Kentucky won the tournament the first year and had an 8-0 season record against other conference teams. Kentucky, Tennessee, Alabama, and LSU dominated the SEC from 1933 to 1960, and Florida experienced only marginal success.

Sewanee left the conference in 1941, and the SEC was comprised of the remaining 12 teams until 1964 when Georgia Tech and Tulane left the league. In 88 games, Sewanee had managed only three conference wins – one of which, unfortunately, was against Florida.

In the 28 seasons prior to 1961, the Gators played 550 games. They won only four more than they lost – 277 wins and 273 losses. In conference play, however, there were only seven winning seasons, and Florida's conference record was 10th overall among the SEC schools with 157 wins and 224 losses.

There were three Florida seasons with only two wins – 1920, '23, and '25. Until 1965, the best season came in 1947 when Coach Sam McAllister's Gators won 17 games and lost nine. During two time periods, Sam McAllister coached Florida teams for 10 seasons – five seasons from 1938 to 1942 and five more from 1947 to 1951. He enlisted during World War II and served in the Navy from 1943 to 1946. McAllister was also an assistant football coach while heading the basketball program, a dual assignment which wasn't unusual in those days.

THE EARLY YEARS

McAllister coached 215 games at Florida, more than any coach prior to 1960. His 55 percent winning average is second only to Lon Kruger's in Florida basketball history. McAllister's second-place SEC finish in 1941 was the highest a Florida team would finish until 1967 when Florida once again finished second.

McAllister's 1941 team, captained by Frank Yinshannis, had an impressive overall record of 15-3. Florida reached the semifinals of the SEC postseason tournament that year before losing to Tennessee (which went on to defeat Kentucky for the championship.)

The only seasons that didn't produce at least one SEC win for Florida were during the war years. In 1943 after McAllister joined the Navy, Spurgeon Cherry coached the Gators for four seasons. Cherry had an 0-6 conference record his first year.

The Gators' most SEC wins before 1960 came during the 1953 season when the

Record of SEC Teams 1933-1960

SEC Teams	Total Wins	Total Losses	Total Games	Winning Percentage	Number of Winning Seasons	Number of SEC-Game Winning Seasons
1. Kentucky	597	108	705	.850	27	25
2. Tennessee	385	204	589	.650	23	18
3. Alabama	367	213	580	.630	22	17
4. Vanderbilt	327	244	571	.570	17	14
5. Auburn	289	238	527	.548	18	14
6. Louisiana State	339	280	619	.547	16	17
7. Tulane	309	280	589	.520	13	12
8. Georgia Tech	296	281	577	.510	14	11
9. Mississippi State	280	275	555	.504	12	6
10. Florida	277	273	550	.503	15	7
11. Mississippi	277	326	603	.460	7	6
12. Georgia	276	340	616	.450	12	3

Kentucky did not play a regular season SEC game in 1944 and was banned from SEC play in 1953.

team won eight games and lost five, finishing third in the conference under Coach John Mauer. It was the first winning SEC season in eight years and the only winning SEC season in the 15 years prior to 1960.

Mauer had deep roots in the game. He was an All Big Ten player at Illinois in both basketball and football. Because of his football background at Illinois, where he was a teammate of the legendary Red Grange, Mauer served as an assistant football coach at Florida as well as being the head basketball coach. Mauer came to Florida directly from West Point, where he had coached Army's football and basketball teams.

His coaching career had begun, however, in 1927 when he headed the University of Kentucky program. He had the dubious distinction of being replaced at Kentucky in 1930 by Adolph Rupp. In 1952 Mauer's inaugural Gator team won its first 10 games which is the school record for most consecutive wins in a season. The Gators' first loss that year was to the man who had replaced him at Kentucky more than 20 years before.

IN THE BEGINNING... 1916-1960

Perhaps Florida's most notable basketball accomplishment in the 41 years prior to 1960 was finishing as runner-up in the SEC Tournament in 1934. The Gators received a first-round bye and then beat Kentucky 38-32. An early account of this game in the 1934 *Seminole*, the University of Florida yearbook, states: "The win was particularly meaningful because the Wildcats had just completed an undefeated season under the 'Baron,' Adolph Rupp." It would be Florida's last win over Kentucky until 1965.

That quarterfinal win propelled Florida into the semifinal game against Vanderbilt, and the Gators escaped with a 24-23 victory. According to the *Seminole*, "Pop" Warner, Florida's "elongated" center, scored the winning basket in the last second of the game. Florida faced Alabama for the title and spotted the Crimson Tide an 11-point lead in the first quarter. Unfortunately, Alabama crushed Florida's conference championship hopes 41-25.

Amazingly, this appearance by Florida in the SEC Tournament finals would be its last for 55 more years. It wasn't until 1989 that the Gators returned to the tournament's final game, only to lose again to Alabama, this time 72-60, for the tournament championship.

Holiday tournaments first became a part of the basketball team's scheduling in the fifties. In 1951 Florida began a long-standing relationship with the city of Jacksonville by becoming the host team for the annual Gator Bowl Basketball Tournament. The competition was held each year between Christmas and New Year's in conjunction with the Gator Bowl football game and was one of the state's biggest sporting events.

From 1951 to 1960, Florida won the Gator Bowl championship three times, beating Florida State in 1952, Georgia Teacher's College in 1953, and the University of Georgia in 1958.

The Gators also played in tournaments outside the state of Florida in Owensboro, Kentucky (1956), and Charlotte, North Carolina (1957), but didn't win either event. It wasn't until 1976, when the Gators won the Big Sun Tournament in St. Petersburg, Florida, that the Gators won a tournament outside the city of Jacksonville.

The first individual Florida player to be honored by the SEC was Jimmie Hughes. In 1934 he became the first Florida player to be named to the Southeastern Conference all-tournament team. In those years, the all-tournament team selections were also the recipients of the league's official All-SEC recognition. Hughes later owned and operated Jimmie Hughes Sporting Goods, a popular Gainesville athletic store.

Center Bob "Pop" Warner and guard Welcome Shearer were named to the second team. Thus the Gators had three of the conference's top 10 selections for that year. Ironically, it was the only year in which Florida has ever placed three players in the league's top 10 All-SEC selections.

It would take 51 more years for a Florida player to be named among the five best in the SEC Tournament. It happened in 1985. The player was Andrew Moten.

Setting the Stage

Richard "Rick" Casares was arguably the greatest athlete ever to play basketball at the University of Florida. At 6-foot-2 and 205 pounds, his body was chiseled like a Greek statue. He was one of the toughest competitors ever to wear the orange and blue and was second-team All-SEC in both 1952 and 1953. Casares came to the Gators from Tampa's Jefferson High School. In 1951, his sophomore season, he made a record 13 straight free throws in a Georgia Tech game.

Vince Dooley, the former Georgia football coach, was a point guard for Auburn when Casares played at Florida. In an interview with the *Gainesville Sun's* Jack Hairston, Dooley recounted playing in the last SEC Tournament in 1953 and watching Casares give a notable performance in Florida's upset of Vanderbilt.

"It was one of the greatest individual performances I've ever seen," Dooley said. "He did it all – scoring, rebounds, the works. Rick Casares carried Florida to a classic victory."

Sam Lankford, the Florida trainer in those years, remembered an incident in Oxford, Mississippi, when Casares and an Ole Miss player were ejected from the game for fighting. Casares, who was also an all-conference fullback in football and an amateur Golden Gloves boxer, wouldn't back down from a grizzly bear.

The Mississippi player had been cut in the scuffle with Casares and went back to his team's locker room to bandage himself up. Casares slipped away from the Florida bench and found his way to the Ole Miss locker room. There he finished the job that was started on the court, and knocked the guy out.

Casares' physical and athletic prowess gave the Florida program a lot of respect. He was named one of the conference's 10 best players in 1952, along with Joe Dean, Cliff Hagen, Bob Pettit, and Frank Ramsey, all prominent names in SEC basketball history. His most notable claim to fame, however, was in football. Casares enjoyed a 12-year career as an NFL running back, 10 of which were spent with the Chicago Bears.

Another All-Tournament selection in 1952 was a Tennessee star named Tommy Bartlett, who would become the head basketball coach for the University of Florida in 1966.

Curt Cunkle, a 6-foot-3 forward who played with Casares from 1951 to 1953, was named first-team All-SEC in 1953 and joined Jimmie Hughes as Florida's only other first-team All-SEC player up to that time.

Cunkle, nicknamed "Kangaroo," was a super leaper. He would take off at the broken circle of the foul line, pull both legs up under him, and dunk the ball. It was a feat not performed by many in those days. Cunkle played with emotion and complemented Casares as an aggressive competitor.

In 1951 the Gator basketball program literally reached new heights. At 6-foot-7, Bill Leach became the tallest player up to that time to wear a Gator uniform. But in 1955, Jim Zinn who also stood 6-foot-7 was the first player to actually capitalize on his height. Some say Zinn was taller than 6-foot-7 but preferred to be listed as smaller.

Zinn could shoot a hook shot with either hand and was the team's leading rebounder. As a sophomore in the 1956 season, Zinn grabbed a school-record 31 rebounds in a win over Wofford College (Spartanburg, S.C.) and again had 31 rebounds against Ole Miss his junior year. It was 1968 before his record was tied by Neal Walk.

Two other notable players for the Gators during those years were Harry Hamilton and John "Sonny" Powell. The 6-foot-3 Hamilton played forward and center, earning All-SEC third-team honors. He led Florida in scoring in 1949 and again in 1951.

Powell was a stocky 5-foot-10 guard from Jacksonville who was a fiery competitor. He delighted the crowd by shouting "defense, defense" immediately after the Gators scored a basket, refocusing his teammates on their next task. Powell was a third-team All-SEC player in 1955 when he scored a total of 355 points for the season. Powell's 487 free throws still rank fourth, and his career free-throw percentage of 77.9 ranks ninth in Florida's record book.

Bob Emrick, a 6-foot-5, 200-pound center from Ashland, Kentucky, became Florida's all-time leading scorer in 1957. He held that record until Neal Walk came along in the mid-sixties. Described as a player who moved with grace, reacted quickly, and defended well, Emrick was a second- and third-team All-SEC selection in 1955 and 1956. He produced 1,544 points during a four-year career from 1954 to 1957.

In his second game as a Gator, Emrick set a single-game scoring record of 32 points against Wofford College. It was the last year in which freshmen were eligible to play on the varsity until the 1973 season, and this freshman went out in style. His 360 points were the most ever scored by a freshman in one season.

A year later, Emrick broke his own record with a career-high 36 points against LSU. During his four-year career, he produced 323 more points than any Florida player preceding him. Emrick was the team captain his senior year, and his prolific scoring established new standards for players in the Florida program.

But the most prominent Florida player in the 41 years prior to 1960 stood a mere 5-foot-10. A guard from Sheridan, Illinois, Joe Hobbs brought a relentless basketball work ethic to Gainesville. Before coming to the university in 1955, Hobbs was featured in a *Life* magazine article about promising high school players. He set ambitious standards for running stadium stairs and spending extra hours shooting hoops in the gym.

SETTING THE STAGE

Hobbs played three seasons – 1956, '57, and '58 – and was named first-team All-SEC in 1958. He was also named a Helms Athletic Foundation Third-Team All-American that year, and became Florida's first basketball player ever to be named All-American.

Hobbs scored 1,331 points in three seasons, had a career free-throw shooting average of 84 percent, and a single-season free-throw mark of 86 percent. He is still the leading career free-throw shooter in the history of Florida basketball and was a ninth-round pick by Minneapolis in the 1958 NBA draft. Hobbs ranks as the No. 14 all-time scorer in the Gator record book. But if you look at three-year careers, he is one of the top five all-time scorers.

Tragically, Joe Hobbs struggled in the years following graduation. He was charged with fraudulent business practices, convicted, and sent to prison in the 1980s.

Another player in the fifties who was a solid performer and developed a passion for Gator basketball was August "Augie" Greiner. A 6-foot forward from St. Louis, Missouri, Greiner was a four-year letterman. He was named the most valuable player of the Gator Bowl Basketball Tournament in his freshman year, 1952, averaging 20 points a game in Florida's wins over Georgia Tech and Georgia Southern. Greiner was the only Florida freshman ever to receive that distinction. He and his wife, Susan O'Ferrell Greiner, and their four children subsequently established Greiner's clothing stores in Ocala and Tampa. He has been one of Gator basketball's most faithful supporters throughout the years.

Two Florida players during the thirties and forties who went on to have notable political careers were longtime U.S. Senator George Smathers and Jacksonville Mayor Hans Tanzler. Senator Smathers was captain of the 1936 Florida team that won five games and lost 10. Tanzler played four seasons from 1947-1950, was the team captain, and was named third-team all-conference his senior year. He was the first Florida player to score 300 points in a single season and the first to record 1,000 points in his Gator career, finishing with 1,219 points.

In June of 1949, the university built Florida Gymnasium at a cost of 1.65 million dollars. At the time, Florida's facility was second to none in the Southeastern Conference with an official seating capacity of 5,500. In contrast, Kentucky's Alumni Gym sat only 2,800. But a year later, "the house that Rupp built," Kentucky's Memorial Coliseum, was completed with 11,500 seats at a cost of 3.95 million.

Florida's first game in Florida Gym was on December 3, 1949, when the Gators met Mississippi State. More than 4,500 people turned out to watch the university's president, Dr. J. Hillis Miller, toss out a new ball, the only visible sign of an official ceremony.

The fans yawned through a first half that saw the Gators take a 21-8 lead and then cruise to an 18-point win 63-45. Junior guard Ted Jaycox, an Ocala native, led the team in scoring with 17 points, and Hans Tanzler had 10 for the only two players in double figures.

IN THE BEGINNING... 1916-1960

In 1951 Florida hosted Kentucky at home for the first time in the new gym. The Wildcats that year were averaging more than 100 points a game. In anticipation of Kentucky's prolific scoring, the university installed new scoreboards that displayed three digits in case a team's score reached 100 points.

Florida's largest basketball crowd to date watched the Gators lose to Kentucky. But Florida fans celebrated the loss as if it were a victory, because Kentucky didn't reach the century mark. The final score – Kentucky 99, Florida 52.

In January 1953, an unofficial 9,000 fans packed Florida Gym to watch Florida take on LSU. The Gators were 10-2 overall and had a 5-1 conference record. It was the second straight year the Gators got off to a great start, and the administration experimented with a new seating arrangement which would allow the record crowd to watch the game.

Florida Gym held two regulation-size basketball courts that were placed end to end in a north-south configuration. The permanent seating was on the north end where the games were played. There was, therefore, an open area to the south end of the building that would hold bleachers and chairback seats.

On this night, the bleachers that normally sat on the south end of the main court were pushed to the far wall on the south end of the building. Folding chairs were placed in front of the bleachers all the way to the south end of the main court. Florida lost the game 68-56, and many fans were upset with the poor visibility. It was the last time chairs were put so deep into the south end of the gymnasium.

For the most part during the 45-year period prior to 1960, Florida basketball failed to capture substantial fan interest or media attention. Floridians thought of basketball as a "sports pacifier" between the end of football season and the beginning of the next year's spring football practice.

Several SEC teams were nationally ranked and produced notable basketball stars. But the Gators continued to operate their basketball program with assistant football coaches who didn't have the time or resources to build a basketball team that could compete in the national spotlight.

A University of Kentucky betting scandal in the fifties created a negative impression of all the teams that competed with the Wildcats in the Southeastern Conference. The league became nationally recognized as a football conference, while its basketball reputation was sliding downhill. For Florida in particular, there was an absolute football mentality when it came to the university's decisions about intercollegiate athletics. Whenever basketball objectives clashed with a football agenda, basketball lost.

This began to change in 1960 when the school hired a coach whose only responsibility was basketball. The frustration, however, of living in a football-oriented environment haunts Florida basketball players and coaches to this day.

Norm Sloan

A Basketball Man at Last
1961-1966

Gators Plaster ...
ors Bounce Back, ... **or 80-59 Cage**
prise Vols, 84-73

Cliff Luyk's 40 points
spark 92-83 Gator win
ators Crush Georgia, 90-5

Gains Valley Products Tomlinson, Vols S...
y SEC Koss to Face WVU Next Week Kentuc...
umph Win, 78

Says Goodbye to Tech, 92
11 Points to Lead
55 Win Over Tamp...

Pound Seminoles,
Gators Down Deacons, Highly G
His Cham

Henderson
Barbee Spark
Fine Triumph

The Turning Point

By 1960 the University of Florida was far from becoming a competitive threat on a basketball court. If you asked basketball fans in Pennsylvania where the University of Florida was, they most likely would answer Miami. Basketball followers up north couldn't even tell you if the Gators were in a conference. There was little, if any, national recognition of Gator hoops. People who loved basketball knew about Kentucky. Some recognized that Mississippi State was making noise in the Southeast. But very few even placed Florida in the same conference with these two schools.

Even on its own campus, Florida basketball was a joke. There was nothing macho about being a basketball player. Tickets weren't necessary, and students wandered in and out of a game in Florida Gym by showing a fee card. Florida had never even sold a season ticket.

On campus, players were rarely recognized. Students attended games primarily to see the opposing team. Cheerleaders viewed basketball games as a waste of time and resented having to support this "other" sport. They had little incentive to create cheers that would inspire fans at a basketball game.

The Gators had never won a conference championship – they'd never even beaten a conference champion the same year it won the conference. The team seldom won a game on the road and was perceived as a doormat. The conference contenders counted the Florida game as a win before most seasons even began.

Ray Graves had recently been hired by UF President J. Wayne Reitz to assume coaching responsibilities from Bob Woodruff, the school's football coach and athletic director. Woodruff wasn't willing to accept the role of just athletic director and departed; consequently, Graves was handed both responsibilities.

At age 42, Graves had earned his reputation as a professional football player with the Philadelphia Eagles and later as a 10-year assistant with Georgia Tech's football program. His leadership skills would now be tested in a much broader arena. His primary duty would be to build a Florida football team which would be nationally competitive. But he wanted to develop an athletic program that would also be respected across the board.

The basketball program had become an embarrassment to UF, a university that aspired to excellence in one of the fastest-growing states in America. As one of the southernmost SEC schools, Florida was a long way from the heartland of the nation's best basketball talent. The recruiting budget was insufficient to finance national recruiting, yet the state's high school programs were woefully inferior to northern competition and couldn't fill the gap. It was a two-fold challenge – not enough money to bring in players from the North or Midwest and an underdeveloped high school pipeline from which to draw quality in-state players. But things were about to change.

Graves had permission to hire a basketball coach who would devote 100 percent of his time to his sport. No longer would the head basketball coach also have to be an assistant football coach. Additionally, the basketball coach would have a full-time assistant.

Graves had his work cut out for him in hiring a coach. In the previous 27 years, the Gators had lost every single basketball game they played against teams that won the SEC title. Even more distressing was the fact that the average defeat was by 31 points. Graves desperately wanted to find a coach who could bring respect to the ailing program.

As Graves assessed the situation, he came to realize that if Florida really wanted to get serious about basketball, the university needed to hire a great salesman and hope that he could coach.

The job attracted plenty of applicants, but none stood out more than the personable head coach of the Citadel, Norman Leslie Sloan.

Sloan had played college basketball at North Carolina State under the legendary Everett Case and was a veteran of the U.S. Navy. He began his coaching career in 1951 at Presbyterian College in Clinton, South Carolina, and after a one-year assistantship at Memphis State, took over at the Citadel in 1956. In his very first year at the Citadel, he received the George Mikan Award for producing the nation's most improved basketball team. His Citadel record twice earned him recognition as the Southern Conference Coach of the Year.

Sloan was handsome, articulate, poised, and passionate about the game of basketball. He seemed to have it all. Graves believed Sloan had all the tools necessary to construct a quality college basketball program at Florida. What Graves could not foresee was that the unrelenting passion of Sloan's convictions would create many unsettling moments in their relationship.

When Sloan was hired, he was 34 years old and eager to meet any challenge put before him. He saw Florida as a unique coaching opportunity. Sure, it was a football school. Yes, it lacked basketball tradition. Certainly, the state was deficient in developing high school athletes who could play the sport.

It was, however, "the" University of Florida. There was only one university in every state which was considered "the" state school, and in Florida at that point it was UF. And it was icing on the cake that the state of Florida was a fantasy island in the minds of many Americans. Sloan knew if he could get things rolling at the University of Florida, the Sunshine State would pave a super highway to basketball heaven for him.

Few people could perceive the kinds of changes necessary to develop a basketball program that could earn a national reputation. Sloan could. He knew things would have to be turned upside down.

At UF, basketball players were accustomed to being treated like second-class citizens. They wore the football team's hand-me-down travel blazers. They had always practiced at night during the preseason because their coach was on the football field in the afternoon. They even missed meals because the dining hall operated on the football team's clock, often closing before basketball practice ended. Although players had plenty of justification for their underachieving performance, Sloan immediately demanded a change of attitude.

Sloan was committed to making every aspect of the Florida basketball program first class, and he had a plan for making it happen. He would give what was necessary. He would accept nothing less in return.

His background at the Citadel had provided a classroom for him to absorb the value of self-discipline. He was determined to transform Florida's performance by establishing rigid standards that demanded excellence.

Sloan's first team meeting was called for a Saturday morning two days after his arrival in the spring of 1960. One of the returning players, Gil Farley, had a social engagement in Miami that weekend and wasn't about to change his plans for a coach he had never met. Basketball season was over. There was plenty of time for the two of them to get acquainted before next fall. Farley felt his plans were too important to be changed.

On his arrival back in Gainesville Sunday night, Farley was informed by his teammates that Sloan wanted him in the basketball office the next morning. By 11 a.m. that Monday, Farley was the first casualty of the new regime. The players got the message that this coaching staff was very serious about basketball. And the message was clear – it would be Sloan's way or the highway.

Sloan believed if players were going to take pride in their program, they would have to make real sacrifices. The experience might be painful, but the results would be worth it. The changes were comprehensive.

Players were taught how to put on their playing socks. They were instructed to keep their jerseys tucked in. They were required to take off topcoats before entering a building. Most of all, they were taught to be punctual for every required meeting – and that meant being there 15 minutes before the prescribed time. When Sloan said to be there at 4 p.m., everyone learned he meant 3:45.

On one occasion, the players were to take a bus from Florida Gym to the airport for a four-day road trip. According to Sloan, the bus was scheduled to leave Florida Gym at 4 p.m. Every player but one was on that bus by 3:45. Bob Hoffmann, a 6-foot-8 center from Chicago, had a room in Weaver Hall, directly across from the southwest end zone of Florida Field. At 3:55, Sloan ordered the bus driver to close the door and head for the airport. As the bus turned left onto Stadium Road heading toward Century Tower, Hoffmann's teammates saw him running down the road carrying two suitcases, trying to catch up with the bus. It was four days before they would see Hoffmann again.

Sloan not only let his players know who was in charge, but he also quickly put the athletic director on the spot.

Sloan had been given his own office, a first for a Gator basketball coach. Unhappy with the linoleum floor in his office – the same dull linoleum floor that was in all the coaches' offices – Sloan had the office carpeted. When he presented the bill to his surprised athletic director, Graves objected, "Look, Norm, even the president of the university doesn't have carpet. When I put carpet down in my office, I paid for it from my own pocket. If you want carpet, you'll have to pay for it yourself." Sloan fumed, but lost the first of what would be many skirmishes.

Scholarship players arriving on campus found a coach who was different from the man who recruited them. The personable, affable temperament Sloan displayed for prospects and their parents radically changed. Sometimes it seemed as though Dr. Jekyll had turned into Mr. Hyde.

This dichotomy in Sloan's personality was the players' first clue that they might be in for a difficult situation. Sloan would now say it was his job to "run the players off," and it was their job to figure out "how to stick around." Many players went through a revolving door during Sloan's years as Florida's head coach. Those who found a way to stay exhibited the toughness of his personality and possessed the same fierce determination to compete.

One of the many changes Sloan orchestrated was the introduction of a highly competitive schedule. In previous years, Florida had its traditional SEC games, but non-conference opponents were teams like Erskine, Rollins, Stetson, Jacksonville Naval Air Station, and Tampa.

Sloan quickly turned that around by scheduling non-SEC teams that included real competition like Duke, North Carolina, Rice, Southern Methodist, and Wake Forest. He believed strongly in rivalries and was intent on developing them with other schools in the state. Sloan was convinced that if Florida was going to be successful, it needed to get high school prospects within the state excited about playing for the Gators. Miami and Florida State became "must wins" for Florida. Sloan wanted it understood that the University of Florida was *the* dominant basketball school in the state.

Sloan worked extremely hard to communicate his objectives to the media throughout the state and was tireless in promoting the program to high school basketball coaches. He was like a shot of adrenaline to this listless program, and he was beginning to win respect for UF basketball. Everyone who interacted with Florida's new head coach knew Florida basketball would never be the same. A new era had begun.

Battle Scars

Prior to Sloan's arrival in the spring of 1960, Florida had won only 14 of its previous 45 games. Sloan inherited a team that had gone 6-16 in the 1959-60 season.

Seven of the returning 11 players who suited up in Gator uniforms in December 1960 were from northern states. In his first Florida ballclub, Sloan was happy to discover a 6-foot-8 raw-boned junior from Syracuse, New York, named Cliff Luyk.

Luyk had a sweeping hook shot, sharp elbows, and overall toughness that delighted Sloan. He was extremely popular with the fans in Florida Gym, who chanted, "Luyk! Luyk! Luyk!" as a reward for the lanky center's contributions in the midst of a home-court tussle.

Luyk became an all-conference player, leading the league in rebounding. He finished as the SEC's fourth best in scoring and field-goal shooting his senior year (1962). Luyk scored a career-high 40 points and had 24 rebounds in a 92-83 win over Tennessee. In the same game, he racked up 24 first-half points, breaking Joe Hobbs' record of 22 first-half points scored against Miami in 1958. (Luyk's record was finally broken by Tony Miller, who scored 28 first-half points in 1972.)

After graduating, Luyk was drafted by the Syracuse Nationals, but elected to go to Spain where he proved a natural fit for Spain's Real Madrid team. Cliff Luyk's outstanding European career culminated in Spanish citizenship, and he was recognized as a national hero.

Luyk's play was complemented on the Florida team by Lou Merchant, a talented point guard, and Bobby Shiver, the team's captain. Shiver averaged 14 points a game. Buddy Bales, Neil Cody, George Jung, Carlos Morrison, and Paul Mosny were the other returning players who comprised the nucleus of Sloan's first Gator team.

The new era began with a trip to Winston-Salem, North Carolina, where, in front of 8,000 fans, the Gators played 11th-ranked Wake Forest right down to the wire before losing 85-79. This was the first nationally recognized non-conference team Florida had ever played at the beginning of a season. Playing Wake Forest on the road and almost pulling out a win was a signal to fans that this coaching staff was serious about Florida's basketball future.

The Demon Deacons had been 21-7 the prior year and were ranked in the nation's top 10. Florida came ready to play from the opening tip and surprised Wake with an "in your face" man-to-man defense.

On the offensive end, Luyk scored five of the first six points and took control of the "paint." Billy Packer, a 5-foot-10 guard who later became a well-known basketball commentator, scored 26 points in the game and remembered the moment this way:

"Florida had jumped out to an early lead, and Luyk was having his way inside. With about five minutes gone in the opening minutes, 'Bones' (Wake's legendary Coach McKinney) called time out. McKinney said, 'Someone better decide they're going to stop Luyk or he's going to kill us.' On the next possession, Jerry Steele (Wake's 6-foot-8 center) landed a crushing forearm against Luyk's nose, pushing it flush to his face. Blood gushed profusely."

Luyk's nose was fractured in three places. He was finished for the night. Florida led the 10th-ranked ACC power 42-40 at the half but just couldn't hold on without the services of its big center. Sloan said, "If we hadn't lost Luyk, I'm confident we would have won the game."

By the next game, however, Luyk was back in action. Despite wearing a protective mask for the remainder of the season, he never lost his competitive edge.

It was this kind of personal toughness that Sloan used as an exclamation point to define the word competitive to his Gator players. In his view, injuries were only an inconvenience. Sloan showed little tolerance for a player's reluctance to play hurt.

Midway through the year, another Florida player, floor leader Lou Merchant, suffered a serious injury.

The Gators had won four in a row and 10 of their first 13 games. They were undefeated in conference play, and 6,500 fans showed up when Florida hosted Auburn. With just over 16 minutes left to play, Merchant had scored 22 points and was single-handedly taking the War Eagles apart. He picked up a loose ball in Auburn's front court and broke away from the pack toward the Gator basket. As Merchant went airborne to score, he collided with Auburn's Billy Tinker, who blindsided the Gator guard to take away an easy basket.

The contact propelled Merchant into a 180-degree flip, and his face crashed into the hardwood floor. The force of impact broke Merchant's jaw, and he was out of action. But the Gators were able to hang on to win the game 58-53. With a semester break, Merchant had 15 days to heal before the next game. A wire brace was designed so that he, too, could play the remainder of the season.

Sloan knew where his Florida program needed to go, but it wouldn't get there with players who couldn't overcome adversity. The players quickly discovered what was expected of them.

By January, there was new energy coming from the heart of the Florida campus. Students began stopping by to watch basketball practice. If they wanted a seat during a game, they would have to start arriving before the tip-off.

Perhaps the defining moment of Sloan's inaugural season came in Nashville late that first year. Florida was in the hunt with a shot at the SEC title. The team had lost only three times to conference foes. With three conference games left to play, the Gators faced Vanderbilt and Georgia Tech on their last weekend road trip of the season.

Saturday night Vandy crushed Florida's SEC title hopes 77-60. After the game, Sloan told his players to be in their rooms at 11 p.m.

When Cliff Luyk, Paul Mosny, and Bob Shiver entered the hotel well after midnight, Sloan was at the front door to greet them. He ordered them to meet him in the lobby at 7 a.m. the next day. The three players weren't late this time and arrived right on schedule. Sloan handed each of them a sack of apples and a one-way bus ticket for the 14-hour bus ride back to Gainesville.

With only eight remaining players, Florida lost to Georgia Tech on Monday night. One week later, with reinstated players, the Gators managed to beat Georgia at home and close out the year with a fourth-place conference finish. It was the best a Florida team had done in conference play since 1953.

Sloan's first team won 15 games and had a legitimate shot at the conference championship. They didn't win it, but Sloan was named SEC Coach of the Year, his third such selection as a major college head coach.

Overall, the '61 season was a benchmark year for the Gators:
- Florida's nine wins were the most SEC wins ever.
- With just five SEC defeats, this was the first winning season in seven years.
- Lou Merchant's 459 points were the second most ever scored by a Florida player in a single season.
- Luyk's 13.5 rebounds a game made him the second-best rebounder in the SEC.
- A record total 50,000-plus fans watched Florida win all eight of its home games.

Basketball fever had begun to grip the campus. Sloan had provided an alternative for the winter months. The team's inspired play and Sloan's fiery courtside personality had captured the imagination of sports-minded people across campus and around the state.

But the sacks of apples and the one-way bus tickets had a far more penetrating effect on the players and the future of the basketball program.

In Sloan's second season (1962), the Gators again had a winning year. They finished 12-11, but the team failed to capitalize on the momentum of the previous year. Luyk replaced Merchant as the school's No. 2 all-time single-season scorer, and his 490 total points fell just 12 short of Joe Hobbs' 502 single-season record.

Merchant became frustrated with Sloan and failed to duplicate his performance of a year earlier. The Gator guard averaged just under 11 points a game and struggled to find a comfortable role.

There were seven upperclassmen with substantial playing experience, but this team won only three of its first 10 games. For the first and only time, the Gators lost twice to Florida State in a single season. The poor start and the losses to Florida State were offset by a strong finish. Florida closed out the year with three consecutive SEC wins and had their second straight winning season.

The final game was a resounding 105-78 rout of the Georgia Bulldogs that sent fans home on a positive note. It marked the first time since 1958 that a Florida team had passed the century mark. It was also the most points ever scored against an SEC opponent.

Developing a Foundation

The development of a strong basketball program happens one small step at a time. While two back-to-back winning seasons may not seem like a major accomplishment, it equaled the most consecutive winning seasons for Florida in two decades.

To sustain Florida's emergence as a conference contender, the Gators would now reap the benefits of having a full-time basketball coach devoted to the year-round task of building the program. In his second recruiting class, Sloan delivered what many believed was Florida's best group ever. Seven highly regarded newcomers – five freshmen and two transfers – arrived on campus in September of 1961 to legitimize Sloan's belief that Florida could compete for the best talent.

Sloan believed if the Gators wanted to contend at the top every year, they would have to beat the Wildcats. Kentucky was not only the premier basketball school in the conference, but also one of the best college programs in America. Prior to Sloan's arrival, Kentucky had won the SEC in 10 of the previous 13 years. Florida's only win against Kentucky ever had come in the second round of the 1934 SEC Tournament.

To beat Kentucky, Sloan had to match the Wildcats in recruiting. He knew that recruiting was the key to making Florida basketball competitive, not only with Kentucky but with the best programs in the nation.

Sloan saw Florida basketball as a diamond in the rough – a beautiful campus, Southern charm, warm weather, and a state that was untapped for its potential to develop talent. Florida represented some of the most virgin basketball territory in America. With newcomers pouring into Florida every day, Sloan had a gleam in his eyes from the belief that it all belonged to him.

Sloan's strategy was to channel all of his energy into building relationships with high school coaches and helping them teach the game. He knew that in time he could capture the best players and build a pipeline of talent for years to come.

There was a considerable difference between the ability of high school players from Florida and those from the Midwest and Northeast. The investment in northern programs was dramatically different, and Florida prospects did not enjoy the same level of competition. Florida high schools had playing facilities that were spartan at best, with many high school teams actually playing games on outdoor courts.

A crucial component in any player's development is practicing during the summer months. But with Florida's hot summer days, the beach was a more likely place to find a high school athlete. There were no lighted courts or summer leagues. Basketball just wasn't a high priority for young people in Florida.

High school basketball coaches in the state were hungry for a relationship with a college coach who would encourage the sport's development. And Sloan was eager to fill that need. He seized every opportunity to promote the Gators by speaking at high school banquets and making himself available for a coach's questions. He held summer camps in Central Florida and at Bolles School in Jacksonville. He persevered in selling the sport year round.

Sloan knew the heart and soul of his teams would initially come from northern players. But once he had that foundation in place, he envisioned Florida's homegrown talent providing the program its long-term success.

In 1962 Sloan hired Perry "Boom Boom" Moore, a native of Belpre, Ohio, as his assistant. Moore, who stood 6-foot-5, was a graduate of the University of Maryland, where he had run track and played center on the basketball team. Moore was a polished communicator and a hard-working recruiter. Florida players nicknamed him Boom Boom because when he challenged players to take the ball to the basket with authority, he would constantly say, "Grab the pass and – boom – take it to the hole!"

Moore had a good feel for coaching. Because of his own size, he communicated well with the big men, and came to play a primary role in working with them. He projected a positive, enthusiastic personality and was genuinely sensitive to a player's concerns. He and Sloan seemed to be a good match for one another. His boisterous nature, however, gave people outside the program an impression of arrogance. Some even viewed him with contempt.

Another important member of Sloan's staff was the extremely popular physical education instructor, Jim McCachren. McCachren was a native of North Carolina and part of a family that earned a legendary reputation for its athletic accomplishments in football, basketball, baseball, and track at the University of North Carolina.

Sloan, Moore, and McCachren provided the core of leadership that served Florida basketball for many years. Their strategy was three-fold: Sloan would establish solid relationships within the state. Moore would travel the nation in search of the best prospective talent. McCachren would coach the freshman team and scout opponents. McCachren's special knack for communicating with young people provided an important transitional relationship for the incoming recruits.

Sloan's second recruiting class was eligible for the 1962-63 season. The group was headed by two transfers who both had roots in the Sunshine State – Tom Baxley and Brooks Henderson.

In 1960 Baxley was the most talked about basketball player ever to come out of a Florida high school. He held all of the Miami-area scoring records and averaged more than 30 points a game for North Miami High in both his junior and senior years.

His 57 points against Clearwater in the 1960 state high school tournament set a single-game scoring record for Florida high school basketball.

Baxley originally signed at Maryland and averaged 32 points a game for the Terrapins' freshman team. When he developed a case of homesickness, Perry Moore was there to persuade Baxley to transfer to Florida.

Baxley earned nicknames like "Tom the Bomb" and "Buckshot Baxley." He had one of the quickest releases with an outside jump shot of any guard ever to play for the Gators. In his first Florida game, Baxley scored 34 points in his hometown of Miami in a losing effort to the Hurricanes. It was a night during which Miami fans packed along the endlines shook the floor-mounted standards that supported the backboards but still couldn't keep Baxley from having a record performance.

Baxley averaged 16 points a game during his first season to lead the team in scoring. Ironically, he never matched his opening-night performance or this season's average during the rest of his career.

Brooks Henderson was a 23-year-old sophomore who graduated from Coral Gables High School and spent four years in the Air Force. When he came out of the service, Henderson signed on at New York University where he averaged 21 points per game as an NYU freshman.

His freshman team was one of the most highly regarded in the nation, with names like Happy Hairston, Barry Kramer, and Bob Patton. But Henderson wanted to play college basketball in Florida, where his talent could be showcased in a program on the rise. Henderson was considerably older than the other incoming players and had the maturity to capitalize on his exceptional skills. He was regarded as one of the finest prospects ever for the Gators.

The two transfers, under NCAA rules, sat out their first year (1961-62). The freshman class they joined in the fall of 1961 included Dick Tomlinson, an athletic 6-foot-5 forward from Wheeling, West Virginia, who had been named all-state in football, track and basketball; burly Bob Hoffmann, a 6-foot-8, 240-pound prospect from Chicago, Illinois; Don Mason, a 5-foot-11 point guard from the Bronx, New York; and myself at 6-foot-8 from Bridgeport, Ohio. Little did I realize at the time that my love affair with Florida basketball would span these 35 years and provide some of the most important moments of my life.

After a fine freshman season, Mason crossed wires with Sloan and departed. The remaining five players formed the nucleus of the Florida program during the next four years.

The 1962-63 team was anchored by three seniors: Buddy Bales, a point guard who led the team in assists; Tom Barbee, a Brevard (North Carolina) Junior College transfer who averaged 11 points a game the year before; and Carlos Morrison, a three-year letterman whose jump shot was rivaled only by his ability with a cue stick.

With wins over Florida State, Jacksonville, Texas Tech, and Wake Forest, the

Gators were 4-2 by the holiday break. Florida's cast of first-year players had stepped into the lineup with substantial playing time. Sophomores Baxley, Henderson, Hoffmann, and Tomlinson were given starting assignments. Taylor Stokes, a third-year junior from Tampa Hillsborough High School, was the fifth starter and averaged 12.2 points a game that season.

In the Wake Forest victory, Henderson played one of his best games of the year, and Barbee replaced Stokes in the starting lineup and responded with a 27-point night. Unofficially, just over 6,000 fans were on hand December 15 when Brooks Henderson, who averaged 14.2 points a game that season, put the defensive stopper on Wake's ace Dave Wiedeman for the 73-67 Gator victory.

"That's the greatest job of defense I've ever seen by one man in college basketball," said Sloan about Henderson's effort. "And what a hustler Barbee is," Sloan went on to say. "He gives you 110 percent all the way."

Barbee was a pressure player with great instincts for the game. He was hump-shouldered and sometimes moved as if every bone in his body was sore, but he could square up and stick a jump shot. In two seasons, he averaged 12.7 points a game and his career high was 32 against Georgia.

With semester exams in the mix, Florida had almost two weeks to prepare for its next game in the Gator Bowl Tournament on December 27. Sloan decided the team needed this time period to practice and scheduled two-a-day workouts through Christmas Eve. For the players who lived in Florida, there would be time to get home after practice on the 24th, but for many on the team, it was a Christmas away from home for the first time.

After the outstanding performance against Wake Forest, Barbee had begun to experience soreness in his foot. The likable, easy-going engineering major from Weaverville, North Carolina, rarely complained. But each day the condition worsened as Sloan pushed him through the pain. Pulling all-nighters while studying for his thermal dynamics final was a breeze compared to the team's blistering two-a-day practices. When the pain was finally too much to bear, Barbee went to the doctor. He returned on crutches with a cast on his foot.

For Barbee, the diagnosis of a stress fracture was an early Christmas present. He could go home for the holidays and get some rest. The rest of the team was not so lucky. Christmas Eve in downtown Gainesville's Happy Hour Pool Hall is a memory none of us will forget.

A Complicated Coach

The longest week of basketball in the 1962-63 season began on a Tuesday in late January as the team arrived in Charleston, West Virginia. With a 10-5 record, the Gators had a Wednesday night game against West Virginia University. Several of Florida's players were from that neck of the woods, and family and friends came to the Charleston Civic Center to see Florida play the Mountaineers.

It was Florida's first game against WVU, which, despite graduating Jerry West, continued to enjoy respect as a national power. The WVU force that blew Florida out of the building 114-67 was like a north wind coming across a West Virginia mountain top.

Flying in a chartered DC-3, the team headed for Lexington and a Saturday night encounter with the Wildcats. Kentucky got 30 points from a relatively unknown Charles Ishmael, and All-American-to-be Cotton Nash added 14 as Kentucky crushed this relatively young Gator team 94-71.

The team left Sunday for Knoxville, where it would conclude the seven-day adventure with a Monday night game against the Volunteers. With two devastating defeats, daily practice, and flying through the Smokey Mountains on the old World War II aircraft, the players were fatigued. But the lopsided losses had Sloan irate.

Arriving about one in the afternoon, the team went straight to Stokely Athletics Center where Sloan put the team through a four-hour practice. They were ordered to return the next morning for a two-hour workout that included a 40-minute game-day scrimmage. Mont Highley hadn't started a game and had only marginal playing time, but he impressed Sloan in the workouts and received a starting assignment that night.

Highley was the only married player on the team. He was a first-year junior college transfer from Oklahoma who was extremely well liked by his teammates. At 6-foot-8 he had a strong, 220-pound body which helped him establish position under the basket. Highley could back down a defender off the dribble and score with a right-hand hook or pump fake a midrange jumper. He couldn't jump a lick, but his instincts with his back to the basket helped him capitalize on his skills as a true center.

In his first career start against the Volunteers, Highley was magnificent. He scored 17 points and broke the Stokely Athletics Center record with 20 rebounds. His performance inside gave Baxley room for a game-high 23 on the perimeter. Buddy Bales also delivered with 12 points and seven assists. It was a stunning 84-73 upset of an SEC rival that Florida had never defeated on its home court since their first meeting in 1927.

These seven days were the most physically demanding that the players had experienced. Arriving back in Gainesville, three of Florida's 12 players were hospitalized with physical exhaustion. What started out to be a great season took a 180-degree turn as the Gators lost six of their final seven games.

The final victory came against Mississippi State in Florida Gym. The Bulldogs had an 8-1 SEC mark and a 17-4 overall record. Tom Baxley sparked Florida with 23 points, while Tom Barbee and Buddy Bales each had 15. It was a satisfying late-season win for a particularly tired and struggling ballclub.

The season came to a conclusion with a defeat in Athens. It was the final game ever in Woodruff Hall, played on a night when weather conditions forced the game to be halted again and again. The decrepit building was on its last leg, and the roof couldn't withstand the violent rainstorm. Buckets of water fell on the hardwood floor throughout the game, making conditions extremely hazardous.

The Gators played Georgia without point guard Tom Baxley, who had been suspended for the season's final game. Baxley had challenged Sloan after the previous game's loss at Georgia Tech, and Sloan let Baxley know who ran the show.

In the wet gymnasium, Tom Barbee, playing his last game as a Gator, made a free throw with 80 seconds left, deadlocking the game at 77-77. Georgia held the ball until there were 15 seconds on the clock, and Billy Rado climaxed a 31-point performance by calmly dropping in two charity tosses for Georgia's 79-77 win.

Florida finished the season with a 12-14 record, Sloan's first losing year as the Gator coach. A win at Georgia would have given Florida a break-even year. As the team returned home late that Saturday night, Sloan told the returning players to report to Florida Gym at 3 p.m. on Monday for one final practice.

The season had ended, but Sloan wanted the returning players to understand that a losing season would not be an option while he was head coach at the University of Florida. For more than three hours that afternoon and on into the evening, the team worked to the point of exhaustion.

The infamous practice was climaxed when Sloan blew his whistle and told the entire group to line up on the south end of the court. Sloan said, "Today's practice is a reminder that we will not tolerate a losing season. When I blow this whistle, you will run from endline to endline, and after everyone has dropped from exhaustion, practice will be over."

As the players began to run, and as some began to drop, Gail Highley, Mont's wife, entered the gymnasium on the second level. Gail had been working late and had come to practice to take her husband home. When she saw the tortuous punishment Sloan was exacting, she verbally unleashed on Sloan the pent-up frustrations that she shared with all the Gator players.

The players had become too exhausted to realize what was happening. With a temperature of 105°, Mont required medical attention. But Mrs. Highley's emotional outburst flustered Sloan to the point that he called things off. The season had come to a terrifying conclusion. Some players look back on that day, amazed that no one was a physical casualty.

Perhaps it is only the players who tried to play for Norm Sloan who can fully appreciate the turmoil and uncertainty that surrounded the program during those years. Sloan was masterful in taking a tough-minded stance toward events that transpired with his players. His interpretation of even the most insignificant issue always placed a player on the defensive side of the question.

People outside the program saw Sloan's dynamic personality and strong convictions. He was in church every Sunday. He had a loving family. He was energetic. His personal charm radiated confidence and congeniality. His press comments usually paid compliments to a player.

But the players knew otherwise. Often players tried to press buttons inside their heads to tune the man out. But he was relentless with his attacking vocabulary of insults and vulgarity. It was all so demeaning, and yet to young minds, he seemed to credibly reflect what players feared to be their most grievous shortcomings. Sloan found the raw nerves of a player's self-doubt and seemed to delight in its exposure.

Norm Sloan had a reputation for using strong profanity. Profanity is often an ugly part of the macho environment that surrounds much athletic activity. Vulgar language in sports is often tolerated to some degree, but demeans both the person who uses it and the person toward whom it is directed. In Sloan's regime, it was a part of the everyday experience his players learned to accept.

Most athletes were accustomed to having a coach bark, "Get your ass over here." Some coaches might say, "Get your lazy ass over here." Another coach might say, "Goddammit, get your lazy ass over here." Sloan would say, "You f...... asshole, get over here."

It wasn't just his profanity. It was the way he directed it that began to take its toll on players' confidence and self-esteem. Sloan not only used profanity that would make a sailor blush, but he directed the acidic words where players could be hurt the most. He was a master at verbal intimidation.

Whenever a personal weakness was exposed, Sloan would seize the moment for embarrassment. A player like Baxley, who earned a Ph.D. in philosophy and psychology, would be chastised for thinking too much. The very tall and not necessarily as bright Richard Peek was often humiliated for his inability to think quickly. Sloan made it his mission to remind Peek of his limitations.

Most of us would like to think that all coaches genuinely aspire to help young people develop character. In the sixties, most athletes held high ideals and respected the authority of the coaching relationship. Seldom did an athlete achieve exceptional results without having benefited from a positive mentor. It seems incongruous to find a successful program where a coach was demeaning to his players.

Norm Sloan's teams at Florida exceeded expectations. The question is, did the program's accomplishments exceed the potential of the players Sloan coached? Perhaps only Sloan can answer that question. But many of his former Florida players felt their teams underperformed and could have accomplished more. Players were disappointed in Sloan's failure to inspire confidence and team morale.

Sloan once asked Buddy Bales what the players thought of him. As a senior, Bales had been through the transition in the program and survived. He was a role model to the younger players as a competitively determined athlete who encouraged others to improve. Bales came to practice with a gritty, good-natured personality that inspired a positive chemistry in his teammates. He also had the self-confidence to tell someone exactly what he thought.

On this occasion, Bales looked Sloan squarely in the eye and said that he couldn't answer the question for his teammates, but as far as he was concerned, he hated Sloan's guts.

My personal experience with Sloan was one of total intimidation. If he said to run through the wall at the end of Florida Gym, I would've broken my skull trying. I seldom had a conversation with Sloan when he didn't convince me that he was right and I was wrong.

A recurring observation from former players was that Sloan's inconsistencies were at the root of fractured player-coach relationships. On many occasions, Sloan would tell a player one thing and then do exactly the opposite. He would tell players he wanted unselfish effort and then give playing time to those who were selfish. He would demand toughness and then reward those who were soft.

"We were all very idealistic in the sixties," said Dick Tomlinson, "and most of us came from family backgrounds where we respected authority. We were afraid to challenge Sloan's many inconsistencies because we might lose our chance to get an education. It would have been embarrassing for ourselves and our families if Sloan kicked us off the team."

Once Sloan met with Paul Morton and me to discuss a certain player's disruptive influence on our team's morale, but then Sloan failed to take the action which he described to us as the necessary remedy. What was most significant about the meeting was our courage to speak up to him at all. Unlike Bales, most of us feared disclosing our personal feelings because we might find our statements the subject of his next team meeting.

Mont Highley said recently, "Bales was the only player with the courage to tell Sloan what we all felt. The rest of us were scared at just the thought of having a confrontation with Stormin' Norman."

Players wanted to trust him, to believe in him, and to do whatever was required to succeed in his eyes. He always seemed so credible in whatever he proposed. The longer you were around him, however, the more you began to distrust him. He would embarrass you in front of others, and his actions were inconsistent with his words.

These observations don't change the record. The University of Florida basketball program began making strides when Sloan was put in charge.

His approach, however controversial, achieved significant results. Former players can question how they might have fared with a different coach, but the fact is no one had ever accomplished what Sloan did with Gator basketball.

Life and Death Experiences

Many feel Sloan's greatest strength was his ability to recruit talented players. Sloan always said that coaching was overrated and that winning was the result of having great talent on the team. His recruiting success inside the state of Florida during those years has not been equaled to this day.

Between 1960 and 1965, Sloan signed 23 players from the state of Florida. He reeled in Florida's first All-American – Neal Walk – as well as players like Andy Owens, Gary Keller, Gary McElroy, Mike McGinnis, David Miller, Jeff Ramsey, Boyd Welsch, and Harry Winkler. These players were the foundation for the program's success after Sloan's departure.

In the 1963-64 season, the Gators won 12 and lost 10. Dick Tomlinson set a new Florida Gym single-game scoring record of 44 points against Tampa University, breaking the old mark of 41 set by Joe Hobbs in 1958. The Gators also won the Gator Bowl Tournament, beating Air Force Academy 74-68.

Florida posted two wins over Florida State and had a record-setting night against Miami. More than 6,000 bloodthirsty fans packed Florida Gym and relished the Gators' 114-91 pounding of the Hurricanes.

Miami had given Florida some extra motivation in the pregame warmups. The Gators came out first and got comfortable loosening up as usual at the north-end basket. The visiting team always has its choice of where to warm up, so when Miami came out, they muscled their way in on the Gators. This forced Florida to start the game on the south-end goal. It was the kind of incident that added just a little more gravy to a mashed potatoes kind of evening for the Florida fans.

Brooks Henderson had a career-high 28 points, and Dick Tomlinson delighted the crowd with 23 points, 14 rebounds, and a crushing forearm that propelled Miami superstar Rick Barry into the third row.

Baxley, Highley, and Peek all joined in with double figures. The 6-foot-11 Richard Peek had a career-high 22 rebounds. The 114 points were the most points a Florida team had scored in a game in the school's history; the fact that it came against down-state rival Miami made the victory even sweeter. The 60 points scored in the second half were also an all-time high. Barry finished with 37 points, but it was a footnote to the occasion.

LIFE AND DEATH EXPERIENCES

Dick Tomlinson was a prototype power forward. He was strong, athletic and agile. At 6-foot-5, 205 pounds, he ran the floor to score numerous fast break baskets. But he could also pull up with perfect form and drill a 15-foot jumper. As a junior, Tomlinson made 52.7% of his field goals to tie the school's single-season record.

Tomlinson was also the team's enforcer. He played with determination and wouldn't allow another team's aggressiveness to take away Florida's competitive advantage. In Florida Gym, Tomlinson was a fan favorite with his physical style of play.

Florida shot down the Air Force Academy to win the Gator Bowl championship in Jacksonville, and Brooks Henderson had the two best back-to-back nights of his career. In the semifinal game against Manhattan, Henderson scored 24 points and had 14 rebounds. In the final game he hit six of 10 from the field and made all five free throws to finish with 17 points and eight rebounds.

Henderson's performance earned him the most valuable player award in the tournament. He was joined on the first team by Dick Tomlinson, who scored 46 points in the two nights. Tomlinson could just as easily have been given the most valuable player recognition.

Fans probably remember these games as the highlights of the season. For the players, however, what happened off the court after beating Air Force in the championship game is the more vivid memory. In the early morning hours, the 13-story Roosevelt Hotel where the Gator team was staying burst into flames.

Along with all four teams, many fans were staying at the downtown Jacksonville hotel. At about 6 a.m., guests awakened and began to realize that the hotel was on fire. Because half the team had gone back to Gainesville after the game with Assistant Coach Perry Moore, only six of Florida's 12 players were in the hotel.

Tom Baxley, Bruce Moore, Paul Morton, Richard Peek, Edd Poore, and I stayed overnight, as did Norm and Joan Sloan and their three children, Debbie, Leslie, and Mike.

Paul Morton was on the sixth floor facing the street. The ladder from the firetruck on Adams Street only reached the fifth floor of the 13-story hotel, so Morton securely tied sheets to the radiator unit in his room and shimmied down the sheets to the top of the ladder.

Baxley and I were also on the sixth floor and headed for a crammed fire exit where we became separated. Baxley ended up on the seventh floor, and I wound up with a room full of people back on the sixth. Eventually the firefighting crew brought all of us to safety through the fire exit we had attempted to use earlier.

Sloan and his family also had a frightening experience. Housed on the top floor in a penthouse suite, the Sloans were terrified as the intense smoke filtered up through the building to the top floors. The fire had been confined to the ballroom on the first floor, but hotel guests on the higher floors felt trapped because they had no means of communicating. Fire exits were crammed with people, and the suffocating smoke made it almost impossible to get out of the hotel.

After at least an hour – and what seemed like an eternity to the Sloans – firefighters finally reached the top of the building. Sloan and his family, along with Donna Axom, the 1964 Miss America who also had a penthouse suite, were brought to safety.

The fire killed 21 people and injured 60 more. Most died from smoke inhalation, although several fell to their deaths attempting to escape the building. All of the players survived, but Peek and Poore suffered serious smoke inhalation.

The hotel fire was an unsettling experience for Sloan's family and the six players, but it was the entire team that was repeatedly unnerved flying to games on a chartered DC-3. It felt like playing a game of Russian Roulette.

The old World War II aircraft was one of the safest and most dependable planes in the air. It was agonizingly slow, though, and without cabin pressure or air-conditioning, each road trip became an ordeal.

In the seventies, the athletic department would purchase its own DC-3, the "Blue Goose," but in the sixties the university leased a plane and crew out of Miami. The players nicknamed the pilot Boris Badinoff and the "stewardess" Natasha after the Bullwinkle cartoon characters. Each trip seemed like a brand new episode in a less than comical experience.

After the traumatic hotel fire, the last thing the team wanted to do was get on that plane and fly anywhere. No one ever reported that alligators had nine lives, but the Florida players were beginning to think they had used up the Gator allotment.

Two days later, however, the team was in the air headed for Louisiana to play Tulane in New Orleans and then LSU in Baton Rouge.

On the way to New Orleans, the pilots discovered they had forgotten the maps. Luckily it was a fairly clear day, so they followed Highway 441 back to Gainesville to start over. Arriving in New Orleans a little late, but no worse for the false start, the Gators polished off the Green Wave 86-79 for their fifth win in their first seven games.

The next morning the plane left for a 30-minute scheduled flight to Baton Rouge. Otis Boggs, the legendary play-by-play voice of the Gators, remembers it this way:

> After being airborne for almost an hour, a fair amount of anxiety had set in among the passengers. The co-pilot finally reported that a warning light indicated the landing gear had not locked into place. There was really no way to know for sure until the wheels touched down if the struts would support the aircraft's landing.
>
> Everyone was instructed to remove all sharp objects from their pockets, put their heads between their legs, and hold onto their ankles in preparation for a crash landing.
>
> After what seemed like an eternity, the plane landed safely. But after the horrifying fire in Jacksonville, and the threatening uncertainty of this plane ride, it was a shaken basketball team that got off the plane to play LSU.

LIFE AND DEATH EXPERIENCES

Boggs reports that once the plane got on the ground, the always quick-witted Tom Baxley said, "Coach Sloan, would it be all right if on our next road trip we went by covered wagon and camped out?"

As might be expected, LSU thumped Florida 87-65. But the team rebounded from its trauma. It came back home to score important wins over Auburn and the record-setting victory over Miami. Unfortunately, the weary Gator squad went into its own tailspin at the end of the season, losing six of its remaining nine games.

The last three games of the season are worth mentioning because after four straight defeats, the team collected itself and pulled a big upset over Georgia Tech. Tech was 17-8 overall and 8-1 in the conference before Florida handed the Yellow Jackets a solid 92-73 defeat. After the game, Whack Hyder, the Georgia Tech coach, said, "Looking out there tonight you'd think Florida would have a better record than it does. Their personnel is as good as anyone we've played this year."

Florida then headed for Athens where the Gators handed the Bulldogs their first SEC defeat in the new Georgia Coliseum. Paul Morton's three-point play rescued the Gators inside the final eight minutes, and Tomlinson scored 22 points and grabbed 15 rebounds to lead the victory. The 69-64 win was redemption for the loss a year earlier in the final game at Woodruff Hall.

The victory was especially meaningful to the players because it meant they would have a winning season and would escape any punishment Sloan might exact for a losing record.

The final game of that season was a 59-58 loss to Tennessee in Florida Gym. It was the final game for Florida's only senior, Mont Highley, who finished the night with 21 points and 17 rebounds. For his senior season, Highley averaged 11.5 points and 10.6 rebounds per game, and he had a field goal shooting percentage of 53 percent. After graduation, Highley earned a medical degree at UF. He became an obstetrician-gynecologist in Montgomery, Alabama, where he and Gail raised their three children.

Achieving a Milestone

As the 1964-65 season unfolded, Florida basketball had at last made a place in the hearts of University of Florida fans. They were used to seeing their team win – Florida had won 19 of the 20 home games they had played under Sloan.

During the entire six-year Sloan period, Florida won 51 of 66 home games – 77 percent. The fans became addicted. The student body was enjoying a genuine love affair with Gator hoops, and standing-room-only crowds filled Florida Gym.

Adolph Rupp began to despise coming to Gainesville where the Florida home court was becoming very difficult for Kentucky. Rupp once observed, "With a thimble full of gasoline and a single match, you could burn the place down – and I'll be glad to provide the match."

In truth, the Florida players would have been only too happy to accommodate the Baron of Kentucky basketball. They also found the building less than adequate as a place to practice and work out on a daily basis.

Florida Gym was the property of the College of Physical Education. Professors and students used the facility both as a classroom and for a variety of intramural and minor-sport activities. The scheduling of the gym made it difficult for players to shoot baskets and work out in unscheduled pickup games. The locker room was shared with everyone but the football team, and the facility was seldom clean.

In 1964 it would still be more than a decade before plans for an improved arena would even get off the ground. Despite its faults, Florida Gym was home, especially to the team's four seniors who had been together for the past four years. They comprised a nucleus that now had the potential to give Florida basketball a great season. With a strong core of underclassmen, it appeared this team could win a conference title.

Sloan had orchestrated the best preconference schedule in Florida basketball history with games against powerful Atlantic Coast Conference foes and the traditional in-state rivals. He challenged the seniors to provide leadership, and he set up a preseason conditioning program to make sure the team would be ready for the first day of practice.

Players worked hard during the off-season to develop their skills, but it was normally the six weeks prior to the start of the regular season when serious conditioning began. Sloan was somewhat ahead of his time in deciding that when the players arrived on campus in the fall, long before the October 15 starting date for preseason practice, they would begin a structured conditioning schedule.

An experimental part of the '65 team's conditioning was a program that would be monitored through a research study in the College of Physical Education and Health. Sloan was looking for a method to help his athletes work through what he considered the glass ceiling of their personal limitations to achieve a maximum level of physical stamina.

The players basically became guinea pigs. The focus of the conditioning program was to run on a motorized treadmill at a prescribed speed and a predetermined angle of elevation for a specific period of time. An athlete's initial time was determined by a ratio of his heart rate to his total running time. When the heart rate approached 35 to 37 beats per 10 seconds, the research attendant would stop the treadmill to record the athlete's total time on the treadmill.

Each player was assigned a goal based on the maximum heart rate that was achieved during the initial screening. For example, a player might have run four minutes to reach a heart rate of 35 beats per 10 seconds. That would be his initial challenge for the coming week.

On Monday, Wednesday, and Friday for the six weeks prior to the start of fall practice, the players would go into the basement of Florida Gym where the experimental training was conducted. Each Monday, a player was assigned a total time on the treadmill that was 20 seconds longer than his time from the previous week. If a player failed to run on the treadmill for his prescribed time with a heart rate of less than 35 beats per 10 seconds, he was required to repeat the attempt.

By the fourth week, the psychological pressure was terrifying. Players would wake up Monday morning fearful of not being able to withstand the physical challenge of the afternoon's training. For some, the entire day became a blur of dreading the 4 o'clock encounter with the treadmill. On more than one occasion, a player would walk into the room and, paralyzed by anxiety, be unable to step on the machine to run.

There were a few who relished the challenge and ran to exhaustion. Tom Baxley and Ed Mahoney could run on the machine until the cows came home. On two separate occasions, Baxley even pushed his heart rate beyond the limit, passed out, and fell off the machine.

Somehow, I survived the ordeal but, like many, experienced the agonizing aftershock of what we went through. For several years, I dreamt about the treadmill and imagined the consequences of not completing the assignment.

Everyone who participated in this study agrees that it was one of the most psychologically and physically excruciating experiences of their lives. In retrospect, some are certain that it's a miracle no one died from respiratory shock.

Not surprisingly, Sloan loved the program. He believed the players were developing the kind of toughness that would give them a competitive edge in the closing minutes of a tight game. In reality, the players were developing a dread of the prospect of enduring another season of basketball.

NORM SLOAN: 1961-1966

Once again, however, Sloan's questionable methods were overshadowed by team success. This conditioned team won seven of its first nine games, beating Wake Forest and the University of North Carolina. These were impressive wins over very good ACC teams and clearly demonstrated the potential for this team to have unprecedented success.

Florida beat Tulane 85-63 and scored 102 points to rout LSU, as they began their conference schedule undefeated. By the second week in January, only losses on the road to FSU and Miami kept Florida from having a perfect 9-0 start.

A trip to Auburn on January 9, 1965, found Florida on the short end of a 74-63 score, but with road wins at Mississippi State and Ole Miss, Florida was still 4-1 in the SEC. Record crowds saw the Gators get back one of their early losses with another emotional 86-69 victory over Miami that sent fans home exhausted. Florida now had won 10 of its first 13 games. These were quality wins which included another Gator Bowl Tournament championship. But the program's greatest test was two nights away.

When Norm Sloan took over the Florida program, one team had distanced itself from the SEC pack. That team was Kentucky. The closest a Florida team had come to beating the Wildcats since 1934 was the previous year, when Kentucky escaped Florida Gym 77-72.

The largest crowd ever to see a Florida basketball home game packed Florida Gym the afternoon of January 23. To add to the excitement, it was also the first televised game in Florida Gymnasium. Unbelievably, people were actually *scalping* Florida basketball tickets outside the building. Inside, the building's temperature was rising to a summer afternoon high. Fans had created a basketball atmosphere like never before, and they weren't disappointed. Florida's 84-68 pounding of the Wildcats gave plenty of evidence that the Florida program was rising to another level.

Brooks Henderson led the victory with 20 points and made 12 of 16 free throws. Gary Keller, Jeff Ramsey, and Dick Tomlinson dominated Kentucky in the paint with a total of 49 points. The Wildcat starting five of Larry Conley, Louie Dampier, Tommy Kron, Terry Mobley, and Pat Riley were known as "Rupp's Runts." Although Adolph Rupp claimed it was probably his worst team in 35 years, the same team a year later would reach the NCAA final before losing in the historic matchup with Texas Western, now Texas El Paso.

Florida had now won 11 of its first 14 games, leaving absolutely no doubt that this was a very good Gator ballclub. "This is the best Florida team Kentucky has ever played," Rupp said, adding as a footnote, "It sure does help to have those bigguns." Rupp was also outspoken about the gym. "They need a bigger place to play," Rupp said. "This gym is the only place on campus that isn't big league. They even keep dogs in better places down here."

Joe Halberstein, the popular sportswriter for the *Gainesville Sun*, wrote, "Thirty-one years is a long time to wait for anything, but Florida's Gators are waiting no longer."

As for beating Kentucky after a 31-year dry spell, Sloan said, "We had so much pressure on our shoulders because it had been so long since we beat Kentucky that it took a fine effort to win. I'm very pleased. I'm thrilled to death."

The Gators went on the road and beat Alabama 67-51 to extend a five-game winning streak. Florida had won 10 of its previous 11 games and was now solidly in second place behind Vanderbilt with a 6-1 conference mark.

Gary Keller, with a redshirt season the year before, was a third-year sophomore who was averaging 13.2 points and 10 rebounds a game. Tomlinson was the team's leading scorer with 13.4 points, and Henderson and Baxley were averaging 10 points per game each. Skip Higley, Bob Hoffmann, Paul Morton, and Jeff Ramsey had joined these five to play in every one of the team's first 15 games. The team was strong and it was deep, but it was still searching for some leadership.

Baxley and Henderson had arrived in Gainesville at the same time, but they had struggled to get comfortable with each other in the back court. Players had difficulty relating to Henderson, who was older than the others and more removed from the team's everyday activities. Both players were extremely competitive but had different perspectives on how they thought the team should operate.

Henderson wanted to use his outstanding skills to control the offense and saw himself as a focal point for the team's success. Baxley was never shy about trying to score but had a team-oriented philosophy and would sacrifice his personal goals for the team's overall achievements.

When Sloan began to use Skip Higley at the point, Baxley's playing minutes diminished considerably from his sophomore and junior seasons. Higley was a consummate point guard but, as a sophomore, was being prematurely injected into the mix. Tomlinson also was beginning to see less playing time, and as the fourth senior, my own contribution was felt less and less.

The senior leadership which Sloan had advocated to all of us prior to the start of the year was becoming badly fractured. In retrospect, some of us felt that Sloan would have accomplished more with this season by giving the seniors the playing time they had earned over the past four years.

Ironically, this was the first year Florida had played Kentucky twice in the same season. Even more unusual was that the second game had been scheduled just seven days after the first matchup. Not only did the Gators have to get by the Wildcats in Lexington, but also two nights later they played Tennessee in Knoxville. This road trip would determine the Gators' conference fate. Kentucky won the rematch 78-61, and Tennessee smashed the Gators two nights later.

Baxley played less than 20 total minutes and scored only two points in two of the season's most crucial games. Tomlinson made only five field goals in the two nights and, after scoring 18 points against Kentucky, Henderson had just five points in the loss to Tennessee.

The crushing 75-43 defeat in Knoxville came on a snowy night in which blizzard conditions made traveling almost impossible. The crowd was sparse. Tennessee's Ron Widby had 22 points and A.W. Davis had 17, handing Florida its worst margin of defeat ever against the Volunteers.

The schedule had challenged the Gators to go on the road and prove their worthiness. The road won. Florida came back home dragging its long alligator tail only to get bushwhacked again by Auburn 83-79. It was the nail in the season's coffin.

In front of 5,000 disappointed fans, the Gators lost for the first time at home that season. Henderson and Tomlinson fouled out with six minutes to play, and Florida trailed 71-60. Baxley, Hoffmann, and Edd Poore cut the lead to 77-75, but Auburn took the momentum back for the final margin of victory. "It's tough to play your heart out and lose," Sloan said as he walked briskly across the court. "This wasn't anything like the game at Auburn. We played much better this time and so did Auburn."

Auburn was the only SEC team to beat Florida twice that year, and the Tigers finished in a third-place tie with the Gators at 11-5. Florida won six of its final seven games, the only loss a heartbreaking 80-78 defeat in Nashville to eventual conference champion Vanderbilt.

One of the final six wins came in the return match with Tennessee at home. The game was one of the most memorable SEC confrontations of that era. The Volunteers' decisive win against the Gators 30 days earlier provided more than sufficient motivation for an emotional night in Florida Gym.

Dick Tomlinson and Tennessee forward Ron Widby had been tooth and nail all night. Their emotions finally came unglued, and late in the contest George Conley, the legendary SEC official (whose son Larry played for Kentucky), had a fight on his hands that emptied both benches.

John Ward, a longtime announcer for the Volunteers, was broadcasting from courtside. Fans stormed the court, and in the melee came right over the top of Ward, smashing his head down onto the metal microphone in front of him. The impact stunned Ward and he was temporarily knocked out. Ward never used a color analyst, but he was assisted by an engineer who grabbed the play-by-play microphone after a period of silence and announced, "Fans, a hell of a fight has broken out in this building, and some son of a bitch has knocked Ward out!"

The stunned Ward came back to consciousness and hearing his engineer's comments exclaimed, "Don't say that. You can't swear over the air." At which point the engineer said, "I'm sorry, folks, please excuse me, but really, some son of a bitch *did* knock him out!"

Capping the excitement, Florida won the game on a last-second shot by Henderson. Passing the ball the length of the floor to Jeff Ramsey, Henderson then sprinted past the Tennessee defense to get the ball back from Ramsey and score a layup for the 58-56 revenge victory. Ward told Conley it was a good thing Florida had won or none of them would have gotten out of Gainesville alive.

The team's 18-7 record was the school's best finish in history. The two losses to Auburn and the devastating midseason road trip kept the Vanderbilt game in Nashville from being played for the conference title. Vandy won the league with a 15-1 record.

For many it was a successful season, but for most of this team's members, it was a year of bitter disappointment. This was supposed to have been a year when the veterans would form a nucleus to win a championship. Even though it was Florida's best year ever, it left a bad taste in the mouths of those who were departing.

Tomlinson averaged only 12 points a game in his final 10 games as a Gator. Baxley averaged only eight points a game for the season and just five points a game in the season's final 10 contests. Tom the Bomb, who had begun his three-year career with a 34-point night against Miami, took only 50 shots in the season's final 10 games.

Brooks Henderson led this record season in scoring with 14 points a game. He finished his career scoring a total of 1,001 points. Florida has never had a more talented back-court player. In a three-year career, Henderson made 83 percent of 406 free-throw attempts and ranks third among all Gator players in career free throw shooting percentage. His career average of 15.2 points per game is one of the top 15 career scoring averages among all Gator players.

Tomlinson played in every single game during his Gator career. After his eligibility was completed his senior season, he still needed two more semesters to finish his degree. Sloan felt Tomlinson had underperformed during his four years and called him in to tell him he was being denied a fifth year of scholarship money to graduate. Tomlinson walked out of Sloan's office and went directly down the hall to see athletic director Ray Graves. Graves reversed the Sloan decision and provided the financial aid for Tomlinson to graduate.

All four Gator seniors on the team earned their University of Florida degrees, and along with Bob Hoffmann and Paul Morton, we were the only six players during those years to play entire four-year careers under Norm Sloan.

Never Say Never

The 1965-66 season was Sloan's last in his first tenure at UF. For the Gator players, it was an understatement to say that the end could not come soon enough. This should have been Sloan's best team, with seasoned senior leadership in Paul Morton and an outstanding front line made up of Hoffmann 6-8, Keller 6-9, and Ramsey 6-10.

David "Skip" Higley, the 6-foot, 165-pound junior from Akron, Ohio, had played in 25 games the previous season at point guard and was a veteran. Without question, he was one of the finest point guards in Florida basketball history. Higley never turned the ball over and each year led the team in assists. He was a solid floor-general and a high percentage 18-foot scorer.

Morton was the consummate competitor, but as a freshman from Rochester, New York in 1960, he found the Florida sunshine more inviting than the classroom. Before he knew it, he was on the outside of the University of Florida looking back in.

Morton had great determination and told Sloan he was enlisting in the Army but intended to come back. Remarkably, he had been the leading scorer on the freshman team despite having to shoot left-handed for more than half the season because of a broken right wrist.

After two years of playing basketball while in the service, Morton returned to Gainesville in 1963 with a mature focus on earning his degree and competing for the Gators. His personal toughness and competitive nature were highly respected by his teammates. His ability to set goals and achieve them led him to become a commercial and corporate airline pilot after his graduation.

Morton was the kind of personality that you would have thought Sloan would eagerly thrust into a leadership role. But, for whatever reason, Sloan played Morton only sparingly, and the team was unable to capitalize on his fiercely competitive nature. Morton had a career-high 25 points in the team's 89-86 loss to Vanderbilt. He averaged nine points a game his senior season and made 80 percent of his 92 free-throw attempts.

Gary Keller led the team in scoring with 16 points per game as well as in rebounds with 12.5 per game. Keller played his best game of the season scoring 20 points and getting 16 rebounds in a 67-63 late-season win over Tennessee. Gary later said, "It was one of my best games, but afterward in the locker room Sloan said to me, 'Take that smile off your face. You had a terrible first half.'"

This team struggled to a fifth-place finish in the SEC with a 9-7 record and was 16-10 overall. Seven consecutive away games in the middle of the season, coupled with three home SEC defeats, brought Sloan's final Florida season to a close.

During Sloan's six-year tenure from 1961 to 1966, the Florida program achieved some significant firsts.

- The best SEC record ever (11-5) and the most SEC victories, 1965.
- Five out of six winning seasons for the first time ever under the same coaching staff.
- The best 25-game season record in Florida history (18-7) and the most wins in a season, 1965.
- Seven out of eight victories over FSU.
- Florida's first win ever against Tennessee in Knoxville, 1963.
- Florida's first win ever against Kentucky in regular season, 1965.
- The most points scored by a Gator team – 114 over Miami – a record held until 1972 when Florida scored 120 points against Chicago State.
- The most points scored against an SEC team – 105 against Georgia. The all-time record was set in 1974 when Florida beat Mississippi State 107-104.

As the curtain came down on the first Norman Sloan era at Florida, he had clearly demonstrated that Florida could have a successful basketball program. In his unrelenting determination to get respect from the university's football-dominated mentality, Sloan won friends who supported his endeavors. He also created adversaries who criticized his methods. Sloan was fond of observing that the longer you coach, the more your friends change and your enemies multiply.

Sloan had been making enemies from the beginning. When Sloan drop-kicked a basketball into President J. Wayne Reitz's lap during a 1961 home game, Dr. Reitz put athletic director Graves on notice that "If Sloan does that again, you are to dismiss him."

In March of 1966, Sloan came into Graves' office with an offer he had received from North Carolina State, thinking he could use the offer as leverage to get more money. But Sloan's profanity and treatment of the players had long upset both Graves and Reitz. Graves took the opportunity to inform Sloan that it was the university's feeling that he should look for another job.

Sloan shot back profanely that Graves couldn't fire him. Graves smashed his fist, shattering the glass covering on his desk. "Norm," Graves retorted, "I'm not firing you. You have just fired yourself."

Graves instructed his sports information director, Norm Carlson, to write a press release which named athletic administrator Perry Moore as the new head coach. Graves would present the release to the athletic board. Sloan and Perry Moore were at odds. Sloan had replaced Moore as his assistant in 1965, but Moore was retained as an athletic administrator. Graves liked him enough to decide to give him the basketball job. Carlson wrote the release, locked it in his drawer, locked his office, and went to lunch.

Working in the sports information office was a young man named Larry Woods. He was an admirer of Sloan and knew about the release. Woods told Sloan what he knew, but Sloan was skeptical. So Woods broke into Carlson's office, broke into his desk, and took the release to Sloan.

Norm Sloan was stunned by this development and was outraged to think that his former assistant would be named as his replacement. Sloan called supporters who were influential with the university. Under pressure, President Reitz directed Graves to hold off naming a successor until there had been a formal search.

Although Larry Woods was replaced for his misdeeds, Sloan's pressure prevented Perry Moore from ultimately being hired as head coach.

The Sloan years had officially ended, or at least that's what everyone believed in 1966. It would have been a safe bet that Norman Sloan would never return to Gainesville, Florida. But you know what they say. Never, never, never say never.

Tommy Bartlett

An All-American Experience
1967-1973

Gators Now Winningest Eve[r]

0th-Ranked Gators Rout 'Cats, 89-[ ]

GatorsWhip
[C]ats 89-72 Big Gators Rip 'Cane[s]

Bartlett's Bunch shows

[Fir]st [T]ime in History — Stung Gato[rs]
[A]re in Top Ten — Look Ahea[d]

Gators Roll As Kel[ly]
Joins 1,000-Point C[lub]

Miller hits 25 in UF's 73-70 win

[Be]nch helps Gators slip by LSU

Defeat Georgia
[For] Third Time

A Breath of Fresh Air

Ray Graves was primarily committed to being the school's head football coach, but he genuinely cared about young people. As director of athletics, he wanted an environment that supported all of the scholarship athletes' efforts to succeed.

Some returning basketball players had spoken with Graves to express their disapproval of the way Sloan ran his program. Graves was determined to hire a coach who would raise the best interests of the players to an equal footing with winning. With Sloan's departure, Graves believed the basketball program could reflect the highest ideals of intercollegiate athletics and at the same time have winning seasons.

Graves was relieved to have Sloan out of the picture, but the fallout from his decision not to appoint Perry Moore as the head coach was disquieting. The interview process continued through more than 100 applicants. Speculation focused on FSU's Hugh Durham, Duke assistant Chuck Daley, Western Kentucky's Guy Strong, and Stetson's Glenn Wilkes.

But Graves finally decided to offer the job to the 28-year-old head coach at the U.S. Military Academy who had played on three outstanding Ohio State University teams in the early sixties. During his visit to the Florida campus, Bobby Knight accepted Graves' offer, shook hands, and headed back to the gray granite walls overlooking the Hudson River. He was greeted by the corps of cadets and other high-ranking brass who, together with the Army basketball players, persuaded him to renege on his verbal agreement to accept Florida's offer. Knight said by way of explanation, "I've only been a head coach here for one year and have an obligation to the people who went with me at a young age."

Graves had planned a press conference for Thursday to announce Knight's appointment and had to scramble for another qualified candidate. This turn of events had created a public perception that Graves was failing to provide effective transition for the program. He was determined to have an appointment to announce. He had considered Tommy Bartlett but had told him the job was Knight's. Bartlett had withdrawn his name from consideration, but he and his wife had planned a Florida vacation beginning that weekend. Bartlett was summoned back to the Florida campus on Friday.

The bizarre circumstances dropped the job squarely in Bartlett's lap. On Saturday morning, June 4, 1966, just 48 hours after Knight had called to reject Graves' offer,

TOMMY BARTLETT: 1967-1973

Tommy Bartlett learned that he would be the 12th head basketball coach at Florida. He celebrated his 38th birthday on June 6 with his first day of work as the Gators' new head coach.

Bartlett brought with him a former teammate and close friend from the University of Tennessee, Dick Davis, who would handle recruiting. Davis was joined by Jim McCachren, who was on various coaching staffs from 1949 until 1973. These three were the program's central coaching figures until Billy Henry was hired by Bartlett in 1970.

Tommy Bartlett, one of the nicest human beings to set foot on the Florida campus, was quiet yet determined. He had been an assistant on Ray Mears' staff at the University of Tennessee for five years and had also been Tennessee's varsity tennis coach. He had been coaching basketball since 1952.

Born in Georgia, Bartlett lived most of his life in Knoxville, where he had been an outstanding high school athlete. In 1952 he was a second-team all-SEC basketball player on a Tennessee team that went 13-9. His wife, Essie Roberts Bartlett, was a warm and engaging woman dedicated to raising three boys. The Bartletts were a sports family who had fun together. Their door was always open, and returning players who thought they never wanted to bounce a round ball again were rejuvenated by the personal hospitality and warmth of the Bartletts.

Bartlett came to town with a Volkswagen convertible and painted it bright Florida orange with blue and white trim. He was excited to be part of the Gator family and wanted others to feel his energy and optimism for the basketball program. With renewed enthusiasm generated by a coaching staff that made basketball fun again, the Gators began a string of seasons that generated some of Florida's most exciting basketball moments.

Tommy Bartlett was just what this psychologically exhausted group of Sloan players needed. He encouraged the players and made them feel valuable to the program's objectives. He treated them like winners and believed simply that they would want to do the things necessary to win. In later years, with less talent, his weak point would be an inability to inspire his players. But the motivation for these players was, at the time, serenity. Bartlett's even temperament allowed everyone to relax and to begin working in a constructive fashion.

Tommy Bartlett and Dick Davis could coach basketball. They helped the players develop fundamental skills that would make them tough competitors. Bartlett's trademark at Florida was a 1-3-1 zone defense. He imported it from Tennessee where he had helped Ray Mears design and refine a system that made defense an offensive weapon.

The 1-3-1 is well suited to a team that has a big front line. This team had more size than any Florida basketball team ever; few college programs could match it. Gary Keller played in the middle and was joined up front by Jeff Ramsey, a 6-foot-10, 240-pound senior, and Neal Walk, a 6-foot-9, 220-pound sophomore.

Florida also had long bodies at the skill positions which added valuable quickness to the team's exceptional size. Gary McElroy, a 6-foot-6,185-pound junior was one forward, and David Miller, a 6-foot-7, 180-pound junior played the big guard. The veteran point guard was 6-foot senior Skip Higley. At times Miller would move to the point, where his size and wingspan gave the zone defense a difficult point defender, and Higley would move off to the wing defensively.

The system suited players like Keller, Ramsey, Walk, and later Andy Owens because it gave the big people good position on the backboards. Those early Bartlett years produced Florida's best rebounding teams through a combination of unprecedented front-line size and Bartlett's ability to complement his players with the 1-3-1 zone defense.

Bartlett continued to promote a family atmosphere and the team responded to it. In June, prior to its first season together, the team embarked on a 17-day goodwill tour through Panama and Venezuela. The experiences of camaraderie and bonding friendships were similar to those of the 1994 team that went to Australia before finding its way to the Final Four. Playing international teams in the off-season helped both teams get better acquainted and gain maturity.

The '67 Gators won all three games in Venezuela by sizable margins, beating Caracas, Caroboda (the best team in Venezuela), and Aragua of Maracay. Of the nine games played in both countries, their stiffest competition came from the Panamanian Olympic team, which handed them their only defeat. Florida committed 42 personal fouls in this game and finished with just three players. The games were a tremendous opportunity for the development of team chemistry, but what the players experienced off the court in rebuilding team morale was even more rewarding than the victories.

No one benefited more from this coaching change than senior Gary Keller. A constant target of Sloan's crucifying coaching style, Keller's psyche was as fragile as crystal. "Coach Bartlett is a winner," Keller said, "and he treats us like winners. We have a lot of confidence in ourselves, in him, and in each other."

Keller came to Gainesville at 6-foot-9 and a thin 180 pounds. He was a much-heralded Florida high school player who had been recruited by the best colleges in the country. Sloan persuaded him to stay home and help build the Florida program.

Perhaps no single Florida basketball player endured more coaching abuse under Sloan than Keller. Keller responded badly to criticism, but Sloan's insensitive treatment was counterproductive. Keller's physical development was a barrier to his conditioning, and Sloan had tried to build his stamina by demanding that he push himself to exhaustion. For most athletes, this was a difficult but acceptable part of the training process. But Keller was tortured by it.

In Keller's sophomore year, every Florida player was required to run a mile in six minutes prior to the start of fall practice. This is tough for any player, particularly for a big man, but Sloan was convinced that every player should be able to do it. He drew a line in the Florida sand and told the team no player would start fall practice if he didn't meet this objective.

TOMMY BARTLETT: 1967-1973

Keller kept coming up short. Sloan knew he was not going to be able to run the designated time. The stormy Florida coach got Keller up before dawn one morning and met him on the cinder track that was at the south end of Florida Field. He pulled his car onto the track with the headlights showing the way and ordered Keller to run or he would be run over.

Keller survived, but the ordeal had little effect on his body's ability to sustain the challenge of a 40-minute game. What Keller needed was a coach who would see his best qualities and teach him how to capitalize on his strengths.

Keller played left-handed and moved gingerly like a long-legged water bird stepping through the swamps. His challenge was to gain confidence while developing the muscle to play inside.

Gary's stature certainly wasn't unique to the team. Several inside players on the basketball team were tall and thin. Allen Trammell, a Gator football player, noted their resemblance to the Florida egrets that strutted near the ponds on campus. He aptly nicknamed the basketball players "pond birds," a name that stuck and was heard often in good-natured teasing.

An illness that caused Keller to be redshirted his sophomore season under Sloan provided an unexpected chance for the resident pond bird to fulfill his personal dreams. As a fifth-year senior, he became the main cog in Tommy Bartlett's system and discovered a basketball experience that was tremendously rewarding.

This was a veteran Florida team with the right mix of under- and upperclassmen. Keller and Edd Poore were fifth-year seniors. Poore had grown up in Knoxville where he was a three-sport star in high school, also excelling in football and baseball. He was a highly regarded recruit in 1963, but like many others, had been burned out by Sloan and quit his senior year. He returned to the '67 team with a remaining year of eligibility. Bartlett gave Poore's Florida career new life, and Edd gratefully contributed valuable leadership in his senior season. After graduation, Poore became Gainesville High School's head coach and guided the team to the school's only state basketball championship in 1969. He retired from the Brooksville, Florida, school system in 1993.

Skip Higley and Jeff Ramsey were veteran four-year players who joined these two as the senior class. With five juniors and three outstanding sophomores, Bartlett had the right combination of experience, depth, and talent to formulate a season of unprecedented success. It was a moment in time when Florida basketball would put all of the pieces together to have its most glorious season yet.

Before the season began, one of my good friends Larry Barnett asked, "Willie, how are the Gators going to do this year?" And I said, "Barney, they're going clean, 25-0." He never let me live down the optimistic prognosis, but those long-legged pond birds made almost everyone else's fondest dreams come true.

The Best Season Ever

The 1967 season began with the Gators crushing Jacksonville University 93-59. After wins over Miami and Florida State, they beat Kentucky on the road and were a perfect 4-0.

The Kentucky win in Memorial Coliseum was huge. Never before had the Gators beaten the Wildcats in Lexington. It was also Kentucky's third consecutive home defeat, which hadn't happened since 1950, and left the crowd in stunned silence. Florida's big front line outrebounded Kentucky 51-40, and Gary Keller tore up a Wildcat man-to-man defense, scoring 17 of his team-high 25 points in the second half. Florida put on a late-game run that had Adolph Rupp and the Big Blue faithful wondering what had hit them.

With just over a minute to play, Florida took the lead for good as Skip Higley knocked down a 20-foot baseline jumper. He then joined teammates David Miller and Gary McElroy, hitting both ends of one-and-ones in the closing minute to ice the 78-75 win. It was a dramatic finish to an award-winning performance, and the knowledgeable Wildcat fans knew this was a good Florida team.

It was also a night when Florida basketball would reveal its secret weapon – Gatorade – for the first time. Developed at UF and named after its team, this thirst quencher's courtside appearance at the Kentucky game was the humble beginning to the product's raging success. Billy Reid of the *Louisville Courier-Journal* wrote, "They call this stuff Gatorade, and whatever's in it, Kentucky should find out."

"You can bet at least I'm going to drink some the next game," laughed Jeff Ramsey. "We beat Kentucky, didn't we?"

Florida played its second rare December SEC game and lost to conference favorite Vanderbilt in Nashville 77-69. The schedule had force-fed the Gators' preparation, and they went on to win seven straight, including the Gator Bowl championship.

Kentucky paid a return visit to Florida Gym in mid-January, and 6,900 fans were on hand to greet them. The crowd began arriving six hours before tip-off and was rewarded with an 89-72 crushing of the Wildcats. Florida rocketed into the nation's top 10 for the first time ever, actually hitting the No. 8 spot.

Sports Illustrated (Jan. 1967) did a feature article titled "Tall, Stoned and Gatoraded," which talked about a lucky tension-relieving stone that Bartlett picked up

TOMMY BARTLETT: 1967-1973

in Venezuela and carried in his pocket and the "extra energized bigguns" that were dominating the league. Florida enjoyed its best season start since the 1951 team had gone 12-1. The Gators next met Tennessee in back-to-back games which, in the final analysis, wiped out a chance for the coveted conference crown.

Ironically, Tennessee's entire team was in the Florida stands to witness UF's Saturday night win over Kentucky. Tennessee's coaches realized their team could not run with the Gators. The Volunteers came out Monday night and controlled the game's tempo from start to finish, beating Florida 66-53. Five nights later, they repeated the victory in Knoxville 56-42. They were Florida's two lowest-scoring SEC games of the season.

These back-to-back losses to the Volunteers were bitter pills for Bartlett to swallow because they came at the hands of his former mentor, Ray Mears. With two losses to the same team, it would be almost impossible to win a league championship.

Somehow, two nights later, Florida squeezed out a 63-61 win at Georgia. The Gators went on to beat Alabama in their third straight SEC road game but then lost their fourth at Auburn. It would now take a miracle to be sized for the championship rings.

Miracles do happen. The team regrouped from the Auburn massacre and upset ninth-ranked Vanderbilt 83-75. That SEC TV game of the week started an eight-game winning streak that went right through to the final game of the season. Miller, the team's second leading scorer for the season, scored 21 points against Vandy. Higley had 20, and Keller's 14 points and 11 rebounds brought Florida back within reach of the contenders. The Gators were back in the league championship picture.

David Miller was one of the best-liked players to wear the orange and blue. At 6-foot-7, he was the tallest player to play guard for the Gators. His wingspan and foot-speed made him tremendously effective in the 1-3-1 zone defense. Miller probably holds an SEC record for the most "clock stops" by deflecting opposing team passes with his feet.

In the summer before his senior year, Miller had broken his neck diving into a shallow spot at the university-owned recreation area, Lake Wauburg. He wore a body cast from the waist up for several months. Still, he was able to captain the team and start all 25 games in his senior season. He recorded a career-high 25 points against Wisconsin and averaged just under 10 points a game.

The unsung hero of this team was Gary McElroy. McElroy grew up in Clearwater and was extremely quick. He had exceptional reflexes and patrolled the baseline in the zone like a panther stalking a fresh piece of meat. He was responsible for covering the corners, which can be the Achilles' heel of a 1-3-1 defense.

McElroy was also a quick leaper who could dunk two balls at the same time. He was a forerunner to Dennis Rodman with long arms, huge hands, and jumping ability which made him an exceptional offensive and defensive rebounder. Like many other players on this team who accepted their roles and contributed unselfishly to the team's success, McElroy came to play every night. He averaged 7.8 points and 5.8 rebounds during his 76-game playing career and graduated from Florida with a degree in nuclear engineering.

With the Vanderbilt win, Florida had proven its worthiness to its fans. But more importantly, the team had finally jelled. All of the pieces came together, and roles were well defined. The team had the best chemistry ever. The Gators won their final 17 games by an average margin of 20 points. The only game that was a contest in the second half was Mississippi State in Starkville, which Florida won 59-54.

Jeff Ramsey was another former Sloan player who was rejuvenated by the Bartlett regime. Big Jeff was an extremely likable guy who genuinely wanted to be successful. He took everything to heart, and a little encouragement went a long way. Jeff set a career field goal shooting percentage of 51.7 that stood for ten years. His 63 percent mark in 1965 is the third best single-season field goal percentage to this day.

Higley, Keller, McElroy, Miller, and Walk, along with Owens, Ramsey, and Boyd Welsch, gave the Gators eight players who were virtually interchangeable. It was a team capable of playing head to head with the best teams in the country.

On March 4, 1967, a Saturday, the final game of the regular season arrived. With 20 wins under their belt, the Gators met the Georgia Bulldogs at home. It was an extremely emotional day, particularly for the four seniors. These players had been through a challenging Florida basketball experience. None of them would have believed 12 months earlier that they would be so personally excited playing their final game for the Gators. Few others could fully appreciate what this moment might mean to these players who had experienced such a turnaround in their college playing careers.

Already the team had surpassed every other Florida team in total wins, winning percentage, most points in a single season, highest scoring average, most field goals attempted, most field goals made, best rebound margin, best overall record in the SEC, and the most wins ever in conference games. They had already beaten Georgia twice, the first time in the Gator Bowl Tournament and again in Athens where they escaped with a two-point win. Beating any team three times in the same season is an accomplishment, let alone a huge rival like Georgia. And not only was this Senior Night and the final basketball game of the regular season, but miraculously Florida still had an outside chance to tie for the conference crown.

The Gators and Vanderbilt had four SEC losses, and Tennessee had just three. However, Tennessee had to go to Starkville on Monday night, where a loss would mean a three-way tie and a chance for the Gators to share in a first-ever title. Florida put the Bulldogs to rest 96-63 in a bizarre game that produced three technical fouls, including one on the crowd. Harold Johnson and Butch Lambert were officiating.

Late in the game Higley was called for a touch foul. Higley put a soccer-style toe to the ball as he returned it to Johnson, who gave him a technical. With a 20-point lead, Jeff Ramsey smiled and shook Higley's hand, and big Jeff got a "T." Then a fan decided to fire a wad of paper, striking Johnson. This put the game on the edge of a forfeit. Johnson told the crowd that any more debris thrown on the floor and the game belonged to Georgia. Fortunately things quieted down, and Florida polished off the Bulldogs.

The team waited out a long weekend and stayed up past midnight Monday with ears glued to a static-filled broadcast on the Tennessee radio network. Unfortunately for Florida, the Volunteers finally beat Mississippi State 78-76 in three overtimes. Florida literally couldn't have come any closer to a share of the SEC crown.

Many felt the play of this team at the end of that season was Florida's best-ever effort. By season's end, Florida was respected as one of the best teams in the nation, but the SEC only permitted its conference champion to play in the NCAA Tournament. This team was supremely confident, and in a *Sports Illustrated* article, writer Frank DeFord observed that the Florida team was loose and very little seemed to trouble them. "It's just a feeling," said Gary McElroy, "and I can't quite explain it. Except all of a sudden it is there and you feel that there's nobody who can beat you and you don't worry."

The season produced some lasting memories:
- Beating Kentucky twice in the same year and for the first time ever in Lexington.
- A Gator Bowl Tournament championship where Skip Higley was named the most valuable player while scoring a total of only 16 points. Higley may have been the best ball-handler in the history of Florida basketball. He definitely was one of the most unselfish players ever to wear a Gator uniform.
- A 95-65 exhibition win over Yugoslavia, which at the time was undefeated and the best amateur team in the world. This Slavic team had beaten a USA team led by Cazzie Russell for the World Championship in Chile.
- The best win-loss record in Florida history to this day, 21-4.

For Gary Keller, it was the culmination of a career that recognized him as the best big man ever to compete for the University of Florida. Keller, in many ways, personified the transition of Florida basketball.

He was a product of Dixie Hollins High School in St. Petersburg and became a catalyst for the Florida program to attract the best talent in the state. He persevered, believed in his goals, and even survived a life-threatening illness that suspended his playing career for one year. Moreover, he became Florida's first legitimate professional athlete. After signing to play in the American Basketball Association for the Minnesota Muskies, he finished a three-year career with the Miami Floridians.

Always emotional, Keller experienced highs and lows in his career, but he left Florida basketball in better shape than he found it. In a profound sense, Gary Keller brought respect to the program as it struggled to survive at a higher level.

Keller was an All-SEC player in both his junior and senior years. He scored more than 1,100 points in three seasons. Through the years, his loyalty to Gator basketball has remained steadfast.

Even though Florida couldn't get its hands around its first-ever coveted SEC trophy, its 21-4 season put this team in the record book for posterity. It was the first Florida team to end the season ranked in the nation's top 20.

Every contributing player was a Sloan recruit. The team's record is a lasting tribute to Norm Sloan's commitment to build the program with state of Florida players. The credit for the success, however, belonged to Tommy Bartlett who touched all the right buttons and coached the players to their potential.

WALKing to the Big Apple

The 1968, '69, and '70 seasons belonged to Neal Walk and Andy Owens. They were freshmen together in 1966 and part of a Sloan recruiting class that was exceptional.

Walk arrived in Gainesville at 6-foot-10, 215 pounds, from Miami Senior High School and, along with Owens at 6-foot-5, 210 pounds, gave the freshman team a front-line tandem that was overpowering. The two big men led the Baby Gators to a 17-1 season. It was the best record for a freshman team ever.

Coming out of high school, most 6-foot-10 prospects need a lot of developmental work. Walk was no exception. He was considered a "project" who needed to work hard to develop his skills. Under the watchful eye of Assistant Coach Dick Davis, Walk worked hard to develop post moves and spent long hours in the weight room. His timing developed through tap drills where the big man bounced up and down while tapping the ball against the glass backboard. He memorized footwork mechanics while shuffling his feet back and forth across the inside of the free-throw line. He jumped rope and shot thousands of 10-foot baseline jumpers.

In Bartlett's 1-3-1 offensive and defensive systems, Walk was well positioned to capitalize on his skills. He was not particularly quick, and he couldn't jump very high, but he developed an uncanny ability to be around the basket when it mattered most.

The summer before his junior season (1968), Walk was at a camp in New York's Catskill Mountains with some of the best competition in the East. The experience matured him and honed his skills against outstanding competition. Walk possessed an inner toughness to succeed that was also often apparent in his attitude. He could never be accused of being shy. In fact some teammates felt he was downright arrogant – cocky, vain, self-confident – but whatever others thought of him, the bottom line was he got the job done.

In 1968 he was named an Associated Press Second-Team All-American – Florida's first ever. Walk also led the nation in rebounding, was 10th in scoring, and was rated the seventh-best player nationwide in an AP poll. As a senior, Walk averaged 24 points and 18 rebounds a game. This time he was named a third-team AP All-American.

Neal Walk set 22 game, season, and Florida career records. He was chosen second in the NBA draft. As the result of a coin flip, Milwaukee won the right to pick first and chose Lew Alcindor (Kareem Abdul Jabbar), and the Phoenix Suns chose Walk. He

TOMMY BARTLETT: 1967-1973

a thunderous ovation. His teammates in the dressing room heard the roar and knew what had happened.

Owens epitomized the ideals of a student-athlete. His commitment in the classroom reflected his determination on the court. He earned a juris doctorate from the Florida School of Law and was recognized in Florida Blue Key. In recent years he has been a circuit court judge in Sarasota.

Where Walk leveraged his 6-foot-10 ability into a professional basketball career, Owens put basketball on the shelf and pursued his professional career in law. His impact on Florida's basketball reputation and the ideals of intercollegiate athletics is a model by which many would like to measure an athlete's success.

The '68 Gators went 15-10 and won 10 of 11 games through the middle of their schedule. Down the stretch they lost four out of the last five to LSU, Auburn, Mississippi State, and Georgia who all tied or finished below them in the final league standings. Florida's 11-7 SEC record was good for fourth place. The Wildcats won the league with a 15-3 mark.

Six Florida players got most of the minutes. Mike Leatherwood, Gary McElroy, [?] Miller, Andy Owens, Mike Rollyson, and Neal Walk started almost every game. Rollyson was a very bright 6-foot-3 forward from Plant City, Florida, who later practiced tax law in Washington, D.C. He had a career-high 17 points in the final game of his senior season in a 97-83 loss to Georgia and averaged eight points a game for the '68 team. Walk and Owens accounted for 40 of the team's 78.7 point scoring average which is the sixth-best team mark in school history.

Another talented player who impacted the team's success at this time was a Gainesville native and former walk-on, Boyd Welsch. Walter Welsch, Boyd's dad, was a respected professor in physical education. Welsch grew up just a few blocks from Florida Gym and developed into one of the Gators' finest perimeter shooters. He was an athlete who could pole vault, shoot par on a golf course, or bury a 25-foot jumper. In his senior year (1969), Welsch averaged 12.6 points per game while shooting percent from the free-throw line. His career-high of 28 points was recorded in his senior season in a heartbreaking 81-80 defeat at Auburn. Welsch averaged 20 points a game in the final three games of that year as the Gators swept their way into their first-ever postseason tournament invitation. Florida finished the regular season beating [?], West Virginia, and Alabama to eventually face Temple in the first round of National Invitation Tournament.

The WVU game had an interesting twist. Florida had scheduled the game in the Gainesville Coliseum as a home game, but the managers had packed their home blue jerseys. Fortunately, the team practiced with reversible blue and white practice jerseys. With the West Virginia players in their road blue uniforms, [?] used the white side of the Gators' practice shirts and inscribed numbers in black magic marker. The makeshift uniforms didn't look very good, but went on to have a distinguished playing career for the Suns and the New [...] in the NBA. Although Walk was never formally honored in a ceremony, [...] 41 is the only basketball jersey ever to be retired by Florida.

Walk has worked to overcome a devastating paralysis that resulted [...] surgery and has been a prominent spokesperson for others with disablin[...] He continues to work in a public relations capacity for the Phoenix Sun[...]

Although Walk and Owens arrived at Florida together, Walk finished [...] Owens because Owens was redshirted his sophomore season. The two b[...] together in 1968 and 1969 and are regarded as the best inside tandem [...] the same time for the Gators.

Andy Owens, a product of Tampa Hillsborough High School, [...] former Gator player Bobby Shiver. After an intense recruiting battle, h[...] over Lefty Driesell's Davidson College.

Owens was the consummate competitor and had the court sense [...] At 6-foot-5, he did most of his scoring in the paint. In the Walk years [...] the high post where his passing and driving skills complemente[...] counterpart. Later as a senior, he found even more room to roam insi[...]

Few Florida post players have ever fought as hard, night in and n[...] Owens. He was a tough, hard-nosed player who punished people on [...] court with his physical play. No one ever wanted to guard Owens [...] sharp elbows and athleticism to beat them up. He had a deadly jum[...] 15 feet, and he could also put the ball on the floor and explode to th[...] point plays.

In three seasons, Owens played in 76 games and averaged 19[...] ranks 11th overall in scoring with 1,445 total points, but he is one [...] players to average 19 points or more per game during his career. O[...] figures in his final 42 straight college games, averaging 27 point[...] year. Almost 25 percent of his career points came from the free-[...] achieved an 80 percent career free-throw average. During his [...] Owens shot 200 free throws and made 81 percent of his chances.

Owens also had a flair for surprising people with his behavio[...] sophomore season, he traveled with the team, dressed out, and [...] away games. In one of the last games Florida played in the Au[...] Owens took a teammate's dare to dunk the ball before the game. [...] before tip-off, when both teams had gone back to their dressing [...] preparation, Owens slipped back onto the court. It was illegal a[...] on either team to dunk during warmups or during the game. Ow[...] on the official roster.

With 3,500 rabid Auburn fans as witnesses, Owens grabb[...] or five times as he drove to the basket, and threw one down in [...]

the team looked good enough to earn a 75-57 win over the Mountaineers.

In 1969 the Gators won 12 of their last 14 games to close out the regular season at 18-8. They recorded successive home wins over Kentucky, Tennessee, and LSU, enjoying the biggest one-week home show in Florida basketball history. The win over the Kentucky Wildcats was again particularly sweet because the Wildcats won the SEC and received the conference's NCAA bid.

"Florida basketball has moved up on the shelf with Gator football," Joe Halberstein wrote in the *Gainesville Sun*, and Gator fans were talking Florida hoops like never before. An appearance at the National Invitation Tournament in Madison Square Garden was arguably Florida basketball's most significant accomplishment to date. A Florida team had never been selected to play for a postseason championship. The trip to New York was a marquee event to acclaim the university's athletic profile in the national spotlight. Florida was one of 16 invited teams, and its opening-round opponent would be the Temple Owls.

The Gators had a solid first half and went to the locker room with a 37-35 halftime advantage over the tradition-rich Philadelphia school. After intermission, Florida was as cold as a New York City winter night. Temple went on a 19-7 run to lead the Gators 54-44 with 14:32 left in the game. Temple's Eddie Mast, who averaged only nine points a game during the regular season, bombed Florida's 1-3-1 zone from the corners and finished with 20 points. Mast was joined in double figures by four other Temple starters who combined for all but two of the team's total points. Temple held Florida to just 29 second-half points to win 82-66.

Neal Walk scored 26 points and had 17 rebounds despite picking up his third personal foul in the first 12 minutes of the game. Bartlett gambled and let Walk play the entire way. Walk didn't foul out until the outcome had been decided. Unfortunately, Walk's performance was not enough to overcome a miserable night of shooting by his teammates who managed a paltry 34 percent.

Tennessee, the other SEC representative in the NIT, was also eliminated by Temple 63-58 in the third round. It was no surprise to either Florida or Tennessee that Temple, coached by Harry Litwak, went on to win the tournament.

The Gator team had been dubbed the "Fabulous Five Plus One," the "One" being Neal "The Hawk" Walk. The Hawk's display of talent in this prominent media market catapulted him into the national spotlight. In just a few short months, Neal would reap the rewards of an outstanding Florida basketball career by being the No. 2 selection in the NBA draft.

There were two Mikes on this team who deserve special mention – Mike Leatherwood and Mike McGinnis. Leatherwood was a point guard who transferred from Pensacola Junior College. Leatherwood's black-rimmed glasses gave him the appearance of Clark Kent in a Gator uniform. His super slinky two-handed jumper seemed to roll off his forehead and somehow find the basket.

With two glass ankles, Leatherwood might have been slow in his black, high-topped Converse shoes. He was, however, deceptively quick and never made a mental mistake. Leatherwood was the general. Leatherwood's first job after graduation in 1969 was to become the head basketball coach at Indian River Junior College. He's held that job ever since.

Mike McGinnis became the true sixth man of this team. McGinnis fought through knee and groin injuries that threatened his career and limited his chances to perform to his potential. He was responsible for many key baskets that helped forge crucial wins. His 14 points in Florida's 82-81 win over the Wildcats in 1969 were his career high.

Fans remember him as the "great white leaper." McGinnis would spring from the floor and keep going up. No Florida player has represented the program with more class or greater fortitude. His unselfish attitude and personal determination distinguish him as another of Florida basketball's unsung heroes. McGinnis became a winning basketball coach at Central Florida Community College where he was also the athletic director. In addition, he became a respected SEC football official.

Kurt Feazel, Leatherwood, McGinnis, Richard Vasquez, and Walk gave the Gators another distinguished group of senior leaders in this magnificent year. It would be impossible to overstate the contribution this group made to Florida basketball. While the 1966-67 team is recognized for its best win-loss record ever, this team was the first to put the program in a position to capture a national tournament title.

The season inspired record standing-room-only crowds in Florida Gym, and its reputation as the toughest place to play in the SEC continued to grow. Beginning in 1967, the Gators won 30 of their next 33 home games, which is the best string of home wins ever in Florida Gym. The Gators beat Kentucky four out of six times and had top 10 upsets of Kentucky, Tennessee, and Vanderbilt.

Neal Walk rewrote Florida's record book in scoring and rebounding. His 31 boards in the January 1968 win over Alabama tied Jim Zinn's 1957 mark as the most rebounds ever in a single game by a Florida player. Walk also had 22 rebounds in the first half of a 1967 Florida State game and holds five of the top 10 single-game rebounding marks in Florida history.

As the only Florida basketball player to have a retired jersey, Walk's remarkable Florida career is prominently noted. He and Owens were also the last of Sloan's recruits to impact the program's accomplishments, and with their departure, Bartlett would become increasingly challenged to demonstrate success in attracting comparable talent to Florida's campus. Although there were some very choppy seas still to come, Florida basketball appeared to be sailing with a strong wind at its back.

The Science of Success

The success of Bartlett's program was raising the expectations of Florida's fans. It was also generating unprecedented support for the team. This was specifically noted by the growth in membership of the Gator Tip-Off Club.

The Tip-Off Club was an initiative of Norm Sloan when he took over the Gator program in 1960. The club was organized to promote interest in Florida basketball and met on a regular basis during the season to bolster the team. Jim Lowry was the club's first president, and men like Tom Dobson, Selig Goldin, Var Heyl, Alan Lederman, Steve Rappenecker, Rabbit Robbins, Herb Smith, and Joe Wittmer, to name a few, contributed greatly to the extra effort to promote the basketball program in the late sixties and early seventies.

The group provided funds for the annual awards banquet and presented gifts to seniors. They also rewarded the coaches with gifts for a job well done. The club took initiative to influence everything from the sale of season tickets to the actual re-engineering of a section of new chairback seats in Florida Gym. Ben and Grace Franklin were Florida basketball's first official season ticketholders in 1961, and by the late sixties Florida had almost 600 season ticketholders. Tip-Off Club members extended hospitality to players which gave them a chance to have homes away from home by knowing local families. By 1970, the club's membership had grown to more than 200.

Not surprisingly, with this unprecedented interest in the basketball team came serious pressure on Bartlett's staff from members of this group to recruit better players. Sloan had left Bartlett with a cupboard full of solid players. But Bartlett and company hadn't been able to expand by adding new players with the same potential. The staff was trying to make lemonade out of some recruiting lemons.

Some felt Florida's great outdoors seduced both Bartlett and Davis out onto the tennis courts and golf courses rather than the recruiting trails. Bartlett was one of the top amateur tennis players in the nation, and Davis had a low single-digit handicap with a golf stick. It would have been difficult for anyone to exchange pretty spring days in Florida for a plane ride to the chilly, rainy East and Midwest. Whatever the cause, after achieving unprecedented success with an inventory of great talent, these coaches had failed to restock the shelves.

As the two full-time staff people, Bartlett and Davis were trying to wear a number of hats and needed another full-time assistant. Graves found the money, and Bartlett called in Billy Henry.

Henry was coached by Bartlett in high school and was a small college All-American at Carson-Newman College. Henry was a ball of fire. He was named the Young Man of the Year by the city of Jackson, Tennessee, where he had a fine record as a first-year coach for Union University. His dynamic, energetic personality provided a stark contrast to the laid-back profiles of Bartlett and Davis. It also caused others to more closely measure the personality differences among the staff and question their effectiveness in selling the program.

More than ever, Florida basketball would have to be sold. The program had lost the momentum which Sloan had created in the early sixties, especially within the state of Florida. Many of Florida's best high school players were leaving the state and going to schools that had a stronger basketball reputation. Part of the problem was that college basketball in Florida received little media coverage. It was natural for the best high school players to picture themselves playing for schools that received national attention.

Another recruiting challenge was the lack of good summer jobs for the players. The city of Gainesville just didn't have the kind of business base to provide athletes with attractive summer employment. A summer job was a permissible perk within the guidelines of the NCAA. The caveat was that the job should pay a salary commensurate with a similar job for any non-athlete. The summer jobs Florida players might look forward to would be washing cars, cutting lawns, or doing odd assignments for basketball supporters. In cities like Houston, Los Angeles, Pittsburgh, and Minneapolis, there were good summer jobs paying young people $12-$15 an hour. In Gainesville, players were lucky to make minimum wage at a fast-food franchise.

It was also a time when southern schools were only beginning to integrate. It was the late sixties, and a black athlete was offered little to do socially on the largely segregated Florida campus. Many of the state's outstanding black players glanced at Florida and went elsewhere. Tommy Curtis had a good visit, but went to UCLA. Otis Birdsong took a look and then signed with Houston. Eddie Johnson grew up 18 miles south of Gainesville, but went to Auburn. His brother Frank went to Wake Forest and Howard Porter signed with Villanova. All eventually had NBA careers.

For players from the Midwest and the Northeast, a recruiting trip to the Florida campus became a Disney World experience. The coaching staff decided to capitalize on the tropical paradise appeal to overcome the negative perception of the university's program with in-state players.

From November through April, prospects would fly out of cold, gray skies and land in warm, sunny Gainesville. They would leave bare trees and a snow-covered landscape to find flowers blooming, birds singing, and warm water for swimming. Recruiting visits might include a trip to Silver Springs or a picnic at Lake Wauburg.

Bartlett would provide his boat and prospects could water ski and get to know players and program supporters. A college football or baseball game was always on the agenda. The coaches knew that just riding around campus and seeing college coeds in shorts gave the impression of a beach party.

It was hard for northern recruits not to have a good time on a weekend in Gainesville, but nonetheless the Florida staff was finishing second in the recruiting battles for out-of-state players. Many gave strong indications that they wanted to come to Florida but ultimately chose to go elsewhere.

Dick Divenzio from Pittsburgh took his shirt off and got a Florida suntan at a Gator homecoming football game but then went back to the "Steel City" and signed with Duke. Kent Benson and Mike Flynn loved the coaching staff and the Florida players but chose tradition-rich Indiana and Kentucky for their playing careers. It was a very frustrating situation for the Florida coaches.

With the departure of Andy Owens, Florida basketball needed a new hot-shot and where better to find one than in the Hoosier state, where the ability to shoot a basketball is a birthright.

The next three seasons can be summed up in two words: Tony Miller. Florida basketball has never known a more devout disciple of the roundball religion. Miller was wrapped up in the game of basketball. He was a freshman in 1969 and quickly earned the respect of those teammates who likewise lived to play the game.

Miller joined two other northern disciples on his freshman team – Mark Thompson from Mt. Pleasant, Ohio, and Tim Fletcher from Evansville, Indiana. These three, along with Jerry Hoover, a sophomore from Benton, Illinois, and Gary Waddell from Lexington, Kentucky, established the team's basketball mentality.

These northern players found a much different basketball environment at Florida than they expected. Their other teammates were not accustomed to working hard in the off-season and rarely invested quality time in the gym. Miller, Fletcher, and Thompson played hundreds of one-on-one games at all hours of the day and night. They ate, slept, and dreamt about basketball.

With Keller, Owens, and Walk, Florida basketball had generated its scoring punch on the inside. During the next three years, Gator basketball rested its fortunes on the perimeter jumper of 6-foot-1 Tony Miller. Miller's trademark was his jump shot. Like Andrew Moten in the eighties, Miller could load it up and let it go from University Avenue. If there had been a three-point line in the early seventies, or if freshmen had been able to compete as four-year players, Miller likely would hold every single Florida scoring record to this day.

Miller holds the all-time single-game scoring mark of 54 points, achieved in Florida's final home game against Chicago State on February 29, 1972. With a 9-13 record, only 2,278 fans showed up for a game against such a lightly regarded opponent. Little did they realize it would be a Florida basketball night to remember.

TOMMY BARTLETT: 1967-1973

Miller had 28 in the first half, and the team scored 67 points, the most points ever scored by a Florida team in a half to this day.

With 10 minutes left to play in the game, Miller had already broken Dick Tomlinson's 44-point record. After scoring his 19th field goal of the night to make it 45 points, Miller went to the bench to a standing ovation. There were still five minutes left to play, and Bartlett was told Tony was only seven points away from Pete Maravich's 52-point Florida Gym record. Bartlett later said, "I remember when Pete set that record and our fans cheered for him. I'd rather see one of our own players' names in the record book than one of theirs."

Fans chanted, "We want Miller! We want Miller!" With three minutes and seven seconds to play, Bartlett sent Miller back in. Tony was almost immediately fouled and hit a free throw. Then Jerry Hoover had an easy breakaway basket and unselfishly handed the ball to Miller for two more. Hoover later joked that he was trying for a new assist record.

At the 1:50 mark, Tony got point number 50. With 56 seconds to play, he was fouled and made both free throws to tie Maravich's 52-point record. With time running out, Florida twice turned the ball over trying to get it to Miller. Just as it looked like Miller would have to settle for the tie, Chicago State fouled with nine seconds left to play. Miller stepped to the line with two chances to break the record. *He missed both free throws!*

But Dan Boe got the rebound and pitched it back to Tony who again got hammered with four seconds to play. This time he converted both charity chances for his 53rd and 54th points, and Florida won 120-69. Tony admitted, "I was lucky to get another chance."

The record is even more remarkable because it was set without the three-point line, and almost all of Miller's shots were made outside the 19-foot arc. Only Pete Maravich's 50 and 52 on separate occasions and Chris Jackson's 53, with the benefit of the three-point field goal in 1990, have come close to Miller's record.

Despite the emotion of that spectacular night, the coaching staff was failing to motivate the team's overall performance. The staff resorted to asking a Florida football coach to light a fire under the basketball program. Gene Ellenson, the Norman Vincent Peale of Florida athletics, took off his helmet and tried to rescue the Gator cause.

Ellenson genuinely enjoyed being around Bartlett's staff. He tried to find a hot button to give the Gator players a lift. Ellenson coined a concept he called "positive molecules." Ellenson believed you could influence the outcome of an event by how you thought and felt about the result you were seeking. He would give emotional talks to the players in which he would implore them to believe in each other.

"In every situation you can convey a positive or a negative message to your teammates," he told them. "There are millions of molecules out there in the air colliding with each other. If you are sending positive thoughts about the outcome of the event, then a chain reaction of the 'thought molecules' will give you the result you desire."

Week after week, Ellenson stoked the players with positive comments. He became a fixture on the Gator bench at home games, staring at the basket when the Gators were shooting free throws, sending positive molecules. When the opponents were shooting their free throws, he would stare at their basket, propelling all the negative molecules he could muster.

Tony Miller particularly liked Ellenson's inspirational talks. But as a football coach, Ellenson didn't know much about basketball. Once he asked Miller, "What position do you play?" Miller said he was a guard. Ellenson replied, "Christ sakes, Miller, you're awful small to be a guard." Tony fired back, "But Coach, I'm meaner than hell."

Ellenson fed off Miller's enthusiasm for the sport and inspired more converts in some of the other players. One night during the '71 season and in the middle of a long losing streak, Florida played at Georgia. Ellenson challenged the team to sign a pledge that said simply "No-No-Bulldogs." Everyone signed it.

Late in the second half, with Georgia leading and Ronnie Hogue filling it up for Georgia from the outside, Bartlett called a time out. In the huddle Ellenson pulled Miller aside and said, "Listen, Tony, the next time Hogue gets ready to shoot, put your hands down to your sides and just stare at him."

When Hogue got the ball, Miller backed off and dropped his hands. Hogue hesitated and then passed off. The next time Hogue got the ball Miller did it again. Unnerved, Hogue asked, "What are you doing, man?" Miller replied, "I'm throwing molecules at you." Hogue stared back and then fired and missed. Then he missed again. On the next possession, he missed yet again.

As Miller described it, Hogue totally freaked out. The Gators went on to win 88-79, one of only four SEC road wins that Florida would record in the four seasons from 1970 to 1973.

The Florida coaches had strong evidence that they were losing their best recruits to financial incentive packages that went beyond what the NCAA permitted. As Bartlett became more and more frustrated, he permitted some avid supporters to influence the recruiting process with a more direct monetary involvement. A group of 12 individuals put some fairly substantial money into a pot and told the coaches to get Florida a college basketball superstar.

The star recruit they got was Troy Walker, a 6-foot-5, 210-pound junior college transfer who grew up in Zanesville, Ohio. Walker was touted as one of the most outstanding junior college players in the nation. To get Walker all the way to Gainesville, the Florida slush fund was manipulated with some "creative banking." Walker was married, so the fund financed an automobile, arranged for an apartment, and bought furniture, including a television set. They found a job for Walker's wife and allowed Walker a monthly stipend.

When the prized recruit arrived in Gainesville, those close to the program were anxious to see him play. Ronnie Neder, one of the Gators' most avid basketball supporters, went into the gym with Walker and some other Gator players. Neder was stunned to see that Walker was extremely ineffective in competing with the group. As the weeks went by, it became obvious that Florida's new recruit would never be invited to commit to the program.

The players nicknamed him "Herman Helicopter" because he was one of the few 6-foot-5 guys who couldn't dunk. One night before the season even began, the Walkers loaded up a U-Haul with everything they had been given and drove off in their new car, never to be seen again.

The late Selig Goldin, a local attorney, had an avid interest in the Florida basketball program. Goldin helped structure some of those special financial arrangements that helped players a little outside the guidelines. Goldin was the Tip-Off Club captain and genuinely wanted to help. Except for the Walker incident, the level of a financial supporter's involvement might be an extra $20 for a date, a "used" pair of shoes or sportcoat, etc. Sometimes a booster would pay more than face value for a player's tickets (although, for the players, just getting someone to buy their tickets was a bonus).

In 1973 freshmen were eligible again for the first time in 20 years, and Florida desperately needed an impact player. The staff was trying to recruit Bill Moody, a high school star from Greensboro, Florida. They felt he could be favorably persuaded if he had a car to drive to his high school senior prom. Goldin had a brand new Lincoln Continental. He drove it to Moody's house on a dirt road outside the Panhandle town.

The home was very humble. Goldin could see through the living room floor to the ground below. He gave Moody the keys and a little money. He told him to have a good time and to call the next day when the prom activities were over. Two days later, Moody finally called Goldin and said, "Mr. Selig, thanks for letting me use your car. But I had a little problem. You see, I'm not good yet at driving cars and on the way down the road I ran through a fence and the car is stuck out in this field."

The good news was Moody signed with Florida. He averaged seven points a game his freshman year, despite (as he described it) "a sprung-out ankle." The bad news was his ability to perform in the classroom was worse than his ability to drive a car. Moody lasted only one year.

Taking a Final Shot

The late sixties and early seventies were the Vietnam War era. On campus, long hair, protests, and "streaking" were the signs of the times. On more than one occasion, a nude male would streak through Florida Gym to screams of delight from the fans. In general, excitement and emotion in the gym continued to provide a home-court advantage.

As popular as Florida Gym was with fans and streakers alike, the building was becoming a handicap to Bartlett's program. The gym was worn out. Some of Florida's recruits were playing in high school gyms that were better than what Florida was trying to sell its college program with.

In 1969 expectations ran high that the Gators might build a new activities center. The dream was crushed, though, when students voted down using the student activity money for a new building. It was a time when the mood of young people was anti-war and anti-establishment. Politics, not sports, had their attention. A coliseum was an artifact of a culture which they rejected, so the proposal bit the dust.

Every other SEC school was constructing or had constructed a modern arena, but Florida couldn't get money for it from the legislature. The students' vote was needed to make it happen. The competition used this as a recruiting trump card to convince potential prospects that Florida just was not serious about college basketball.

As the second assistant, Billy Henry spent a lot of time on the recruiting trails and worked overtime to find a positive spin to sell Gator hoops. Driving from Ft. Lauderdale to Naples late one night on a recruiting mission, he tried to think of ideas to counteract the negative image of Florida's outdated gym. He thought about the raucous crowds and some of the notorious fights. He knew opponents feared playing in the cramped facility. He remembered how dark the building seemed in contrast to more modern arenas.

Driving along dark, narrow Highway 84 through the Florida Everglades, he noticed the sign that said "Florida's Alligator Alley." Henry thought to himself, "No one wants to pick a fight with the Gators in the Alley! Alligator Alley!" Thus Billy Henry coined the term used to described the old gym until it was finally replaced by the O'Connell Center in 1980.

There were several players who distinguished themselves in this era despite the failure of their teams to achieve any notable success. Jerry Hoover and Gary Waddell came to Florida as freshmen, and both earned University of Florida diplomas.

Hoover was a 5-foot-11 point guard who was among Bartlett's first recruits in 1967. Hoover turned down schools like Davidson, St. Louis, and Western Kentucky. He loved the university from the moment he arrived on his recruiting visit and quickly rejected other offers.

During his career, he averaged 10.5 points and led the team in assists all three seasons. His 307 total assists rank fourth all-time and his 16 assists against Alabama in 1971 are the most ever in a Florida game. Hoover's most memorable game came during his senior year (1972) when Florida played fifth-ranked Kentucky. With a packed Alligator Alley and a regional television audience, Hoover scored the game-winning basket. With nine seconds left, he took an in-bounds pass and worked loose off a high-post screen to score a layup for Florida's 72-70 upset of the Wildcats.

Hoover started every game from 1970 to 1972 and ran Florida's disciplined half-court attack. His ability to break down opposing defenses permitted him to get the ball to a wide-open Tony Miller for uncontested shots. Hoover always guarded the opponent's best perimeter player and often sacrificed his own scoring opportunities to give teammates the ball for easier baskets. After earning his juris doctorate from UF's law school, Hoover went to Houston to practice law.

Gary Waddell was a 6-foot-10 first-team all-state player who grew up in Lexington, Kentucky. He was coached for two years in high school by the son of the Baron himself, Adolph Rupp, Jr. His family had vacationed often in Florida, and the Gator program had made a good impression on him early in his high school career. Waddell turned down a number of SEC schools, including the Wildcats, to be a Gator.

Waddell led a 15-8 freshman team, scoring 21 points a game, and had a fine sophomore year with a 10 point per game average. Unfortunately, he developed a dislocated lumbar vertebra, an almost identical injury to the one that hampered Boyd Welsch a few years earlier. The injury required complete inactivity, and Waddell ballooned to 250 pounds. This severely affected his mobility in his final two seasons of play. Waddell never became the dominating center who could carry the torch that Walk and Owens left behind.

As Bartlett's staff failed to adequately attract quality four-year players to the campus, they began meeting their immediate needs with transfers. Two of the more outstanding transfer students were Tom Purvis and Earl Findley.

Purvis, an Ocala native, transferred from Jacksonville University, and Findley transferred from West Palm Beach Community College. Purvis was extremely athletic but became a difficult Gator teammate whose attitude never quite got adjusted. Late in his senior season, Purvis twice had career-high nights of 27 points. But they came too late to impact Florida's overall success.

Findley had the tools to be a great major college player, but two years was not enough time to perfect his skills. His career high was 34 against Ole Miss in 1970 which caused fans to fantasize about his potential. At 6-foot-7, he had deceptive quickness and phenomenal leaping ability.

Unfortunately for him and the Florida fans, Findley played during a period when dunking was illegal in NCAA games. One night in Morgantown, West Virginia, during the 1970 season, Findley scored 26 points and was called for goaltending twice in a double-overtime loss to the Mountaineers. The game clock had mysteriously malfunctioned, and the time was being monitored by an official who would use a starter's gun to signal the end of the game.

The basket interference calls had given the Mountaineers a chance to take the lead. As the teams traded baskets in the closing seconds of the one-point contest, the official holding the gun was seated at the end of the scorers' table next to the Florida bench.

As the seconds wound down, the gun-toting timekeeper began to raise the pistol, moving his arm in the direction of the action on the floor. The entire Florida bench was on its feet. Standing directly next to the moving pistol was Assistant Coach Dick Davis.

Davis' full attention was directed to the action on the floor. When the clock ran out and the timekeeper fired the gun, it went off directly next to Davis' ear. The Florida coach thought he had been shot in the head and grabbed his ear screaming loudly as the game ended in Florida's dramatic 88-87 loss. No one else had any idea what had happened. It took several minutes for Davis to gain his composure and for others to realize that Davis' anxiety was coming from something other than the Florida defeat.

This episode developed into one of those memorable insider stories for the Florida players of that era. The team delighted in watching the action on film over and over again, running the projector in reverse and then back again over the final few seconds to watch Davis grimace in stunned surprise. Each time the film showed the timekeeper's arm moving to a point directly below Davis' ear, someone would stop the projector and run it back again before finally letting it roll to the end.

As SEC schools began to integrate in the late sixties, Florida's first black athletes began arriving on campus. Bartlett had been engaged in a bitter recruiting war with Florida State University to attract Rodney McCray, a promising 6-foot-11 black player from Pensacola Washington High School. McCray was regarded as one of the best big men in the country, and Bartlett's staff spent untold hours driving between Gainesville and Pensacola to persuade McCray to become a Gator.

One of McCray's high school teammates was a 6-foot-1 senior, Steve Williams. Every time the coaching staff visited McCray, Williams would show up at the meeting. Williams would appear wearing an orange and blue tie or shirt, clearly demonstrating he wanted to be a Florida Gator. Bartlett offered a package deal, hoping it would be the key to a positive decision from McCray. But McCray signed with Florida State for what some believed to be those "extra incentives." Steve Williams, true to the orange and blue, still wanted to be a Gator.

TOMMY BARTLETT: 1967-1973

On March 4, 1970, Steve Williams, a member of the 1970 Class AA state basketball championship team at Pensacola Washington High School, became the first black athlete to receive a basketball scholarship to Florida. Williams was later joined by Malcolm Meeks, a black 6-foot-3 forward from Daytona Beach.

Steve Williams opened the door for an integrated program at Florida, and few others could have performed this feat with more class or dignity. Williams faced life in the proverbial goldfish bowl. Society's prejudices created profound challenges for him. Many Florida high school players had never had a black teammate, and some held deep resentment toward Williams because of his race. He suffered the indignity of rooming by himself at times because the process of integrating athletes was handled awkwardly by those in charge.

Players who had come to Florida from up north comfortably embraced Steve as a personable teammate, but they also recognized his traumatic struggle for acceptance. Williams earned the utmost respect of everyone associated with this transition in Florida's athletic history. His integrity as a young man provided a model which inspired other outstanding black athletes in this time period to choose the Florida program.

Williams' historic place in the program's archives came three years after Perry Wallace had broken the conference color barrier as a freshman at Vanderbilt. Wallace played the 1968-70 seasons to pioneer the sport for black athletes in SEC arenas.

With the recruiting loss of Rodney McCray, Bartlett was in desperate need of a big man. He found Florida's first 7-footer in Ft. Wayne, Indiana. Doug Brown came to Florida as a 170-pound project. He needed time to develop his potential. Sadly, his knees caved in during his sophomore year, and he never again wore a Gator uniform.

In 1972 Bartlett's staff found Chip Williams, a 6-foot-8, 220-pound center from Dunedin, Florida. Billy Henry convinced a skeptical Bartlett that this big kid could play. "He has a great attitude, is as tough as nails and loves the Gators," Henry said. "What more can you ask?"

Williams' sophomore season (1973) was Bartlett's final year as head coach. The curly-haired school boy from Central Florida had the best first year of any previous Florida center. He scored 30 points in his first varsity game, a 100-76 thrashing of Valdosta State, and he had a season-high 31 in an 81-78 loss to Georgia. Williams finished the year with a 16.5 scoring average and 12 rebounds a game. It wasn't enough to save Bartlett's job, however, as the Gators finished seventh in the SEC with an 11-15 mark.

Perhaps the highlight of this year was Florida's first SEC basketball championship. Florida won an SEC basketball junior-varsity championship in 1973. Since freshmen were now eligible to play for four years, there was a transition year for the players on SEC rosters. Don Close and Curt Shellabarger led the JV team to a

9-2 season, the best record among the 10 SEC schools. They beat Tennessee's JV 70-65 to clinch the mythical title.

There were a number of noteworthy accomplishments during Bartlett's seven seasons. Florida beat Kentucky and Tennessee in the same season three times (1968, 1969, 1971), a feat they had achieved only once previously (1965). They recorded upsets of ranked opponents like the 70-69 win over eventual 1972 Final Four participant Louisville. In Alligator Alley, they won 60 of 79 battles – 76 percent.

On the road, however, Bartlett's teams won only 35 of 101 games – 35 percent – and could only manage five wins in the final 39 SEC road contests. Beginning in the 1970 season, Florida won only 41 of Bartlett's final 103 games and only 25 of 72 SEC games. The Gators finished in the cellar of the conference in 1972 for the first time since 1959, the year before Norm Sloan's arrival. After an 11-15 season in 1973, the fourth consecutive losing season, the epitaph was written for Bartlett's UF career gravestone.

Tommy Bartlett, Dick Davis, and Billy Henry were three of the finest men ever to coach basketball at the University of Florida, but they never had the recruiting ability to sustain the momentum from those early years. They made a genuine effort, and the program enjoyed immense success with the inherited talent. The record shows, however, they just couldn't sustain the program at the next level.

Apathy in the media, a second-class playing facility, changing demographics in the basketball culture of southern schools – all these contributed to the coaching staff's failure to capitalize on their early success. They were never able to sustain the momentum that was created by the three best back-to-back seasons in Florida basketball history.

The natives were once again restless because the basketball program had fallen to an all-time low. Bartlett realized the end had arrived, held a press conference, and said, "Nobody asked me to resign." However, he added, "It looked like we were turning the corner and getting back to winning, but when we turned the corner, somehow I fell off." Florida's President Stephen C. O'Connell ordered athletic director Ray Graves to once again begin the process of searching for a new coach.

John Lotz

Basketball Blue Bloodlines
1974-1980

Lotz SEC's Top Coach

BY ANDY COHEN
Times-Union Sports Writer

Florida Hires Lotz, Of North Carolina

Over Vandy
'Biggest Upset'

sports

Gene Shy no hero; 'It's a team thing'

Alligator Alley: The No Way Can Ran...

At Florida

'Own Identity'
'Heckuva Finish—Lotz

Gators Gun Down Kentucky

Angles for Points

Gators cr... PC, 79-6... in titl...

Lotz Fired as UF Basketball Coach

The Carolina Connection

He was one of four children, all boys. The sons of a preacher man. If you knew the preacher, you would have had a good idea about the makeup of the sons.

The preacher had big hands. He could have been on the receiving end of a hot sheet of steel as it rolled off a conveyor belt in a Pittsburgh mill. Strong hands – the kind you want to feel when a loved one dies or when you need a friend's compassion.

At 6-foot-5, 250 pounds, he was a large man with strong facial features, penetrating and caring eyes, and a deep voice. When he spoke, it got your attention. With his New York City accent, he would ask people in a playful way, "What's da secret of yer success?" His was a genuine faith in a loving God. In a Bronx Baptist church every Sunday morning, his sermons spoke the language of a common man.

It wasn't surprising that his four boys would be tall. And there was never a doubt the four brothers would be dependable – no one would ever have reason to question their character. One of the brothers became a senior executive with Dow Chemical. Another earned a doctorate of divinity from Harvard and is one of the world's most respected theologians. The youngest played college basketball and in 1957 in three overtimes helped the North Carolina Tar Heels defeat Kansas and Wilt Chamberlain to win a national championship. He became a dentist and married the daughter of evangelist Billy Graham.

The tallest one had his dad's name, and at 10 years of age, he blew a trumpet on a New York City street corner for the Salvation Army at Christmas. He was the one who always wanted to coach. His life was anchored in his faith, and his passion was to help young people. As an assistant to Dean Smith at the University of North Carolina, he observed a philosophy of coaching that produced success in the context of those high ideals.

The UNC assistant coach's only notable vice was an affinity for clothes, and his closet resembled the men's fashion section of Bloomingdale's. Bob McAdoo, the former North Carolina All-American and All-NBA star, put it succinctly: "Coach, you outrag them all."

On March 15, 1973, UF President Stephen C. O'Connell named John Calvin Lotz the 13th head coach in the school's basketball history. After four consecutive losing seasons, Dr. O'Connell had seen enough. He had asked some people close to the program to help him find a new direction for the basketball team. All roads led to Chapel Hill.

There were many similarities between the University of North Carolina and the University of Florida – both provided outstanding academic environments; both were rooted in strong alumni support; both reflected their individual state's commitment to academic excellence; both offered highly competitive intercollegiate athletics; and both held immense respect for the other.

There was, however, one big difference. The Tar Heel wore short pants and bounced a ball. The Gator wore a helmet and kicked the stuffing out of one. Florida basketball fans saw Lotz as the medicine to cure a floundering program. A transfusion of Carolina Blue bloodlines was injected into the Florida program. Unfortunately, like oil and water, the University of Florida and John Lotz didn't mix in the end.

The search for Bartlett's successor had produced some well-known finalists including Bill Musselman of Minnesota and Frank Mulzoff of St. Johns. But Lotz was one of the most prominent assistant coaches in America. He had turned down jobs at Cincinnati, Georgia Tech, and VPI while patiently helping Dean Smith build the Tar Heel program.

Dan Murr, a sportswriter for the *Gainesville Sun*, wrote in the spring of 1973, "If you're asking yourself, 'Is John Lotz for real,' he is. And when you get to know him, you'll probably get excited, too."

For some, Lotz was not easy to get to know. His manner was forthright, but his convictions were intimidating. After all, this Yankee was in the deep South where people didn't often say what they meant. Southern hospitality was an art form of demonstrating interest but remaining politely skeptical. With Lotz there were no hidden agendas. The man told you exactly what he thought. He didn't know how to do otherwise.

Gainesville was a radical change in the life of Florida's new coach. At 38 years of age, he brought to campus the image of one of America's premier basketball programs. He also brought a new bride. A bachelor for longer than usual, Lotz married Vicki Joyner, 10 years his junior, shortly before coming to Gainesville. In an interview with John Quincey of the *New York Herald Tribune*, Lotz said, "We're almost as excited over our new house as we would be if we had signed a seven-footer."

Florida's new staff would have a North Carolina flavor. Dick Grubar, one of the most popular players ever to play at North Carolina, was a great competitor and came to Gainesville after one year as the coaching assistant at Virginia Commonwealth University. Terry Truax, a Converse shoe representative who was a longtime friend of Lotz, also wanted to get back into coaching. Truax had been an assistant to Morgan Wooten at famed DeMatha High School in Washington, D.C. and later was a graduate assistant for Dean Smith at North Carolina. Grubar and Truax balanced Lotz' personality and, most importantly, were loyal and trusted individuals.

John Lotz never met a detail that he liked. His management style was to build relationships and trust people to do the right thing. He didn't believe in instituting a lot of rules. Instead, he focused on developing character. Lotz was a self-motivated individual who shared inspirational stories with his players while reading their responses. He was a disciplinarian, and the program once again reverted to principles that would breed success.

Sitting beside Dean Smith for seven years, Lotz had been schooled by a master of coaching strategy. He was eager to communicate the x's and o's and make basketball an enjoyable experience. Florida's returning players were hungry for leadership. They were energized by the new staff, and they responded like pieces of clay in the hands of a sculptor.

First and foremost came conditioning. North Carolina's program prided itself on conditioning, and Lotz and his staff knew how to get a team in shape. To Lotz' surprise, Florida teams had never run a suicide – a drill run inside the lines on a basketball court. Players line up on one endline and run to the nearest free-throw line which acts as an imaginary line across the court. Then, it's back to the starting baseline and then to half court. Next, it's back again to the baseline and then to the extended free-throw line at the other end of the court. Players then run again to the baseline, and finally all the way to the other endline on the far end of the court and back again to the starting baseline.

In a Lotz suicide, there were three rules. First, the player's foot had to touch each line or imaginary line before he turned to go the other way. Second, he had to accomplish this within a predetermined time, say 30 seconds. Third, everyone who was running had to finish within the designated time.

Suicides definitely got the players' attention. If the team was not particularly focused in practice, Lotz would blow the whistle, and everyone would run a suicide. Most of the time the suicides came at the end of practice when players were most tired and just the thought of additional running was like, well, committing suicide.

The players quickly got the message. They were learning what it meant to take basketball seriously again. "My whole game went downhill my first three years as a Gator," fourth-year player Steve Williams said. " In the past we'd play games in the locker room and at times wouldn't take a serious attitude toward the game. You can compare my first three years with this year's first week of practice. Coach Lotz is so organized it's unbelievable."

Players also discovered that this coaching staff would emphasize objectives that challenged each player to take responsibility for the team. In prior years, little consistency was shown in dealing with team issues. Under Sloan and Bartlett, players were disciplined at the extremes. At one end of the spectrum, Sloan was heavy handed without rhyme or reason. On the other end, Bartlett chose not to know if a player's conduct was inappropriate.

In the Lotz program, if a player strayed outside team guidelines, the entire team

JOHN LOTZ: 1974-1980

paid the price. The coaching staff wanted the players to know that when one of them let down, everyone suffered. They wanted every player to take ownership for the best interest of them all.

For example, if the coaches were instructing the players on the court and a player on the sidelines wasn't paying attention, Lotz would blow his whistle and ask the guilty player to stand there and watch his teammates run a suicide. That kind of situation would not likely occur more than once.

For the returning players, Don Close, Tim Fletcher, Mike Lederman, Gene Shy, Mark Thompson, Chip Williams, and Steve Williams, this was a basketball dream come true. They had wanted to be part of a program that would emphasize ideals that inspired excellence. These were players with character. They would have tried to run through a brick wall for this staff.

Most of these players came to Florida with basketball roots in tradition-rich midwestern states. They were frustrated that the basketball program had slipped in recent years, and they were eager for a new direction. Seven years earlier, the players were proud to be Gators but wanted out from under Sloan's Gestapo leadership. Then the situation was reversed. The team liked Bartlett and his staff, but they just didn't have a fundamental respect for the lack of discipline in the program, and they felt little team pride.

Of course, optimism is likely to be the case with any change in coaching staffs. The new coach will bring in a new approach, and the players become energized with renewed interest. The Florida players couldn't get enough of the refreshing mentality of this new staff.

The 1973-74 season began with a stunning 81-69 upset of a South Florida team which came into Florida Gym favored by 18 points. This was a good Bulls team, but no opponent should be favored by 18 on Florida's home court.

Whereas Bartlett's teams ran set plays and worked out of a half-court offense, the new Florida team ran and ran and ran and ran. Players dove for loose balls and took charges. They boxed out their men and rebounded with a vengeance. They fought through screens and played tenacious man-to-man defense. They showed the fans they were serious about playing together.

Players pointed fingers at teammates to say thanks for the assist. When a player took a charge making a great defensive play, the other four guys rushed over to help him up. When a player came out of the game, the whole bench stood up to greet him. It was all for one and one for all.

Chip Williams could hold his own in the middle, but more importantly, he could run the floor. Two of Florida's other big men, Doug Brown and Gary Waddell, were dealing with injuries, so Williams had played a lot of minutes his sophomore season. His lifelong dream was to play for the Gators, and his passionate wish had come true. The 6-foot-8, 225-pound junior would play in a system where teamwork and hard work were synonymous. Chip Williams was a blue-collar type competitor who was well suited to both.

The Gators ran a lot of motion offense, which meant they had to be able to get up and down the court. In the offense they were never stationary. As a center, Williams could be down low, at the top of the key, or in the corner, all in one offensive possession. He led the team in scoring and rebounding and was named first-team All-SEC. For the fifth time in the previous eight years, Florida had a first-team All-SEC selection.

The cohesiveness of this team was testimony to the leadership of the three seniors. Steve Williams, the first black athlete at the University of Florida, had experienced challenges for which there was no play book. He had struggled through his junior year, making only 32 field goal attempts in 24 games for a 3.2 point per game average. He just never found his niche in roles that would permit him to capitalize on his potential.

Steve could, however, play basketball. Tony Miller once said, "No one ever defended me better." He could also score. But once again, he was most effective in an open-court style of game. Most of all, Williams would respond to motivation. Lotz and his staff touched all the right buttons. Along with seniors Mark Thompson and Tim Fletcher, Williams was a tri-captain as the coaching staff challenged him to accept responsibility for the season.

Steve Williams never did less than what was asked of him. He worked hard every day and dedicated himself to the team's objectives. His career-high 19 points and 10 rebounds in a 92-81 win at Auburn highlighted one of Florida's best-ever road wins against the War Eagles. His 249 career assists rank him high among the all-time Florida players.

As Williams came out of his shell and began to capitalize on his ability, he found support from his senior running mates, Tim Fletcher and Mark Thompson. No two athletes have ever given more of themselves every single day in Florida basketball uniforms. Fletcher and Thompson had come to Florida with those inbred midwestern basketball values. Neither had been highly recruited, but both were major college material. Both had benefited from redshirt sophomore seasons, and as fifth-year seniors they had the maturity to be exceptional leaders. This was their final season, and they put everything into it they could muster.

When the coaching staff asked the team to run three miles, Fletcher and Thompson ran six. When they told the team to run suicides, Fletcher and Thompson did double suicides. The two compatriots were the first players to arrive and the last to leave the practice floor.

This type of leadership set the tone and gave the program its standards. By the end of the season, others had emerged who would carry the team to some great moments. But this team owed its success to the character of its senior leadership.

One of Lotz' first recruits was Bruno Caldwell from New Jersey who quickly demonstrated that he was a fine prospect. Caldwell turned down Notre Dame and Southern Cal to come to Gainesville and scored in double figures in 16 games his first season. He led the team in assists with an average of four per game. In the last four

JOHN LOTZ: 1974-1980

games of the year, his play was spectacular as the Gators beat fifth-ranked Alabama and fourth-ranked Vanderbilt, along with Kentucky and Ole Miss.

The Kentucky win was in Memorial Coliseum – only the second time Florida had won in Lexington. The Gators could have beaten just about anyone that night. Florida broke the Coliseum record set by Notre Dame in 1939 for free throws made in a game. The Irish had made 23 of 24, and Florida made 25 of 26. To this day, that record stands as the best free-throw team percentage (96) in a Wildcat game.

This 1973-74 team posted a 15-11 mark, reversing those same numbers from the previous year. After Florida beat Jacksonville in the Gator Bowl Tournament, the *Gainesville Sun*'s Jack Hairston said, "I've been watching Florida basketball teams for seventeen years and this is the most courageous win I've seen a Gator team collect." It was a team with heart and pride and, yes, it was a team with courage. The fans were coming back. Once again, hope had emerged that Florida could have a nationally competitive program.

Having Fun Again

This staff knew that the process of running a major college basketball program required a 12-month commitment. Whereas Bartlett and Davis were drawn off the court and into the outdoors during the spring and summer, these new coaches were focused year-round on basketball activities which would improve things the next year. Theirs was a pure-bred basketball mentality which had a single-minded mission. Basketball was their game, and recruiting was their middle name.

At North Carolina, Lotz had been the designated recruiter and helped Carolina land All-Americans Bill Chamberlain, Walter Davis, George Karl, Mitch Kupchak, and Robert McAdoo, among others. Although Lotz had a personal knack for appealing to the egos of promising high school athletes, the UF program lacked prominence in the eyes of Florida high school prospects.

The Bartlett years documented the frustration of losing the state's talented players to out-of-state recruiters. It was now becoming very apparent that widespread financial incentives outside the guidelines spelled out by the NCAA were influencing young athletes' decisions.

Tates Locke, the former Jacksonville University coach, in his book *Caught In The Net* described the extremes to which a coaching staff would go to sign a talented player during this time period. The Florida program neither seriously competed "outside the lines," nor had the resources to be competitive if it had been so inclined. Sportswriter Dan Murr also wrote, "If there is one item in the success story of John Lotz as a highly qualified successful recruiter at the University of North Carolina and now as the coach at Florida, it's honesty."

One of Lotz' early disappointments came when he was recruiting Mychael Thompson, a talented forward from the Bahamas who eventually had a 12-year NBA career. As Thompson was leaving the campus after his recruiting visit, he told Lotz he wanted to be a Gator. As an afterthought, Thompson said, "By the way, Coach Lotz, who handles my trips home?" Lotz told Thompson the university could only assist with travel that was related to the team's games. Thompson signed with Minnesota and told Lotz it was because he "liked the cold and the snow."

Lotz' staff absolutely would not cheat. In fact, the closest John Lotz ever came to a rules violation was in the recruiting of the state's most-heralded talent ever, Darryl

Dawkins. In 1975 Dawkins was breaking every record at Orlando Evans High School and was recognized as one of the best high school prospects in the nation. Lotz was determined to make him a Gator.

For almost three years, Lotz had worked to build a personal rapport with Dawkins. The relationship seemed to solidify through both individuals' Christian faith. Dawkins and his mother belonged to the Antioch Primitive Baptist Church of Orlando. Lotz would attend services at the church and became friends with Pastor W. D. Judge. The key to Dawkins' future, Rev. Judge convinced Lotz, was in the pastor's hands. "The Lord wants Darryl to play for a Christian coach," Rev. Judge was fond of saying.

With Darryl and his mother in regular attendance, Lotz would drive to Orlando for Wednesday night and Sunday services. Lotz believed his strong Christian faith had given him the inside track.

As the decision time was approaching, the recruiting had become intense. It appeared Kentucky, Florida State, and Florida were the leading contenders. Lotz had heard his two rivals had offered Dawkins everything from the governor's mansion in Tallahassee to the Calumet Farms in Lexington. When the Rev. Judge told Lotz the church had a need, Lotz went into action. He asked some supporters to come up with $75 to buy the church a gold-wrapped bible.

But even the Lord couldn't deliver Darryl Dawkins. Like Moses Malone, Dawkins decided to forego college, instead becoming a first-round NBA draft pick of Philadelphia. Lotz' financial incentive package graced the church sanctuary for years to come. Florida basketball lost another great in-state player who could have, might have, but never did become a Gator.

Chip Williams had a respectable senior season in 1974-75, even though his scoring average dropped to 13 points per game. More of the scoring came from the efforts of Bruno Caldwell and Gene Shy. Florida had all the competition it could handle that year because the SEC was extremely strong. Kentucky reached the national championship game before falling to UCLA, and Alabama also had a good year with a 22-5 record and a trip to the Big Dance.

Overtime wins against Vanderbilt and Mississippi State gave the Gators four consecutive SEC wins by early February. But down the stretch, with back-to-back one-point losses, the team lost five of its last six games.

The highlight of the season came in the final home game when Florida managed to beat fourth-ranked Kentucky, handing the Wildcats one of their five season losses. For the third time in two years, Florida knocked off a top 10 opponent.

Florida exploded for 16 points in a nine-minute second-half stretch during which Kentucky never scored. Mike Lederman stole an in-bounds pass and scored six points in 19 seconds to break a 54-54 tie. Gene Shy had 20 points and six rebounds in the 66-58 Gator victory. It was a thrilling moment for Florida fans to see this scrappy, hustling bunch of Gators upset another Kentucky applecart.

"We wanted this one for Coach Lotz and the seniors," Lederman said after the game. "We played our best game of the season, and it's just a super win." The baton of inspiration had been claimed by the 6-foot-1, 170-pound junior from Leo, Indiana, Mike Lederman. Lotz later said, "I have never been associated with a player who gave more of himself and capitalized on every segment of his potential as Lederman did."

Where Fletcher, Thompson, and Steve Williams set the tone the year before, Lederman and Don Bostic, a 6-foot-2 sophomore from Ballard High School in Louisville, Kentucky, would key it up a notch. The combination of "Bos" (Bostic) and "the Fireman" (Lederman) became the backbone of Florida's ballclub. No two guards had ever played with better chemistry in a partnership and with more tenacity. Their play was mirrored by Craig Brown and Dan Cross in the 1994 Final Four year.

Each player had a sixth sense for the other on the court and together they made plays that neither could accomplish alone. They double-teamed opponents and made game-winning steals. They took charges that changed a game's momentum. They set screens and helped teammates score easy baskets. But most of all, they never quit. When Winston Churchill said, "Never, never, never give up," he could have been talking about Bostic and Lederman. They loved being Gators and fought their hearts out every game to win.

Bostic made game-winning free throws twice in his career and had a career-high 16 points against Montana State. Lederman got a career-high 25 against Georgia and averaged 10.4 points a game during his three years. An injury midway through his senior season was a setback, but he finished the year with five straight double-figure nights.

Both were also strong Christian men who reflected the spiritual dimension of Lotz' life. In the summer months, they traveled abroad with a Christian-oriented basketball team, and after graduation they played for Athletes In Action. They were both highly respected by their teammates.

Gene Shy from Akron, Ohio, emerged as the team's leading scorer, averaging 16 points per game his junior and senior years. Shy was a young black athlete who had grown up in eastern Ohio and was stunned to experience the cultural prejudice in the South in 1972. He seriously considered transferring during his freshman year, but when the coaching change took place, he experienced a change of heart and fell in love with being a Gator.

Shy was a bright, sensitive, and hard-working athlete. He excelled on the offensive end of the court where his perimeter-range jumper was a trademark. Shy scored in double figures 20 times his sophomore season, had 32 points and 13 rebounds in a home win over Auburn, and scored 30 points in a road win over Kentucky. Shy was also voted the most valuable player in the Gator Bowl Tournament that year, scoring 45 points and getting 29 rebounds.

The "Quiet Man" scored double figures in 69 of 79 games his sophomore, junior, and senior years. His 28 points in the 107-104 double-overtime win in Starkville propelled Florida to one of its greatest wins ever against Mississippi State. Shy became the second all-time leading scorer to Neal Walk, falling just 27 points *shy* of Walk's 1,600-point mark.

"Four years is a long time," said Shy. "I really hate to leave Gainesville, but I'm grateful to Coach Lotz for helping me graduate this term and teaching me a lot about life as well as basketball." Today he is a successful attorney in Miami.

Despite a somewhat disappointing 12-16 record, the 1974-75 team averaged the most points per game of any Gator team – 81.8 – a record which wasn't broken until the 1987 team averaged 84.2. Chip Williams finished a stellar Gator career by being named third-team All-SEC. He was the first Florida player to receive All-SEC honors in each of his three collegiate seasons.

The other two seniors, Don Close and Joe Repass, finished their Gator careers without seeing much action because the coaching staff had begun to give younger players more of the playing time. However, both Close and Repass displayed unselfish attitudes and worked hard to help lay the groundwork for the future of the program.

The Lotz program didn't have a lot of rules, but the ones they had were never bent. Lotz believed his responsibility was to build a total person, and basketball was the venue to help him construct better men.

The departure of Bruno Caldwell was the program's first setback. Jack Hairston, the *Gainesville Sun*'s sports editor, said Caldwell's dismissal was one of the most unusual stories he had encountered, and to his knowledge, it was unique.

Lotz had told the players to pay attention to their academic progress and if they needed tutoring, the staff would arrange it. If the player demonstrated he was doing all he could, summer school would be available. But if a player failed a class without raising a red flag and asking for help, then he was on his own and took the consequences.

Caldwell never asked for help and subsequently failed eight hours. Lotz refused to bend his rules. His best player, who had led the nation in free-throw shooting and was a sensational passer, bit the academic dust.

Hairston said, "I believe the majority of coaches I have known would not have hesitated to excuse Bruno Caldwell and pay his way to summer school." He went on to say, "Lotz is not like the majority of coaches. He is a man of admirable moral fiber."

"I hate to lose him," Lotz said. "But I'm coaching fourteen men and I have to do what I think is best for fourteen men, not just one man."

Several years later, Caldwell penned a poignantly touching letter in which he thanked Lotz for making a gutsy decision and expressed deep appreciation for what Lotz had done to help him better prepare for life.

LOTZ to Overcome

Even after two years in Gainesville, the Lotz staff still sometimes felt like fish out of water at the University of Florida. Their North Carolina backgrounds gave them a jaundiced view of the football mentality which permeated this athletic program. These Florida coaches were all basketball. None of them had the slightest inclination to get excited about college football. Grubar, Truax, and Lotz had basketball bloodlines to match those of any football elitist. They quickly became frustrated with the over-zealous football people who seemed condescending.

Out of one side of the administration's mouth came the words "we want first-class basketball." Out of the other side came phrases that made basketball people realize they were considered second rate. The athletic board and the athletic administration were virtually all football people, and athletic association employees were primarily accountable to football. The rest of the sports got what attention and resources were left over.

Florida brought Rick Robey in for a recruiting visit. Robey, who later signed with Kentucky, told the coaches that he had a great weekend. He said, "Coach Lotz, Florida is terrific and I'm having a hard time choosing, but there's one thing I can't get out of my mind." "What's that?" Lotz wanted to know. "Coach, when we went into the A.D.'s office, all I saw was football stuff and mounted fish. Are you sure they play basketball at that school?"

There was little recognition ever given to the challenge that existed for Florida basketball because football was the dominant concern. Florida's fans were trying to hold basketball accountable to football's same very high standard without providing the basketball program with sufficient resources to do its job.

These coaches had a lot of class and never exhibited visible dissatisfaction. But inside, it tore away at their personal motivation to fight the system. On a national platform, both sports attracted equal attention, and the competition was intense at the upper Division I level. Florida had the resources to build facilities and fund programs, and it seemed logical that the university would want both programs to succeed.

Nationwide, people looked at Florida and were surprised that the school did not achieve a national ranking in both sports. What they couldn't see was the lack of continuity in the school's leadership. Just about the time a university president was getting serious about basketball's success, there would be a leadership change.

JOHN LOTZ: 1974-1980

Lotz had been hired by UF President Stephen O'Connell. Ray Graves had signed the contract, but it was O'Connell who demanded that the basketball program be taken seriously. Then in 1974 O'Connell retired, and Florida hired Dr. Robert Q. Marston, who cared very little about sports, let alone college basketball.

Everyone at North Carolina had treated basketball as the premier sport. Lotz had been a Carolina bricklayer, and the Tar Heels constructed a basketball temple to athletic excellence. He just couldn't understand why Florida didn't want to focus its resources to help basketball excel.

One of Lotz' first conflicts was over a media guide. Florida's basketball and football media guides were like comparing a high school term paper and a Ph.D. dissertation. In addition, the logo that was used to project Florida sports was a football helmet. Lotz designed a basketball logo that became a trademark for the team. He even went to the book store and bought post cards to put together a recruiting piece out of his own pocket. There were so many obstacles to overcome, yet so few people really understood or cared enough to change things.

The biggest challenge was Florida Gym – it truly was the pits. The hardwood floor had been sanded so many times that the nails were visible. The ceiling had been replaced, but they left the same old incandescent lighting. Jacksonville contractor Bill Gay and Gainesville builder Chuck Perry had donated the resources to construct a new players' dressing room, but the same broken tile was in the moldy showers. Fire doors and exit ramps for the handicapped had been added, but the worn-out floor and dirty backboards told the story of how tired the place had become.

If Florida Gym had been a bad dream for Bartlett's staff, it was John Lotz' worst nightmare. Lotz was trying to recruit the nation's best players with one of the nation's worst facilities. When Adrian Dantley came for his recruiting visit, he had a great weekend and seemed very impressed with the university. But as the coaches were taking Dantley to the airport, he said to Assistant Coach Terry Truax, "Hey, Coach Truax, we forgot to go in the arena." Reluctantly, Truax turned the car around. Dantley signed with Notre Dame.

As a home court packed with fans, Alligator Alley was the best. As a place to work each day both individually and as a team, it was depressing. The fans loved the atmosphere for the 12 home games each year, but the players were disgusted with the place the other 353 days.

Everyone who competed against Florida used Florida Gym to discredit the program. With the largest student body among SEC schools, Florida had a football facility that was second to none in America and a basketball arena that was the embarrassment of the SEC. After the student referendum in 1968 had voted a new building down, the passion to construct a new arena was extinguished and the idea lay dormant for another few years.

Lotz knew Florida had to build a new building if his program was to have a chance to be successful. The university had undertaken a study to build a mass-seating arena. They wouldn't call it a coliseum or relate it to athletics because they thought it might kill the project. It was going to be built with student funds and had to serve student needs.

Lotz grabbed the structure's first rendering and beginning in 1976 prematurely slapped a color picture of it on every media guide. The caption referred to "the building which is to be constructed." But the wait seemed interminable.

Another major obstacle in the seventies was the media. Seldom would the state's newspapers give college basketball much attention. The southern sports fan was a football fan, and the sports pages reflected that interest. During the sixties, the *Gainesville Sun*'s sports editor Joe Halberstein did a super job of covering all the sports, including basketball. Halberstein left in 1971 to work in Pennsylvania, and the *Sun* hired a new sports editor, Jack Hairston.

Hairston was a sportswriter who had worked in both Atlanta and Jacksonville. As president of the Football Writers' Association of America, he had an interest in three sports: football, spring football, and football recruiting. Hairston was an excellent sportswriter, but in writing about basketball, he tended to be critical. Basketball people found him divisive because his interest centered on issues that were mostly controversial. Rarely was the personality of Florida basketball reflected through feature stories that captured the program's substance.

Dan Murr covered basketball in those years for the *Sun*, but his time was spread among all the other sports. Murr loved the Florida basketball program but had difficulty giving it the attention he felt it deserved. On many occasions during the heart of the basketball team's season, an important victory would be a secondary sports page story to items like the heights and weights of the football team's next recruiting class.

As a result, the one newspaper in the state that might potentially have provided insight into the program's development became another of its major obstacles. Competing schools would subscribe to the *Gainesville Sun* and clip articles to send prospects. In effect, the Gators' hometown newspaper was used as a weapon against them.

Breaking Through Barriers

Despite the problems behind the scenes, Florida was gaining respect around the SEC, and no one wanted to play the Gators in the Alley. But most of all, the players were feeling pride in their basketball program. Lederman and Shy were co-captains for the 1975-76 season and gave tremendous senior leadership. A cast of younger players began to develop. This team was similar to Lotz' first season when the players exceeded their potential.

Bob Smyth, a 6-foot-8, fourth-year junior from Xenia, Ohio, took over at center. Smyth played sparingly as a sophomore, attempting to overcome severe cartilage and ligament damage to his left knee which caused him to be redshirted for a season. Smyth was considered the most improved player in the conference, averaging 13 points and almost 13 rebounds a game. His 17 points and 18 rebounds led the Gators to an upset win over eventual SEC champion Alabama.

Len Sanders was a junior college transfer from Bradenton who started 19 games. His breakaway basket in the closing seconds of Florida's 72-69 win over eighth-ranked Tennessee sealed a big home-court victory over a Volunteer team that would only lose six games. Sanders was the consummate defender. At 6-foot-4 he was perhaps Florida's best-ever defensive small forward. He became an eighth-round pick of Denver in the NBA draft.

The coaching staff elected to bring sophomore Al Bonner off the bench as a sixth man, and Bonner filled the role to perfection. Bonner had played at Pensacola Washington High School, and his sister Quientella was one of the most successful players in the history of Florida women's basketball.

Bonner had one of the sweetest jump shots ever seen in Florida Gym. It was a high, arching one-hander with perfect backspin and exceptional range. Bonner averaged 12 points a game, but would have really benefited if there had been a three-point line.

Alabama was the SEC champion in 1976 with a 23-5 season. The Tide crushed North Carolina in the NCAA Tournament before losing to Indiana in the Sweet 16. Bernard King and Ernie Grundfeld led Tennessee to a 21-6 season and an invitation to the NCAA Tournament. Florida beat both Alabama and Tennessee during the regular season, giving the players and the fans tangible evidence for optimism.

The 1976-1977 season proved to be Lotz' best and would bring him the Adolph

Rupp Award as the conference's Coach of the Year. He also was recognized as the National Coach of the Year by the Fellowship of Christian Athletes for Division I coaches in all sports. It was the first such national recognition for any basketball coach at the University of Florida.

The season began with wins over Mercer and East Tennessee State. Then the Gators went to the Gator Bowl in Jacksonville to face Al McGuire and the Marquette Warriors. It was the same Warrior team that would go on to win the national championship. Mick Elliott, writing in the *Gainesville Sun,* said, "Marquette won the game, but Florida won some friends and influenced a lot of people."

The lead changed 29 times, and the score was tied on 16 other occasions before Butch Lee dropped in two free throws in the closing seconds to give second-ranked Marquette the win 64-61.

Al McGuire, the Marquette coach, said, "I wouldn't have minded losing this game, it was a pressure cooker. I don't think we were off our game. I thought we played pretty good." Florida's Don Bostic said, "Maybe it looks good to come close, but I'd rather have the mark in the win column."

Florida would go on to win six in a row, including the championships of both the Big Sun Tournament and the Gator Bowl. Florida defeated Memphis State in the Big Sun final which was held in the ThunderDome, St. Petersburg's new arena. Florida's win was the first time a Gator basketball team had won a tournament outside the city of Jacksonville. In the Gator Bowl Tournament, Florida posted its second win in three tries over Jacksonville University and earned a victory over Holy Cross in the finals.

One of Florida basketball's continuing challenges was developing a schedule that exposed players to the national media. Many players dreamed of professional basketball, and the national exposure during the college career was part of the formula in the NBA equation. Whether they were shooting hoops on the side of a backyard barn or rattling a netless rim on a neighborhood playground, basketball players everywhere were drawn to the glamour and money of the NBA. It was becoming a major motivation to the best players of this era.

Schools that recruited well made the investment to travel long distances to games. Tournaments sprang up in Hawaii and Alaska. No longer was it just the Holiday Festival in New York or the Sugar Bowl Tournament in New Orleans, but now there was the Rainbow Classic in Hawaii, the Rebel Roundup in Las Vegas, and the Great Alaska Shootout in Anchorage. Television was beginning to play a more important role in the sport's projection, and schools used televised games to prominently display their programs. On the recruiting trails, it was important to tell the best players who and where you were playing.

The coaching staff at Florida was creating inroads to the state's talent pool. They had tapped into Edison Junior College in 1976 for Len Sanders. This year they found another Edison player, a point guard, Richard Glasper. Lotz predicted Glasper would be one of the greatest players ever to sign with Florida, and Glasper's performance on the court soon proved Lotz correct.

Glasper was the first player to wear jersey number 00. He was lightning quick off the dribble and had a 38-inch vertical leap. At 6 feet tall, he was difficult to guard and in his first season averaged 11.9 points a game with a field goal shooting percentage of 53.5 percent.

Even more valuable was Glasper's passing skill. With the ball in his hands, his court awareness and quickness made him a real threat. He averaged 4.5 assists in an average of 31 minutes a game and had 226 assists and 91 steals over his two seasons as a Gator.

Smyth and Bonner were the leading scorers in 20 of Florida's 26 games in the '76 season. Bonner was now in a starting role. He shot 58 percent from the field for the year, making him UF's highest percentage shooting "three man."

Al Bonner and his younger sister, Quientella, left a legacy of basketball achievements in Florida Gym. Both had exceptional character and distinguished the university through their accomplishments. Like the Lawrence brothers in the eighties, these two members of the same family provided many thrills for Florida fans, while at the same time representing themselves with tremendous class.

Off to a 9-1 start, the Gators were riding high on confidence when they hosted Alabama. Unfortunately, the Tide, coached by C.M. Newton and led by Reggie King and T. R. Dunn, handed Florida a stunning 83-71 upset as a payback for the year before.

Florida rebounded to crush Georgia, scoring more than 100 points for the third time that season. Then the Gators lost a huge game to the Kentucky Wildcats at the buzzer in what at the time was the biggest official crowd (5,712) ever inside Alligator Alley.

Florida broke the official crowd record three weeks later. With 5,794 in attendance, Florida beat the Volunteers, who were 16-3 overall and 10-0 in the SEC. The 80-76 win sent shockwaves throughout the Southeast. Al Bonner scored nine of his 19 points in the last 7.5 minutes. Glasper scored 12 of Florida's final 20 points which prompted Tennessee Coach Ray Mears to say, "His one-on-one play killed us. Glasper is the key to their ballclub."

Lotz' dad came down from New York City to see the game and saw that a congregation of raucous Gator fans could really raise some hell. The Bronx Baptist minister got the flavor of a Florida crowd which granted no biblical mercy to the Volunteers.

Bernard King had been charged with marijuana possession which inspired the crowd to chant, "Smoke a joint, Bernie, smoke a joint," intimidating one of the greatest players in the history of the league. King missed an uncontested layup that would have tied the game in the closing seconds.

Ray Mears, the Tennessee coach, was devastated and actually had a nervous breakdown after the Florida win. King complained about the chanting, declaring that

Gator fans didn't have any class. But Bob Smyth responded, "We don't have great players, we can't rely on talent, we must play hard every night out. Tonight we were ready. Hallelujah."

King was one of the best basketball players ever to play in the SEC. Were it not for his problems off the court, he might have been recognized as the best player ever in a conference with names like Issel, Maravich, Malone, Barkley, and O'Neal. In a 14-year NBA career, King was an All-Star four times and had a scoring average of 22 points a game.

Florida finished the year winning just three of the final seven games, but the 17-9 season rewarded Lotz. He was named SEC Coach of the Year. It was the third straight year a Florida team averaged 81 points a game, which represents the best scoring average in any three-year time period. This team averaged a team-high 51.5 field goal percentage, also a best-ever mark. In Lotz' first four seasons, his teams averaged 74.2 percent from the free-throw line, which is the best four-year mark in the record books.

At the time, some would argue it was Florida basketball's best season. A three-point loss to Marquette, the eventual national champion, and wins over Tennessee and Vanderbilt helped substantiate that claim. The groundwork was coming along nicely, and there was a bright glow to Florida's basketball future.

A Fatal Blow

A distinguishing element in the development of the Lotz program was the character of the athletes competing for the Gators. Lederman, Shy, and Smyth were Bartlett recruits who had made the transition beautifully to the new style of play. Al Bonner, Don Bostic, Larry Brewster, Malcolm Cesare, Ric Clarson, and Len Sanders were Lotz players. The personalities of these players blended well together, and friendships developed both in and out of the locker room.

In the spring of 1977, Lotz finally hooked a big fish. Not since Andy Owens had chosen to stay inside the state had Florida basketball been able to reel in its recruiting line and find such a prized catch.

Reggie Hannah was a first-team high school All-American from Titusville, Florida. He was named the Florida High School Player of the Year. At 6-foot-8, Hannah brought an athletic body and a high school reputation that earned Lotz' coaching staff immense respect for finally turning the corner in the recruiting wars.

The single missing piece that had been haunting the Gator program in recent years was the inability to attract a recognized name player from a Florida high school. The signing of Hannah put away the microscope under which Florida's past recruiting failures had been examined.

Along with Hannah, Florida added four others, including Jerry Bellamy, a 6-foot-6 Pennsylvania native, and Bob Van Noy, a 6-foot-8 forward from New York City. This was Florida's best recruiting class since Walk and Owens had signed in 1966 and reflected the progress of the Florida program under Lotz' leadership.

The 1977-78 team had four seniors. Bonner, Brewster, and Glasper started every game, and John Coy was a reserve who saw limited action.

Larry Brewster was attempting to overcome potentially career-ending knee surgery. At 6-foot-11, he hoped to emerge in the post after a summer of traveling in Europe with teammate Chuck Fritz on a Fellowship of Christian Athletes team. Cesare and Clarson were juniors and added veteran offensive power to a team that had a legitimate shot at Florida's first conference crown.

Cesare, 6-foot-9, had played in every game his freshman and sophomore years. And Clarson, a 6-foot-6 forward from Jacksonville's Bolles School, could shoot the perimeter jumper and rebound hard on the offensive board.

The coaching staff continued to add non-conference opponents that provided an exciting format to the program's attempts to earn recognition outside the southeastern states. This season's schedule had Manhattan, Brown, Marquette, George Washington, St. Bonaventure, and Indiana as warmups for its SEC format.

The Gators opened the season 3-0 before losing again to Marquette, but this time at the Mecca in Milwaukee. That Marquette team finished the year ranked third in the nation. Clarson had 21 to lead the Gators, but Florida couldn't overcome a 41 percent shooting night and 26 points by Marquette's All-American Butch Lee.

The Gators then won four straight, including the Vermont Classic, before losing to Indiana in the finals of the Gator Bowl 73-60. Malcolm Cesare made all eight field goal attempts and led the scoring with 18 points. Indiana eventually made it to the Sweet 16 in the NCAA Tournament and was ranked 13th in the final AP poll that season. The Hoosier victory kept Florida from winning its fourth Gator Bowl championship in seven years.

In the season opener of his freshman year, Reggie Hannah came off the bench to score 20 points against Manhattan. His first start was in the loss to Indiana. Hannah was averaging double figures – his high school press clippings had accurately portrayed his potential.

Malcolm Cesare had gotten off to a great start through the first nine games. The junior from Hicksville, Long Island, was affectionately called "Fonzie" because he looked like the TV character played by Henry Winkler. Cesare was a good student and had two loves – basketball and fishing. The Fonz could pull bass from Lake Alice almost as well as Buddy Bales had in the sixties.

The Marquette game was his coming-out party. Cesare led Florida with 18 points and he "stuffed and mounted" a Jerome Whitehead jumpshot like the 20-pound bass on the wall. In the professional scouting circles, his name was on everyone's list. He was emerging as the best forward Florida fans had ever seen. Cesare had the coordination of a ballet dancer. He got himself open and scored with precision-like movements that froze defenses. He had a soft touch and used every inch of his 6-foot-9 frame.

As the Gators took a 7-2 record on the road to open conference play, this team looked like, played like, and acted like the North Carolina prototype that Florida had envisioned when Lotz was hired.

The Gators exploded for a resounding 92-79 trouncing of Tennessee and posted the season's first SEC victory. The game in Knoxville was decided by halftime when Florida took a 10-point lead. Glasper with 26 and Cesare with 21 led four Florida players with double figures.

With an 8-2 record, Florida headed for Athens, Georgia, exuding confidence. It appeared this was going to be the best basketball team ever. There was no way for anyone to forecast that on January 4, 1978, the Gators would experience another defining moment in the program's prolonged struggle to achieve prominence. In retrospect this game marked the beginning of the end for a coaching staff that was on the doorstep of unprecedented success.

Through the years, the Florida-Georgia rivalry had produced some of the program's most violent struggles. This game was no exception. The Gators were in command with a 34-30 lead at the half, but Georgia set the game's tempo by playing a zone that forced Florida to more patiently handle each offensive possession.

In the second half, with the Gators holding a seven-point lead, Georgia decided to go man to man. So, Florida began to run its four corners offense. But the Gators' tactic backfired, and with 13 seconds left on the clock, Georgia had taken a 53-50 lead.

Glasper missed an outside jumper, and as Cesare turned to go for the offensive rebound, Lucius Foster cocked his right arm, planted his right foot, and landed a devastating unsuspected blow that exploded in Cesare's mouth. It was the most vicious, intentional blow ever recorded against a Florida player. Teeth, bone, and blood went everywhere, and Florida's season went in the tank.

Georgia won the game 57-54, shattering not only Cesare's jaw but also the confidence of a Florida basketball program that seemed poised to move to a higher level.

Cesare's mouth required extensive reconstructive oral surgery to repair a broken jaw and shattered teeth. Somehow, the junior continued to play the rest of the season, but because his confidence was badly shaken, his performance was compromised.

The Florida coaches were disappointed by the defeat, but Lotz was furious that Lucius Foster had not been ejected on the spot. Film of the incident showed Cesare turning to compete for the rebound and Foster, in a premeditated posture, taking dead aim for his target.

The league's commissioner, Boyd McWhorter, a former president of the University of Georgia, asked Georgia Coach John Guthrie for a full report on the incident. Guthrie said that Foster had been provoked into the confrontation. "Foster's contact with Cesare was not deliberate," said Guthrie, who later became commissioner of SEC basketball.

Lotz wanted Foster suspended for the season and was incensed that the conference office, after a lengthy deliberation, would permit such a violent blow to go relatively unpunished. Newspapers across the Southeast carried stories on a daily basis about the incident. The *Gainesville Sun* wrote extensively about the injustice, including a published frame-by-frame sequence of the event. Jack Hairston wrote in a *Gainesville Sun* editorial that "Foster's punch had nothing to do with the game of basketball. It belonged in a charge up Porkchop Hill or a Roman bread riot. Vicious mayhem like that should be eliminated from the game as soon as possible, even if it means getting rid of the perpetrators of such violence."

From the Florida perspective, the SEC office had a reputation for failing to treat the Gators fairly. This was another glaring issue which Lotz wasn't going to let them sweep under the carpet. Everywhere Lotz went in the next few weeks he targeted criticism at the Bulldogs and SEC officials.

On January 22 at an early morning breakfast in Oxford, Mississippi, Lotz told a couple dozen Rebel basketball faithful that a major indiscretion by a player ("who, when they passed out brains, thought they said trains, and caught a bus") had derailed his team's season. "On top of that," Lotz said, "the commissioner of the SEC doesn't have the guts to do anything about it."

It was immediately reported back to McWhorter by someone at the breakfast meeting that Lotz had made the uncomplimentary remarks. From that moment, the entire episode took a new spin, and Florida was now being reprimanded for its coach's tasteless comments.

The incident ended with Foster receiving a one-game suspension for the season's final game against Florida. The Gators won 86-68. But from that early January night, the team went on to lose 10 of its remaining 17 games and finish the season at 15-12. After starting with what appeared to be a run for the conference championship, Florida found itself finishing in a fifth-place tie with Auburn in the final standings.

At one point, a *Gainesville Sun* headline had suggested that Foster's punch could earn a criminal prosecution. As it turned out, it was Lotz and his Gator program that in the end were punished.

In the previous 54 games under Lotz, Florida had won 32. With a veteran team and a strong recruiting class, people believed Florida basketball had finally turned the corner. But after the Georgia loss, Florida won only 19 of the next 54 games and had a 1-5 record against in-state schools. In the final 54-game stretch, Florida played 11 overtime periods and achieved only two victories.

Perhaps just as significantly, Dick Grubar and Terry Truax, who had formed the foundation of Lotz' staff in 1973, became disenchanted with the Florida basketball environment. In successive seasons, both of them resigned. Both coaches' marriages had disintegrated, and they just weren't enjoying a school where many lacked a sophisticated perspective on the sport. Grubar and Truax had outstanding coaching skills. Grubar left the game for good, but Truax moved on and is recognized by his peers as one of the sport's top college coaches.

It was a huge loss for Lotz, but he quickly moved to find replacements. Florida hired its first black assistant basketball coach, James Brown, to replace Truax as a recruiter. With Grubar's departure, Lotz turned to a longtime friend from the high school ranks of New York City, Ed Visscher.

Visscher was an ordained Lutheran minister who had been the highly successful head coach of Long Island Lutheran High School. His program was recognized nationally as one of the best in the country.

When Lotz was at North Carolina, he had successfully recruited Lutheran High School All-American Bill Chamberlain. In 1978 he convinced another Lutheran High School standout, 6-foot-5 point guard Mike Milligan, to become a Gator.

Lotz knew he needed help in the day-to-day administration of his program. He believed Visscher's maturity would make him a valuable addition. Dean Smith told Lotz that the success of any program depended upon staff loyalty and that he should choose his associates carefully to maintain a solid working relationship.

Visscher was known as "the Rev," short for the Reverend Edward Visscher. He was clever in his ability to recognize when it was to his advantage to adopt his ministerial profile and when to present himself as a knowledgeable basketball coach. Visscher made a significant personal sacrifice to leave the security of Lutheran High. After being there for 17 years, moving to Florida with a wife and five children took a great deal of courage.

Visscher was comfortable making decisions and recognized that Lotz needed help with the many details involved in running the program. Visscher hoped this job would lead to a head coaching job at the Division I level. Moving to Florida, Visscher reasoned, might be a stepping stone in his career's upward mobility.

In the spring of 1977, Lotz himself turned down several invitations to leave Florida. The University of Richmond and Duke were each pursuing him heavily, and the Richmond deal included a compensation package that doubled his salary. But Lotz' wife Vicki had recently given birth to their second daughter, and the family was putting down roots and becoming very comfortable in the community. Vicki was involved in church and community affairs. And Lotz himself had become something of a Madison Avenue public relations salesman for Gator hoops.

At the time, the late Bill Elmore was UF's vice president for university operations and gave Lotz a four-year extension to his contract. Elmore told him, however, that his salary would be viewed the same as that of any other university professor. Lotz would get the standard cost-of-living increase.

Elmore operated the university checking account with a tight fist, and his insensitive failure to appreciate the Florida program's accomplishments would eventually contribute to Lotz' undoing. In a two-page letter of understanding on March 21, 1978, Lotz was given a four-year extension with a salary of $30,400. He was provided a $2,500 expense account and a medium-priced automobile.

In one of the letter's paragraphs, Elmore stated that "good cause for termination of this contract is understood to mean repeated failure to effectively perform or neglect the duties of your position. Any conduct that brings discredit upon the university will also result in your appointment being terminated. If you are terminated for cause, you will be notified in writing at least two months prior to the effective date of such termination." These words would come back to haunt the university in the months ahead when a change in athletic directors led to a decision to fire John Lotz.

In turning down the Richmond and Duke jobs and spurning other overtures, Lotz affirmed his confidence in the progress the program had achieved. He genuinely thought he could see a light at the end of the tunnel. It turned out to be a train.

Blindsided by Faith

A substantially reconstructed coaching staff saw the 1978-79 season as a transition year. With Cesare and Clarson as seniors, the staff believed Hannah, Bellamy, Van Noy, and two freshmen, Mike Milligan and Maurice McDaniel, held promising keys to the program's future.

The conference continued to be extremely competitive. Kentucky had won the national championship in 1978, and Alabama, LSU, and Tennessee were all ranked in the top 20. With a new coliseum finally on the horizon, Lotz was battling to recruit players who could take the program forward.

No doubt about it, Florida basketball was competitive. No one took the Gators lightly. In the Alley, Florida had a good 10-point advantage and could clip any team in the country. But the tired old gym continued to be the cause of recruiting problems, and Florida could not realistically expect a top 20 program until it built a new facility.

The "study" had progressed to a timetable for completion, and Lotz could visualize the impact of a new building. The process was moving slowly, and many campus departments still had their fingers in the pie. But a new arena for basketball now appeared to be more than just a fantasy.

Reggie Hannah continued to be a marquee player but frustrated the coaching staff by failing to manage his personal life. Hannah had been the big fish in Florida's high school pond, but his lifestyle choices were compromising the whole team. Hannah was not a bad kid – he was just immature and lacked personal discipline. Lotz was required to spend too much time as a baby sitter for his team's most irresponsible talent.

Hannah was suspended for the season's first three games for not attending class, and Lotz told him that every class he missed would result in an additional one-game suspension. "Reggie has a lot to learn about self-discipline," said Lotz. "I didn't recruit him to be a savior for our program, or just so he could stay eligible to get to the pros. He's got to follow the guidelines set down for every member of this team."

The highlight of the 1979 season was Florida's championship in the Industrial Classic in Providence, Rhode Island. The opening game against Fairfield provided a benchmark against which to measure Florida's come-from-behind victories.

Florida had trailed by as many as 20 points but kept chipping away. With five seconds remaining, Fairfield led 91-88, but turned the ball over attempting to advance

JOHN LOTZ: 1974-1980

it into its front court. Ric Clarson picked the ball up and was inadvertently fouled by Fairfield's Mark Young with two seconds to go. Clarson made the first of a one-and-one. His second shot was a hard miss to the right-hand side of the rim, and Jerry Bellamy slid around from the second free-throw line position to grab the rebound. His soft one-hander at the buzzer tied the score. The Gators had climbed the mountain and were rewarded with overtime.

Florida controlled the opening tap and held the ball for four minutes and 25 seconds before Cesare drove the baseline. He scored his 22nd point, and Florida now had a 93-91 lead. Fairfield answered with a last-second basket and tied the game at the end of the first overtime period.

With the score 93-93, Milligan opened the second overtime with a layup, and Clarson converted two free throws to put Florida in front 97-93. Fairfield scored to cut it to two, and Clarson made two more free throws. Fairfield again scored, and it was 99-97, and Clarson made two more free throws. Fairfield made it 101-99, and Clarson made four more free throws to lead the Gators to a 109-99 victory. Ric Clarson had a career-high 26 points and made 12 out of 13 free throws in one of his greatest games as a Florida Gator.

In the finals, Lotz used the four corners offense, and the Gators easily defeated Coach Dave Gavitt's Providence Friars 79-61. It was one of Providence's few losses ever on its home court.

The Gators' one-point loss to Jacksonville in the Gator Bowl final was the beginning of the end of what became a very disappointing season. Florida would go on to lose 16 of its final 18 games. Seven were decided by six points or less.

Everyone began pointing fingers in reaction to the poor season. Fans will accept your program's bumps and warts if you are winning. But when your team wins only three conference games and ends up dead last, they start looking under rocks for answers. Florida just hadn't recruited enough blue-chip players to pull the program forward. People were more interested in "wins" than "whys."

Lotz and most of the Florida basketball faithful still had reasons to be optimistic. The coaching staff landed a 7-footer, Jim Grandholm, and received a verbal commitment from Tampa High School senior-to-be Jeff Turner. With Grandholm signed and the public commitment of Turner, Florida had players who embodied the high standards Lotz had set for the team.

Turner wanted to play for John Lotz and, more importantly, wanted to stay in the state and help put Florida basketball on the map. Turner shared Lotz' ideals, and Jeff's entire family was excited about the prospect of helping Florida basketball reach higher goals.

Turner was one of the biggest names to come out of Florida in years. He was a high school All-American who was an honor roll student. Lotz knew that with Jeff Turner his program had the cornerstone for its future. Turner's announcement was also attracting the state's other quality prospects. Vince Martello, an exceptional perimeter shooter from the Panhandle, told Lotz that he wanted to be a Gator. The coaching staff knew that a nucleus was developing that could anchor a team to wipe away the disappointment of the previous year.

There were storm clouds on the horizon, however, in the offices of Florida's athletic administration. After 20 years, Ray Graves had retired the previous year, and President Marston had appointed 35-year-old Bill Carr as the new athletic director.

The athletic director's job is to employ coaches who the A.D. believes can win. At the same time, the A.D. must be sensitive to the framework which challenges the coach to do his best job. As a former Florida All-American football center, Carr dreamed about the chance to run the athletic program. Like everyone else, he wanted to win. But Carr was naive about the dynamics that influenced a basketball coach's chances of being successful at Florida.

Bill Carr had high ideals and strong principles. He appeared to be a natural ally for John Lotz. Although Carr had great respect for Lotz as a man, he had begun to question his ability to coach. Carr also believed Lotz lacked the skills to manage the program at a higher level, and he began listening to some who found Lotz abrasive. He began to focus on idiosyncrasies that some people found annoying. Before long, Carr was convincing himself that Lotz was not his man.

Visscher also began to distance himself from what he sincerely believed were Lotz' weaknesses. This separation gave credence to the growing criticism of Lotz. Lotz was unaware that Visscher might be posturing himself to survive any possible blowup in the program. Lotz never even considered that a blowup could occur. What transpired in Lotz' firing can best be described as the tragic undoing of the friendship of Lotz, Visscher, and Carr, who became enemies in the belief that the shortcomings of one another were the cause for the program's demise.

Lotz' last season, 1979-80, opened with LSU – the first and only time Florida has ever started the season with an SEC game. In Baton Rouge the Gators were pounded 112-81 by an LSU team that went on to have a 26-6 season.

The Gators were experimenting to find a formula for success. The team had two transfers and three freshmen in uniform for the first time. Florida's most talented player, Reggie Hannah, was lazy. His lifestyle was pulling apart a team fabric which had been carefully woven of hard work and high ideals.

Lotz knew the pressure was building to improve the win-loss record, but he would not sacrifice the program's integrity. After losses to Florida State and Mississippi State and a 69-67 defeat by Mercer, he suspended several players, including Hannah, for not attending class.

Playing short-handed, the Gators were embarrassed by a stinging loss to a Division II opponent, Florida Southern, 98-75. That loss tipped the scales for Bill Carr. In Carr's mind it was simply unacceptable that the University of Florida could

JOHN LOTZ: 1974-1980

lose a basketball game to a Division II opponent. Alumni from the central part of the state expressed outrage, and the rope around Lotz' neck began to tighten.

Florida beat Iowa State and Illinois Wesleyan but then lost the finals of the Gator Bowl once again to Jacksonville. On Sunday, December 30, Carr told Lotz to come into his office after church. It was then and there that Carr informed Lotz he was fired.

No man was ever so fully unprepared to receive this news than John Lotz. There was no doubt his program had struggled in the previous two years. But he was more confident than ever that his recruiting had fallen into place. After he had proclaimed the building of a new arena for six years, the ground had finally been broken for the O'Connell Center. Lotz had tangible evidence that his program was on the threshold of a University of North Carolina basketball future.

Moreover, in spite of the grumbling, there was really no groundswell of support for Lotz' ouster. He was beginning the second year of a four-year contract, and former players and loyal supporters had not yet considered reaching down to pull the plug. Lotz had faith that the university respected his moral and ethical leadership. He genuinely believed people understood that the responsible profile he had maintained as a coach uniquely distinguished the University of Florida on a national platform. Most of all, Lotz trusted Bill Carr completely.

With two and a half years remaining on Lotz' two-page contract, Carr exercised the option in the paragraph which absolved the university from any additional expense by claiming that Lotz would be fired "for cause." In the letter handed to Lotz on December 30, Carr said, "I am required to give you notice of your failure effectively to perform your duties as head basketball coach. Repetition of or continuance of this failure after your receipt of this notice is basis for termination of your contract for cause. The principal manifestations of your lack of effective performance are: (1) Failure to provide a basketball program of competitive character, either in the Southeastern Conference or in the state of Florida. (2) An inadequate state of development for a program in its seventh year of leadership under the same head coach. (3) General lack of organization affecting all areas to include assistant coaches and players. (4) Failure to recruit effectively, particularly in the state of Florida. (5) An apparent failure to provide adequately for game strategy, and in particular, for special situation plays and adjustments. (6) A failure to develop student support or booster support. (7) A failure to develop positive relationships of value to the program with alumni, high school coaches, and media."

Some questioned Carr whether "for cause" meant a material indiscretion. Were there NCAA rule infractions? No. Were there financial indiscretions in the management of the basketball resources that meant Lotz and his staff had their hands in the till? No. Were there material misrepresentations of fact? No. Did they falsely keep players academically eligible to compete? No. Did Lotz publicly embarrass the university with his manner of conduct and vocabulary? No.

"Lotz' firing caused the Gators' integrity to drop another notch," wrote Larry Guest in an *Orlando Sentinel* column. "The decision smacks of high-handed backroom alumni politics."

Florida had put Lotz in a financial straitjacket. With a young family, a $30,400 coaching salary, and very little in the bank, Lotz felt totally betrayed. The university contended that it would pay him a salary for six months, and the remaining two years of the contract would be nullified.

Lotz refused to coach. He stated emphatically that if he was being fired in April he might as well be fired now. After all, if Carr had made up his mind, there was nothing Lotz could do to reverse the process. But, if he walked and if Florida stopped his salary, he couldn't buy groceries. He wasn't about to swallow such a deal.

Negotiations began in an environment that was more explosive than a Gainesville electrical storm. Four days later an agreement had been reached, but without any public disclosure of the unfolding crisis. Lotz would receive $40,000 of the remaining $86,000 in his contract.

Revealing nothing of the situation, Lotz had coached Florida to a 57-52 win over Georgia at home the previous night. There was not a hint to the players, the staff, or the media that Lotz had been fired. Two days later, on Saturday afternoon, January 5, Florida's athletic director drove to the Gators' next game in Auburn, Alabama. Following Florida's 82-62 defeat, Carr announced to the media that Lotz' tenure was over. Ed Visscher was appointed on an interim basis to fill the head coaching void until season's end.

In a brief press conference inside the Auburn arena, with tears in his eyes, Lotz thanked everyone involved with the university who had supported his efforts. He told the players that he "appreciated their effort and desire and hoped they continued to play good basketball."

"I really can't say what I'll do from here," said Lotz. "It's like a golfer who breaks his arm. He can't say what he's going to do the next day."

As Lotz was leaving the parking lot in a rental car, his radio was tuned to the Auburn postgame show. Lotz heard Sonny Smith, the Auburn head coach, publicly break down and cry when he was handed the Florida release that described Lotz' firing.

Smith would not weep alone. Many of the Florida players, former players, and people around the nation who respected Lotz cried also. Basketball observers had admired the dignity with which Lotz conducted his program and were stunned by Florida's judgment in the decision.

The desire to win had consumed the Florida faithful. With football Coach Charlie Pell leading the charge for victory and promoting the Gator football program in every nook and cranny of the state, fans expected Florida basketball to follow right along.

In February of 1980, Bill Kastelz, a noted sportswriter for the *Florida Times-Union* in Jacksonville, had written, "I think the University of Florida would be doing itself a long-range favor of sorts if it worried a little less about its spotless basketball 'image' and a little more about its won-lost record. The only accepted image in college basketball today is a winning image."

Money talked, and big egos with deep pockets throughout the state delighted in influencing what took place in Florida's athletic affairs. If high-profile university supporters wanted to see a change in basketball, UF President Bob Marston saw no reason why Bill Carr shouldn't take steps to make a change.

Many of Florida's well-documented problems with the NCAA violations in football and the national disgrace that was created by Lotz' firing could be laid at Marston's feet. As the university's president, Marston, more than anyone, victimized Florida's athletic reputation by failing to display the courage of responsible leadership during these times.

This sad event epitomized the University of Florida's failure to understand the dynamics of its college basketball program. A football mentality drove a public perception that Florida basketball should succeed in commensurate fashion with Florida football.

Try as he might, Carr, an ex-All American football player, could never empathize with Florida basketball players. Basketball and football players received the same basic athletic scholarships. They were housed together. They ate together. But for all other practical purposes, basketball was a stepchild in Florida athletics. With the dismissal of John Lotz, a football mentality once again took control of the fortunes of Florida basketball and for that, in the very near future, the university would pay dearly.

Norm Sloan

A Painful Taste of Glory
1981-1989

Gators record another sport 1st in Lexington

Gators SECure 1st-ever tit[le]

Schintzius' career always interesting

A typical UF rall[y] defeats LSU 104

...atches
...C lead
...oes overti[me]
...p Vandy 83-8[?]

Lawrence sinks TCU 77-

Good things come in 3s for UF, [?]

...T victor[y]
Sloan's [?]
...est hour

Bobby Tyler

Gators break Ole Miss jinx

Gators get bi[g]
face N.C. Sta[te]

...ators send
...rdue home
...om NCAA

East region[al]

INSIDE
- Complete NCAA brack[et] D-4
- Memphis State toos [?]

Norman Stormin' Again

As Florida basketball moved into the eighties, former Florida players were further distanced from the program than ever before. In firing Lotz, Bill Carr had performed radical surgery on the program, and many questions remained. What was the athletic association's vision for basketball? By what standards would the next program's leadership be measured? Was winning at all costs really the objective? Did the athletic director understand the dynamics which uniquely characterize college basketball?

There were two things which were certain. A Florida basketball team had never participated in the NCAA Tournament nor won an SEC basketball championship. There were no glass slippers in the trophy case, and years of trying were no longer going to be considered good enough. The words "Florida never" were starting to be the prefix to a lot of basketball sentences.

As Carr began searching for John Lotz' replacement, he was influenced by several factors which had little to do with basketball. He had been named athletic director in 1978 after UF President Marston had completed the deal to hire football Coach Charlie Pell. Carr's responsibilities normally would involve a chain of command where the head football coach reported to the athletic director. But in Pell's case, the football coach's office was connected directly to Tigert Hall. Pell enjoyed the kind of power that, when the president had questions, he called Pell directly. Carr was not in the loop.

Another issue for the A.D. was the growing differences among the football faithful. There were people who loved Ray Graves and were "Graves people." There were those who supported the different approach of former football Coach Doug Dickey and were "Dickey people." Now, Pell was out in the state trying to bring all of these people together to form one big happy family.

Some of the longtime Gator football people were whispering in Carr's ear that he should bring back Norman Sloan. Jimmy Keynes, Red Mitchum, Fred Montsdeoca, and Witt Palmer, among others, were all football Gators who liked Sloan in years past and were now showing some interest in basketball by lobbying Carr on Sloan's behalf. Carr believed that their interest in Sloan might fast-forward the healing process of the divided politics affecting Florida's athletic programs.

Lotz' dismissal was Carr's first major coaching change, and he had gone out on the end of the limb to chop off Lotz. He knew the successor would need to be someone who had recognizable coaching credentials. He wanted a coach who would take charge and run with Florida basketball. If the coach could heat up some of the lukewarm Gator faithful, that would be a real bonus.

The search was not going particularly well. The overtures Carr made to Dave Bliss of Southern Methodist and Jim Boeheim of Syracuse brought negative responses. He flew to Washington, D.C., to meet with John Thompson, who then used the Florida inquiry to negotiate a better arrangement with Georgetown.

Two other names surfaced in the search for Lotz' successor. The late John Randolph, Florida's track coach at the time, had recently come to Gainesville from West Point. Randolph stopped by Carr's office one morning to offer a candidate.

"Bill, there is this guy at the Point who is really doing a super job," Randolph said. "I think you should meet him and find out for yourself." Randolph said the only negative he knew about the coach was the difficulty people had pronouncing his last name: Krzyzewski. Carr rejected the suggestion.

Another last-minute candidate was coaching at Appalachian State. The morning Carr made his decision to hire Sloan, a call came from a man with a thick Brooklyn accent. The caller wanted the Florida job but gave Carr the impression he might find it difficult saying "you all." The Appalachian State coach was Bobby Cremins.

With the controversy over Lotz' firing still smoldering, Carr wanted to move quickly so the media would refocus on the Gators' future and not their past. Carr believed a prominent head coach like Norm Sloan, who was at North Carolina State, would answer Carr's own prayers for finding a notable coaching personality to credibly assure others about the program's future.

North Carolina State people reportedly were not sad to see Sloan considering another job. Fans in the golden triangle of college basketball's most intense rivalries, North Carolina, N.C. State, and Duke, measured Sloan's program first and foremost by how it performed against Carolina. After leading N.C. State to a national championship in 1974, Sloan's teams were competitive but just didn't meet the increasingly higher expectations of State's fans.

North Carolina State worked in the shadow of the University of North Carolina and the success crafted by Carolina's Coach Dean Smith. Sloan won only 14 of the 40 matches between the two schools and only two of the previous 10 meetings in which State faced the Tar Heels. Even with a 20-8 season in 1980, what State fans wanted most was to beat Carolina. Perhaps it was time for N.C. State to change coaches, too.

Carr knew that in Sloan's first stint in Gainesville, he had ruffled more than his share of feathers, but he also felt Sloan's accomplishments at N.C. State made him an especially strong Florida candidate. Carr was scheduled to meet with UF President Robert Marston to update the progress in the coaching search, and as Carr headed out the door to see Marston, he received a phone call. On the line was Gator supporter and businessman Witt Palmer from Ocala, who once again promoted Sloan's virtues. It tipped the scales, and 10 minutes later, Carr reported to Marston that Sloan was his choice.

On February 24, 1980, Norm Sloan officially became Florida's 14th head basketball coach. With the second coming of Sloan, many were hopeful that he would deliver the program to the promised land. Little did anyone realize that when Sloan and the Gators reunited, there would be just a brief vision of the pearly gates before the program landed in purgatory.

Sloan had always had a deep desire to return to Florida. He longed to cement his identity with the Florida program by giving it the type of success it had never tasted before. At 53 years of age, his 14 years of ACC coaching had been enough pressure-cooker basketball for awhile. He needed a change, and he knew the state of Florida had players. He was ready for a reunion with Gainesville.

Sloan expressed delight in having the opportunity to "put Florida basketball back in the national spotlight," and on accepting the position, said he had "left unfinished business when he departed Florida in 1966."

One of the ironies of the change in coaching staffs was that Sloan and Lotz were longtime adversaries and had little regard for each other. Both were outspoken in their contempt for how they perceived the other's motives. Lotz had recruited against Sloan while working for North Carolina and was convinced that Sloan cheated. Sloan portrayed Lotz as a malicious rival attempting to sabotage his career.

Sloan took every opportunity to emphasize Lotz' failures with the Florida program. Anyone who found Lotz attractive for any reason was given a litany of reasons why Lotz was rightfully fired. Lotz couldn't coach. Lotz recruited poorly. Lotz was naive about what it took to be a successful head coach. With the poor results that had been achieved in recent years, the message wasn't hard to sell.

Sloan's first mission was to salvage Jeff Turner. In the fall of 1979, Turner had made a public commitment to play for John Lotz. But now he was having second thoughts. His previous announcement was motivated by his relationship with Lotz. This new regime would have to convince Turner that he fit into the program's redirected future.

The Turner family, however, could not get comfortable with Florida's change in direction. Vanderbilt's Coach C. M. Newton stepped into the picture, and another opportunity for Florida to capture one of the state's classiest basketball prospects fizzled when Turner signed with Vandy. Turner became a Commodore All-American, won a gold medal competing in the 1984 Olympics for the USA, and had a distinguished NBA career.

A rough and tumble beginning to Sloan's first season saw the departure of several players from the prior year. Sloan would describe these players as misfits who had little possibility of representing his program constructively.

Two of the prominent casualties were Reggie Hannah and Jim Grandholm. It was obvious to most that Hannah was an exceptional talent, but it was equally apparent that he had been a disciplinary problem. Hannah's failure to manage his schoolwork and personal life provided plenty of ammunition for a new staff to say good riddance. Hannah took his junior season's 17 points and nine rebounds and transferred one remaining year of eligibility to South Alabama.

Grandholm was a 7-footer and, in contrast to Hannah, was a good student with the right priorities. Grandholm did not like his first impressions of Sloan and transferred to South Florida. He had a fine career under Bulls Coach Lee Rose and eventually played in the NBA.

Shrugging off the disappointment of Turner's rejection and the loss of Grandholm and Hannah, Sloan brought in a marvelous freshman class that included Vernon Delancy, Mike Moses, Marty Perry, Tim Strawbridge, Chip Watts, and Ronnie Williams.

These six players, together with three holdovers from the previous season, provided the team nucleus for Sloan's first year. The three former players who stuck it out were Mark Giombetti, Mike Milligan, and Ken McCraney. The seniors, Giombetti and McCraney, were named co-captains.

Milligan was the most athletically gifted of the three holdovers. He was a polished offensive player who, at 6-foot-5, 200 pounds, was poised to become an exceptional college performer. As a sophomore, Milligan averaged 10 points a game and led the team in assists. Lotz had compared his point-guard skills to those of Richard Glasper and Bruno Caldwell. Milligan was taller than these two and had a potential NBA future. A coach's dream, he was also a good student who came to Florida with both academic and athletic motivations.

Giombetti was a blue-collar player who had an effective 18-foot jumper. He started 25 games the previous year, averaging 12 points and 35 minutes.

McCraney, a walk-on as a freshman under Lotz, may have been the least athletically gifted of the three. But he made himself invaluable with his attitude. McCraney woke up every morning thanking God for letting him be a Gator.

The 6-foot-8, 215-pound Strawbridge was Sloan's first signee. An honor-roll student who led Lakeland High School to the state's top ranking, Strawbridge fulfilled a lifelong dream when he earned a scholarship to play for the Gators. Sloan said of his new recruit, "Strawbridge will be one of the hardest workers at any school in the country."

The two most noteworthy players in this first class would become 40 percent of the starting lineup for the next four years. Ronnie Williams and Vernon Delancy were exceptional high school prospects and immediately brought the program the type of player that could effectively compete in the conference.

Williams had attended St. Johns Prep School in Wisconsin where the team held the No. 1 ranking in that state. His home, however, was New York City, and the previous summer he had led Riverside Church of New York to the national AAU championship.

Vernon Delancy was the Miami Player of the Year at Miami Senior High School and grew up in the inner-city area of Miami known as Liberty City. He told Sloan never to drive alone into his neighborhood because a white man in a nice car would probably not get out alive.

Mike Moses, a 5-foot-11 guard who led his New York City team to a state championship; Marty Perry, a McDonald's All-American from Indiana; and Chip Watts, a 6-foot-10 player from the Florida Panhandle, rounded out Sloan's first recruiting class.

Florida won five of its first six games that first season, including a wing-ding of a ballgame with Florida State in Jacksonville. The game re-energized the magic rivalry that Sloan had hoped to script with his return as the Gator mentor. The Jacksonville Coliseum acted as a neutral site and both teams gave inspired performances. Williams and Delancy combined for 35 points. Hayes Dickens was a walk-on who made his most notable Gator contribution, scoring 15 points in a dramatic 81-74 double-overtime victory.

The long-awaited new arena, the Stephen C. O'Connell Center (nicknamed the O'Dome), was christened December 30, 1980, as Florida easily beat Tennessee State 72-54. The arena's opening night was a rerun of the Florida Gym opener four decades earlier. Fans began leaving the game early as Florida pounded a much less talented opponent.

The season highlight was a dramatic 97-91 win over Alabama for one of three SEC home wins that season. Vernon Delancy dazzled 7,500 O'Dome fans with 38 points. It was the most points ever scored by a Florida freshman in a varsity game and a national season-high point total for a freshman. Delancy finished the season as the sixth leading scorer in the SEC and was one of Florida basketball's most exciting rookie players. He was named to the SEC All-Freshman team, and several publications made him a freshman team All-American.

Playing in their new arena, the Gators recorded several firsts:
- The first SEC win was over Auburn 63-59.
- The first SEC loss was to LSU 92-66.
- The first non-conference loss was to Florida State before 8,300 fans 82-71.

The season also saw Florida suffer its worst defeat ever by Kentucky 102-48.

Sloan promised Ronnie Williams the opportunity to score, and Williams responded by averaging 19 points a game. He was named the SEC's Freshman of the Year. At 6-foot-8, 215-pounds, Williams was compared to former NBA great Wes Unseld. Williams was efficient in his movements and scored with surprising quickness. He became one of Florida basketball's most prolific offensive players.

Giombetti and McCraney finished their careers and provided valuable senior leadership. Giombetti helped Florida get a first-round SEC Tournament win over Auburn in Birmingham when he scored 14 points and made crucial baskets down the stretch in the Gators' 50-48 win.

NORM SLOAN: 1981-1989

The game became infamous because the SEC television network had put a live mike in the late-game Florida huddle and had caught Sloan in his typical raging style, exclaiming, "Do you suppose we can stop them from making any more f...... layups?" Sloan's profanity was broadcast to households all across the Southeast.

McCraney was the team's captain in 1981, and in four seasons played in 57 games. Giombetti and McCraney, though caught in the unsettling transition of the Florida program, both took Florida diplomas with them and left behind value-added reputations.

McCraney's enthusiasm extended beyond his playing days. In 1983 he replaced James Brown as an assistant coach on Sloan's staff. He is remembered for his Magic Johnson smile, his tremendous sense of humor, and his deep love of Gator basketball. McCraney also added occasional touches of inspiration by composing poetry to reflect pride in the Gator program. He was always looking for a way to make a positive contribution.

Florida finished Sloan's first season a disappointing eighth in the conference standings with only five SEC wins and an overall 12-16 record. Fans, however, knew this was a building block year and were comfortable in extending Sloan's staff a honeymoon attitude.

The standing was, however, unacceptable to Norm Sloan. His timetable for building the program showed little patience for players' shortcomings, and he didn't hold back when it came to criticism. It wasn't long before Dickens, Milligan, Perry, Strawbridge, and Watts all became disgruntled. They left when the season ended. The loss of Milligan was the most damaging.

When Sloan recruited Milligan for North Carolina State in 1978, Milligan turned him down and chose Florida. When Sloan took over the Florida program, Milligan found himself in a meatgrinder. Sloan was not enamored with Milligan's performances and browbeat the sensitive athlete. Milligan felt Sloan was making him pay for the previous rejection. Whatever the reason, a disgruntled Milligan transferred to East Tennessee State, and his defection left a dent in the program.

Sloan brought assistants Monte Towe and Biff Nicholls to Gainesville and retained James Brown from the previous coaching staff. Both Towe and Nicholls had close ties to Sloan, and Sloan hoped Brown could help smooth the transition of the coaching change.

Towe was the point guard who engineered Sloan's national championship team at N.C. State in 1974. He was extremely loyal to Sloan and loved the game of basketball. Towe had been on Sloan's staff at N.C. State and dedicated all of his energy toward helping Sloan build the Florida program. An extremely popular college player, Towe related very well to young people and often competed with the players in pickup games. He was personable, enthusiastic, and totally supportive of Sloan's objectives.

James Brown never seemed to quite get his feet planted in the Florida job. He was the school's first black assistant basketball coach, and from the moment he replaced

Terry Truax on Lotz' staff, his working relationship was unsettled. First Grubar left, and Ed Visscher came in. Then Lotz got fired, and Visscher took over. Then Sloan took over, and Towe and Nicholls came in. Within a year, Brown was dismissed. Some felt Brown was only a marginally effective recruiter. But in Brown's defense, he was the victim of a difficult period in Florida's basketball history.

Biff Nicholls married Sloan's daughter Leslie and came to Gainesville to perform administrative duties for the program. Nicholls had played for Sloan at N.C. State and coached in junior college before coming to Florida. He coordinated Sloan's summer camps and managed many of the details of the team's travel. Perhaps most importantly, he became the academic watchdog for the players.

Also stepping into the Florida program during the first year was Sloan's secretary Sharon Sullivan, who then became the right arm for every Gator basketball head coach from 1980 to the present. Sloan's first secretary had left, and Sullivan applied for the job. She had worked for Arizona State's head football coach Frank Kush. Her husband had retired from the military, and after moving to Gainesville, she began working in Florida's athletic administration offices.

Sullivan told Sloan she had been out of the work force for about 10 years. "My shorthand is a little rusty," she told him, "but I have an understanding of working for a high-profile head coach." Sloan told Sullivan that he had never been comfortable dictating letters anyway. He admired Sullivan's confidence and hired her on the spot.

The unsung hero of Sloan's entire coaching career was Joan, his wife. Joan Sloan reluctantly returned to Gainesville the second time around. She had made many close friends in Raleigh and loved the college basketball atmosphere that surrounded N.C. State. Fourteen years was the longest the family had lived in one community during Sloan's career. This time, the roots she had to cut went deep.

Joan didn't dislike Gainesville, but the Raleigh years had produced many happy moments and it was hard to welcome a change. The family had enjoyed a comfortable lifestyle in an environment where people respected their accomplishments.

The Sloans were a very close family. When all three of her children indicated they would make the move to Gainesville, it softened the edges of her husband's decision. Once Sloan had cut the N.C. State cord, the family all pulled together to help make this career move a success.

Joan Sloan had the poise and kindness to counteract much of the controversy which surrounded her husband's career. She was his staunchest supporter. Joan defended every accusation leveled at her husband and tactfully disarmed his critics.

She had one of the most beautiful voices ever to sing the national anthem. In 1956, she began singing the anthem at the Citadel and performed at every home game that Sloan coached thereafter. Through the years, Joan earned deep respect from those who knew her personally, and she gracefully weathered many stormy seas throughout the coaching journey.

Building a Base

The national publications had begun rating college recruiting classes, and in Sloan's second season (1981-82), the Florida staff brought in what the *Sporting News* described as "the eighth-best recruiting class in the nation."

The first major prize came from Cross City, just 25 miles west of the university campus. At 6-foot-8, 220 pounds, Eugene McDowell was considered the top high school prospect in the state. McDowell was named a *Parade* third-team All-American and was ranked one of the top 50 players in the nation.

McDowell was a gifted athlete who looked strong enough to lift a derailed train car back onto the track. His size and strength made him a powerful competitor in the SEC. McDowell became a crowd favorite with his incredible slams and was soon nicknamed "The Dunking Machine."

McDowell was joined by Rob Harden, Randall Leath, Nabe Palmer, Tony Rogers, Rodney Williams, and a transfer from Providence College, George Jackson. Six of the seven players had roots in the state of Florida.

Harden was the only out-of-state player and was the all-time leading scorer at Valparaiso High School in Indiana. Because he idolized Monte Towe, he decided to come south for his college playing experience.

Sloan had kept his word to the state's high school coaches that he would build this program with Florida kids. As he had done 20 years before, Sloan was making an investment in Florida high school relationships that he hoped would pay recruiting dividends in the future.

In Sloan's second year, the SEC introduced an experimental 45-second clock and put in a 20-foot coaching box. Neither rule change appeared to deter Florida's wide-open style of play or its animated head coach on the sideline.

Florida won four of its first five games, but the roof caved in and the season fell apart when Vernon Delancy broke his right hand during the season's fifth game, an 81-65 victory over Florida State. Delancy returned several games later, but Florida unbelievably lost 21 of its remaining 22 games. Ten of those losses were by three points or less. They lost all nine SEC road games and, with a 5-22 record, finished last in the conference.

A 47-46 double-overtime loss to Vanderbilt in the first round of the SEC Tournament accurately reflected the agony of that season. Five victories were the fewest wins since the 1937 team went 5-13, and Florida's 22 losses that year are the most ever in a single season.

There was one record-setting high point in this miserable year. Randall Leath made all 10 field goal attempts and all eight free-throw attempts, scoring 28 points to lead the Gators to a season-opening 91-80 victory over Biscayne College. It remains the only time a Florida player has scored 20 or more points with a perfect shooting night from both the field and the free-throw line. Ironically, Leath's opening-night performance was the best of his four-year career.

Once again the program was rattled by defections. It was rumored that Delancy, Moses, and Williams were receiving some financial incentives to help jump-start the Gator program. Moses felt he wasn't being "adequately appreciated." He was a good student and a fine player. Sloan said Moses was homesick, and the talented point guard transferred to St. Johns.

For the players, memories of those years under Sloan remain intense. "Playing for Sloan was the worst experience of my life," said Hayes Dickens. "I was very unhappy and just felt things weren't going to get any better," said Mike Moses. "Sloan drove me to a mental breakdown," said Marty Perry. "It was my senior year but I had no choice. I had to get out of there," said Mike Milligan.

Harden, whose brother Roger played for Kentucky, also defected. Harden had a career high of 24 in Florida's win over Florida State and scored 20-plus points against both Kentucky and Tennessee. His departure left the Gators with only 10 scholarship players for the next season.

Sloan was always aggressive in the face of controversy. With the departure of players in these early years, he was quick to take the offensive.

In a *Boston Globe* article by Michael Madden, Sloan contended, "People have said there were personality conflicts here. Every kid who doesn't like his daddy has a personality conflict, and every kid who doesn't like his coach has a personality conflict. Well, I was in the service where they were shooting real bullets at me, and I wanted to transfer out of there. But I didn't. I hung in there."

In his second tour of duty in Gainesville, Sloan faced a very different attitude in the athletic administration than what had confronted his predecessors. When he first came to Florida in 1960, one of his first acts of exorcism of the football demons was to remove the picture of football Coach Ray Graves which was enshrined on the wall behind every coach's desk. Lefty Driesell was fond of chiding Sloan about his football boss who would always be looking over his shoulder from up above. This time around, the athletic administration had a major stake in the program's success and made efforts to break down the barriers that had made basketball feel second class in the past.

A vital component in constructing a first-class program is hiring quality people to support the effort. Three people who would add immeasurably to the program's future assumed roles in the 1983 season.

Chris Cameron, Jim Mackie, and David Steele brought credibility and professionalism to Florida basketball, and their respective roles strengthened the program tremendously.

Cameron brought an unselfish creative marketing talent from Lexington, Kentucky, where his love for roundball was a birthright. Cameron won professional awards with a flashy new look for the Gator Media Guide. He began compiling data that more accurately documented the program's history. Most of all, he projected Florida from the viewpoint of a basketball mentality.

Mackie had been a Florida trainer since 1975 but assumed full-time responsibility for basketball in the 1983 season. Mackie was serious about his responsibilities. He initiated systems to improve players' physical well-being and managed every aspect of their conditioning, from what they ate to how they trained. He implemented stretching and running programs to minimize injuries and was on the leading edge of innovative therapy.

One of the biggest changes came behind the radio play-by-play microphone. Otis Boggs had been the voice of Gator football and basketball since 1948. After 34 years as the voice of the fighting Gators, he was retiring. Boggs was employed by WRUF, the university's radio station, but was as much a part of the Gators as any coach or player. His heart was orange and blue, and he enjoyed a love affair with Gator fans.

In Florida Gym, Boggs would broadcast from a crow's nest balcony behind the north-end glass backboard – a terrible vantage point from which to observe a game. In a quiet pressure-filled moment, many an opposing player's free-throw attempt was disrupted as he peered through the glass backboard to both see and hear Boggs' commentary. Boggs tried to get the location's best view by positioning himself to the far side of the seating area, but he still had an awkward look at the game. When the action went to the far end of the court, he had one of the worst seats in the house.

For all those many years, though, Boggs' words created the game's best picture for the many fans across the state who could not attend Gator games. Boggs was legendary as the voice of Florida football, and although basketball enjoyed a much more limited statewide coverage, he had delivered the play-by-play of both sports for over three decades. Replacing him would be a tough assignment.

The task went to Richard Giannini, the associate athletic director. Giannini wanted to accomplish two major objectives with the new announcer. First and foremost, he wanted a broadcasting talent who could articulate the action of both sports with energy and accuracy. Second, he wanted a full-time staff member who would help build a statewide network for both sports. Giannini believed it was imperative for the athletic department to control the products they were marketing and decided Florida would create the new position of network coordinator. The job demanded a talented broadcaster who could also administer a network of station affiliates.

David Steele was one of over 200 applicants for the job. Steele was born in

Jacksonville, grew up in Knoxville, and graduated from the University of Georgia. His selection was greeted with skepticism by many loyal Gator fans. It would be a huge challenge to follow in the footsteps of a legendary figure. Steele handled the transition beautifully, quickly winning the respect of Gator fans.

The network part of the job became an even bigger assignment. Carr and Giannini had made a commitment to Sloan that the new radio network would deliver games to every major market in the state. Florida football was an easy sell, but not all stations wanted to carry Florida basketball. Steele had to craft a network arrangement with stations that would carry both sports.

It was a major turning point in athletic department policy. Basketball would be given a chance to have increased statewide exposure at the expense of losing some stations carrying Florida football. Several longtime station affiliates severed their relationships with Florida by refusing to carry Gator basketball. It proved to be a critical departure from the football mentality of the past.

Cameron, Mackie, and Steele were valuable off-the-court additions, and people around the Southeast began to notice that the University of Florida was no longer just giving lip service in its struggle to successfully compete in basketball.

The reconstruction of Florida basketball continued to labor under the yoke of disquieting events as the 1983 season opened with the suspension of four players, Vernon Delancy, Tony Rogers, Rodney Williams, and Ronnie Williams. The players' unauthorized use of an athletic department telephone credit card was the grounds for their suspension, and they failed to make the trip to the Great Alaska Shootout.

Ironically, this event went substantially unnoticed in light of even more dramatic allegations of impropriety surrounding Florida athletics. The breaking news story was the investigation of Charlie Pell and University of Florida football. Little was mentioned about the absence of the four basketball players as the team lost two of three games in Alaska. Even their return to the lineup was almost a footnote in light of the controversy swirling around football.

Sloan recorded his 500th career win when Florida beat Jacksonville 56-47 in the Gator Bowl final. It was the Gators' ninth Gator Bowl Tournament title and a night for everyone to celebrate Norm Sloan's remarkable accomplishment.

He had begun his coaching career in 1952 and five times was named coach of the year in a conference. At N.C. State, Sloan won 266 of 393 Wolfpack games. Now, his overall record was 500 wins and 306 losses. Delancy and McDowell celebrated with Sloan. They were named Gator Bowl Co-MVPs.

The Gator Bowl championship was followed by the season's best win – an 89-85 upset of fifth-ranked Alabama. Nabe Palmer had 18 points and dueled Alabama's Enis Whatley straight up all night long.

Florida also got a 92-79 overtime win against South Florida, which had the nation's leading scorer, Charles Bradley. Bradley finished with 38 points, but Florida's Randall Leath held him scoreless in the overtime period.

The season's most heartbreaking defeat came in double-overtime at Alabama. The Tide had long since lost their fifth-ranked status and were struggling to the finish with a 7-9 conference mark. Florida trailed by 16 points before coming back to tie the game. Nabe Palmer hit a clutch shot with seconds left in regulation to put the game into overtime. But Alabama held on to win 106-99. The loss extended the Gators' consecutive losing streak in Tuscaloosa to 14 games.

Once again, the Gators ended the season dead last in the SEC with a 5-13 mark. They also finished the season with a road loss to Mississippi State and extended a record SEC streak of 22 straight road losses. Ronnie Williams dislocated his shoulder but played in every game as he passed Neal Walk as Florida's all-time leading scorer. He also led the league in scoring with 21.3 points per game. He joined Tony Miller (1972) as the only two Florida players ever to lead the SEC in scoring.

It was the Gators' fifth straight losing basketball season and the fourth time in five years they finished in the cellar of the SEC. Sloan was finishing his third season of a five-year contract, and the basketball faithful were once again getting restless. After three seasons, this was not the kind of progress that Bill Carr envisioned when he fired John Lotz. With the controversy surrounding player defections, the Florida program was receiving the wrong kind of attention. Carr had been told that Sloan had mellowed since his early years as the Gator boss. But it certainly didn't appear that the old dog was performing with any new tricks.

Sloan got some breathing room, however, with a change at the top of the university's administration. Robert Marston resigned, and Marshall Criser moved into Tigert Hall as UF's eighth president.

Although it's new athletic directors, not new presidents, that make coaches particularly nervous, Sloan took the initiative to meet with his new boss. President Criser questioned the student part of the student-athletes Sloan had recruited. Sloan told Criser that to win, Florida had to bring in some marginal students. He told Criser that if Florida wanted to "look like Vanderbilt," he would recruit accordingly. But if Florida wanted a nationally competitive basketball program, it would have to accept student-athletes that were more athlete than student.

It would take time for Marshall Criser to better understand his head basketball coach, but in this meeting he formed some first impressions that would crystallize in the years ahead.

Trying Times

Prior to the start of the 1983-84 season, the university purchased a $50,000 portable hardwood floor for the O'Dome. The new floor would be easier on the players' legs and it would give the basketball a better bounce.

A hardwood court is where the game is really meant to be played, but when the O'Connell Center opened in 1980, a tartan floor had been installed as the playing surface. The surface had been used during the seventies in arenas all across America because it required less maintenance than traditional hardwood. The rubberized material, approximately one inch thick, was poured directly over concrete and, while fairly wear resistant, was devastating to the players' legs.

Big men seemed to have the most difficulty with the high-tech material. Eugene McDowell's legs had paid the price of practicing on the concrete-like surface, so he was a major beneficiary of the change. Sloan hoped the hardwood floor would restore some resiliency to Eugene's prematurely aging legs and give the Gators the bounce they needed to finally have a successful season.

In three seasons, Ronnie Williams had become Florida's all-time leading scorer. Coming into his senior year, Williams was also the SEC's leading scorer. There wasn't a better power forward in the league.

Vernon Delancy, playing at the small forward position, had become one of the most electrifying players to wear a Gator uniform. He had a unique, one-hand stuff that came over his back, and his flair for the sensational captured fans who nicknamed him "Fancy Delancy." Delancy's passing skills made him the leading returning assist player in the SEC. A lefty who fired bullet-like missiles to his teammates, Delancy broke the Florida single-season assist record with 165 assists his junior year.

Nabe Palmer was the team's point guard whose fan club, "Nabe's Navy," provided the Ocala native with a special lift. Palmer started every game the previous year. At 6-foot-1, 185 pounds, he was physically strong and a team-oriented competitor.

Sloan brought in three freshmen who some believe comprised Florida's best backcourt recruiting ever. Joe Lawrence, Andrew Moten, and Darryl Gresham gave Florida three players with the ability to shoot the basketball. The team had a strong front line, and it was anticipated that these talented guards would quickly impact the Florida program.

Lawrence committed during the early November signing period and graduated as the valedictorian of his high school class. He was from Crestview, Florida, and at 6-foot-5, played the point-guard position for his high school team which lost in the finals of the Class 3A state championship. Moten had shot a phenomenal 78.1 percent from the field and 77 percent from the free-throw line in his final season at Quincy Shanks High School. Gresham was an All-American high school guard from Decatur, Georgia.

Florida struggled to a 4-4 record prior to the start of conference play, and on January 3, 1984, opened the SEC part of its schedule in Tuscaloosa, Alabama. You couldn't blame the players for feeling some serious pressure. After all, Florida had lost 22 straight SEC road games, and Alabama had handed Florida 13 consecutive defeats in Coleman Coliseum. Unfortunately, the losing streak would not end that night. Darryl Neal, a transfer from Oregon State, canned a 22-foot jumper with seven seconds to play, and the Tide handed Florida another stinging loss 63-61.

The shell-shocked team picked itself up to try again two nights later at Mississippi State. With the Bulldogs leading 55-54 and time running out, Ronnie Williams rebounded a long-range desperation jumper by Darryl Gresham and scored. The basket finally stopped the bleeding, and the 56-55 win gave the Gators their first SEC road win in three seasons.

Breaking the 23-game losing streak finally got the monkey off the Gators' back and was going to make the five-hour plane ride back home a little more tolerable. At least that's what most were thinking.

Florida was one of the few schools in the country that owned its own airplane, a DC-3 vintage World War II aircraft. Captain Jack Frost was the chief pilot and was responsible for flight operations. Everyone referred to Frost as "Captain Jack." The crusty veteran of World War II felt tremendous pride in working for Gator sports. He was also extremely proud of this airplane.

Frost maintained the equipment in first-class working order. He spit-shined and polished the old warhorse from top to bottom. He found spare parts in surplus depots around the country and kept the "Blue Goose" in the air long after its brothers and sisters had been retired. Frost flew Gator teams across the Southeast in this weathered aircraft for more than 10 years. The plane was loud and it was slow, but it had always been dependable.

Undoubtedly, it was a luxury for the team to have an airplane. They could almost always get back home immediately after an away game. They might not get to Gainesville until 3:00 or 4:00 in the morning, but the players could be back in class the next day. If Florida had depended on commercial airlines, many classroom hours would have been lost.

Former Florida players have delighted through the years in telling "war stories" about their travels on the Blue Goose. While most of those tales had a basis in fact, the danger players felt from any seemingly threatening circumstance was usually more perception than fact. It was, however, unnerving to bounce along through thunderstorms during four- and five-hour road trips. The plane didn't have the speed, climbing ability, or cabin pressure to reach high enough altitudes to provide a smoother ride. For the most part, the Goose pointed toward its destination, climbed to altitude, and took on whatever weather was in its path.

After the "historic" Mississippi State victory, the team boarded the Goose about 4:30 in the afternoon with John Castronover as the chief pilot. As the plane took off, David Steele joked, "Well, now that we've finally broken the road jinx, it wouldn't surprise me if the Goose got up in the air, caught fire, and we crashed and burned."

The words were hardly out of Steele's mouth when passengers were horrified to see flames in the plane's left engine. At 300 feet, the pilots put the plane into a steep left turn to attempt a return to the airport runway. With full power and a hard 90-degree turn, the plane dove toward the ground. Somehow, with only one engine, Castronover managed to land safely. Everyone hurried off the plane. Eugene McDowell may have spoken for all the passengers when he said afterward, "We weren't very high up, but if I had a parachute I would've jumped."

A manifold exhaust system shield which protected the engine compartment had come loose, and what everyone observed was the actual combustion inside the engine itself. Castronover was determined to repair the Blue Goose with a replacement shield from a retired DC-3 that was parked on the airport grounds. He told Sloan that a red indicator light on the instrument panel had come on to indicate a fire in one of the engines, but he had found that hard to believe. Sloan shot back, "The f...... red light came on because there was a f...... fire in the engine." Sloan had taken his last ride on the relic plane. He bussed the team back to the hotel and booked seats the next afternoon on a commercial airline.

Frost's affection for the Blue Goose was greater than it might have been for one of his own children, but he reluctantly agreed to put her out to pasture and begin looking for a more modern airplane. Several months later, the athletic association purchased a 32-seat Fokker F-27. The plane's pressurized cabin substantially improved both the quality and flight time of future trips. The new plane was named "The Captain Jack" in recognition of Frost's dedication to the university.

Florida's best weekend of basketball in six years came against Vanderbilt and Kentucky in the O'Dome. Florida got rolling by beating the Commodores 73-59 and then took on the third-ranked Wildcats. A record crowd of 12,074 fans and a national television audience saw Florida upset the Cats 69-57.

Delancy, McDowell, Moten, and Williams combined for 58 of Florida's 69 points. Kentucky's Sam Bowie, Jimmy Master, Melvin Turpin, and Kenny Walker clearly were no match for the Gators on this occasion.

With the weekend's victories, the Gators recorded seven wins in their next nine games. Kentucky eked out a 67-65 win in Lexington, and Tennessee came to Gainesville and beat Florida 75-74 in double overtime. Six of Florida's seven

SEC losses that season were decided by an average of 2.67 points.

More than 7,000 fans came to the O'Connell Center for Senior Night and the season's final game against Mississippi State. Action adventure writer Tom Clancy couldn't have scripted a more exciting finish to this thriller. The Bulldogs led 59-58 with seven seconds to play. Florida's senior captain Delancy fired one of his patented one-handers to Ronnie Williams who buried a six-foot turn-around jumper as time expired. It was a dramatic 60-59 victory and a triumphant farewell for these two seniors.

Florida won 16 regular-season games and, with an 11-7 conference finish, produced the best comeback in the 51-year history of the SEC. The Gators went from 10th place in 1983 to a third place tie with LSU in 1984. It was Florida's best SEC season since 1969.

Florida's NCAA dreams were dashed when Tennessee's freshman guard Tony White scored 30 points as the Volunteers beat Florida in the first round of the SEC Tournament in overtime 80-74. It was a sudden and dramatic end to what many had hoped would be the year Florida would make its first NCAA Tournament appearance. But, after five straight losing seasons, Florida was content with any postseason bid. The invitation came from the NIT, and for the first time since 1969, Florida would keep playing.

Florida was paired with South Alabama in Biloxi, Mississippi. The Gulf Coast Coliseum was a home-court advantage for the Jaguars, and South Alabama nipped the Gators 88-87 to end the season. Dexter Shouse and Michael Gerren contributed 56 points to lead South Alabama.

Individual efforts leave no doubt about the achievements of this team. Ronnie Williams set career records with 722 field goals and 546 free throws. He became Florida's all-time leading scorer with 2,090 points. Ironically, in a four-year career, Williams was never picked to the first team of the SEC. He was named to the second-team for the third time in four years.

Vernon Delancy set a four-year Gator record with 427 assists and tied Richard Glasper with a career average of 4.2 assists per game. Delancy's 13 assists in his final game against South Alabama were also a career high.

These two players became Florida's first two basketball players ever to be drafted by the NBA together in the same year. Williams was a second-round pick of the Boston Celtics, and Delancy was a third-round choice of the Milwaukee Bucs.

These two players had successfully produced most of the program's highlights during the past four years. But they were also the first Florida players to complete four years of athletic eligibility and fail to earn University of Florida degrees.

A Five-Year Assessment

With a winning season and a trip to the NIT, expectations for the 1984-85 year were the highest since Norm Sloan's return to Gainesville.

Despite the fact that Williams and Delancy had moved on, Florida returned five experienced players for the season. Eugene McDowell and Randall Leath were up front and could compete with any front line in the SEC. Joe Lawrence, Andrew Moten, and Darryl Gresham played key roles the year before, and their sophomore status belied the experience they had gained from the prior year's success. Francisco Leon and Danny Sheldon had been played sparingly and were entering their final season.

Sloan had recruited what at the time was arguably Florida's best freshman class – Cornelius Brodus, Pat Lawrence, Vernon Maxwell, Ken McClary, and Ronnie Montgomery. All five new players were from the state of Florida, and 12 of 14 players on Florida's roster played their high school basketball inside the state.

Maxwell had received the state of Florida's Mr. Basketball award and was a standout in both football and basketball at Gainesville's Buchholz High School. Lawrence followed in the footsteps of his brother Joe and was touted as being even more talented. Brodus, McClary, and Montgomery had all been recruited by the best schools in America.

Florida won its first seven games, beating six in-state rivals: Central Florida, Florida State, Jacksonville, South Florida, St. Thomas, and Stetson. The Gators scored 120 points to rout St. Thomas on the road, and all 12 Florida players saw action. The win resulted in career highs for Danny Sheldon with 15 points and Rollie Castineyra with 10. With a high-powered offense and an intimidating full-court pressure defense, this team was averaging 88 points a game and putting victories on the scoreboard.

The Gators had a setback in the Hoosier Classic when Indiana provided a lesson in team defense and picked Florida apart possession by possession for an 80-63 victory. It was the first time Florida had played the Hoosiers in Indiana, and Bobby Knight was now 3-0 against Florida teams.

Florida took a 3-2 conference mark on the road to Lexington where they had never beaten Kentucky in Rupp Arena. In a regionally televised game, Andrew Moten scored 26 points and made eight of 10 crucial free throws to lead Florida over the Wildcats 67-55. Maxwell and Leath both finished in double figures. It was only the 13th time Kentucky had lost in Rupp Arena since its opening in the 1976-77 season.

It was also a night when Darryl Gresham made only one of 10 field goals after averaging double figures through a brilliant first 13 games. It was later reported that Gresham had failed drug tests and was battling a cocaine problem that would soon end his Florida Gator career.

This Gator team teased the fans into believing it could have a great season. At one point the record stood at 16-5, but Florida lost five of its remaining six regular-season games to finish at 17-10.

The team gathered itself and pulled a big surprise in the SEC Tournament. In the first round, the Gators drew Kentucky. Florida trailed at the half, and Assistant Coach Monte Towe suggested they try putting 6-foot-10 Francisco Leon at the point of Kentucky's 2-3 zone to get better offensive ball movement. Leon handled the assignment beautifully and got the ball to Randall Leath in the paint for three key second-half baskets. The strategy made the difference in Florida's 58-55 upset win. The Kentucky victory took some of the sting out of the team's late-season collapse. It was only the second time in school history that Florida had beaten the Wildcats twice in the same season. Auburn eliminated Florida in the second round 43-42, and the Tigers went on to win the tournament title.

The season's second-half tailspin once again dispelled any chances for an NCAA Tournament bid as five conference teams – Alabama, Georgia, Kentucky, LSU, and tournament champion Auburn – were on the quest for the Final Four. Alabama, Auburn, and Kentucky made it to the Sweet 16.

Tennessee and Florida received invitations to the NIT, and for the second consecutive year, Florida was sent on the road. This time the opponent was Southwestern Louisiana in Lafayette, Louisiana. Blackham Coliseum looked like an expanded World War II mess hall. It was dark, with exposed rafters and an ancient hardwood floor, but it provided a great college basketball atmosphere.

Someone must have bought the fire marshal an all-expense-paid trip to Hawaii because 7,300 ragin' Cajun fans squeezed their way in to witness the final game ever played in this Louisiana antique.

The game had nine lead changes in the last six minutes. Andrew Moten kept the Gators alive as he answered every Cajun basket and scored Florida's final nine points.

With 38 seconds to play, the Gators trailed 65-64 and called time out. They elected to run the clock down, and with six seconds, Maxwell drove into the lane, but his running 12-footer came up short. Moten rebounded the ball on the right-hand side of the basket.

David Steele was broadcasting the game and later said, "I can still see Drew rebounding the ball. He was wide open – no one within six feet." But with time about to expire, and rushing to beat the clock, Moten curled a right-handed shot around the left side of the goal that rolled around the rim and fell off at the buzzer. It was heartbreaking for Moten. He had given such a clutch performance. "I had to put it up fast, I never heard the buzzer," Moten said despondently. "I thought it would come down to an outside shot, but I was right there under the basket. How did I miss it?"

The 65-64 defeat was another dagger in the heart of a Florida team that had lost its final two games of the season in the closing seconds. Florida finished with an 18-12 record and posted back-to-back winning seasons for the first time since the John Lotz years. The Gators also earned their first back-to-back postseason tournament invitations. Fan attendance was up by over 2,000 per game, and Florida averaged a record, season-high 8,745 fans.

Randall Leath and Eugene McDowell started every game. McDowell averaged 14.2 points and 9.8 rebounds a game. He was a unanimous choice for first-team All-SEC and the first Florida player to be named to the conference's first team since Chip Williams received the honor in 1974. McDowell became Florida's fourth all-time leading scorer and second all-time leading rebounder. His career field goal shooting percentage of 59 percent was also the best ever for a Florida player and the best that year in the SEC. McDowell was an iron man, starting a school-record 117 consecutive games. He set the O'Connell Center record for most points in a game by a Gator (40 against Biscayne, 12/21/82) and most rebounds (21 against Georgia, 1/6/82). More importantly, he graduated in four years with a degree in communications.

Eugene McDowell was an icon of Gator sports in the eighties. Growing up in nearby Cross City, he was a highly visible talent who was heavily recruited. His parents had seven children, and his father worked in the limerock mines of Central Florida. Gene's dad, James, was a determined and rugged individual who felt immense pride in his son's athletic accomplishments.

Mr. McDowell cut and sold blackjack oak to help pay the expenses of the large family, and his old beat-up "pick-em-up" truck wore out the road between Gainesville and Cross City. James McDowell sold hundreds of cords of wood to Gator supporters who were only too happy to support the efforts of the McDowell family. When Eugene was being recruited, an unofficial competition began between FSU and Florida to see whether it would be Gainesville or Tallahassee that would buy the most wood.

The Gators pulled out all the stops and enlisted one of their most fervent fans, Sonny Tillman. Sonny owned a regionally famous chain of barbeque restaurants, "Sonny's Real Pit Bar-B-Q," and he was delighted to be enlisted as a customer. He happily discovered that McDowell's wood was far superior to what he had been getting. Florida won the contest, and more importantly, big Gene. The final score: Florida 350 cords – FSU 0.

Academically, McDowell was a marginal admission with an average high school transcript. But he had determination enough to swim the English Channel, and no one before or since has worked harder to earn his Florida degree. McDowell had a warm, engaging smile and a personality that was infectious. He truly loved the University of Florida. McDowell's tragic sudden death from a defective heart valve in 1995 stunned everyone. Eugene McDowell proved that even at a school as academically demanding as Florida, you can achieve your dream if you never give up.

Randall Leath also had strong family ties to the Gainesville community and had a lifelong dream to play for the Gators. But he failed to really capitalize on his 6-foot-9 potential, and some felt the quietly reserved big man would have responded more productively in a different coaching environment.

Randall's career high came in his first Gator game when he scored 28 points and never missed a field goal or free throw attempt. As a senior, his season high was 19 points in Florida's NIT loss to Southwestern Louisiana.

Leath earned his Florida diploma and entered the coaching profession where he is recognized as one of this state's best high school coaches. As head coach at Gainesville's P.K. Yonge High School, Leath coached his team to the state high school basketball championship in 1991. One of his key players that championship year was a future Gator, Clayton Bates. Leath joined Gators Steve Williams and Edd Poore who had also coached high school championship teams in the state.

On paper, it appears that the 1985 year was a highlight for Florida basketball. But for those who were part of the program, it was actually a traumatic season. The departure of Gresham, the disquieting questions about Gator players using drugs, and the erratic play down the stretch made this another dispiriting year.

Norm Sloan had completed the fifth season of his second tenure. Sloan's overall record was 64 wins and 81 defeats. In the previous 70 seasons of University of Florida basketball, there were eight time periods during which a coach had guided the Gators for five seasons or more. One of those eight was Sloan's first stop in Gainesville during the sixties. Of these eight coaching time periods, Sloan's record from 1981 to 1985 was the worst since Brady Cowell coached Florida 60 years before.

COACHES' RECORDS IN THEIR FIRST FIVE SEASONS

Coach	Tenure	Win/Loss	Winning Percentage
Brady Cowell	1926-1930	35-60	.368
Sam McAllister	1938-1942	56-36	.608
Sam McAllister	1947-1951	63-60	.512
John Mauer	1952-1956	58-52	.527
Norm Sloan	1961-1965	69-53	.565
Tommy Bartlett	1967-1971	74-55	.573
John Lotz	1974-1978	71-62	.534
Norm Sloan	1981-1985	64-81	.441
Lon Kruger	1991-1995	92-64	.589

Some might wonder how Sloan's job could have survived such a disappointing period in Florida hoops. With some of Florida basketball's most talented players and the total backing of the athletic administration, why wasn't someone demanding more accountability from Sloan? He had a modern, new arena. The program had a statewide radio network and a televised basketball show on the weekends. There were more than adequate recruiting budgets and award-winning media guides. Sloan had been allocated more administrative support than any coaching staff before.

Perhaps the answer could be found in the same place that coaches in the past had complained about so bitterly. Florida was a football school, and few people really cared about the fortunes of the basketball program. It was also a football school that had its neck in the wringer, and the university was trying to survive serious fallout and the national repercussions of that situation. A possible NCAA death penalty for football indiscretions was a lot more serious than a marginal basketball program which, according to Sloan, was digging itself out of a very deep hole and needed more time and talent to begin winning more games.

Fighting for Respect

Despite the problems, there was room for optimism about the future. The program was beginning to win more games than it was losing, and more talented players were arriving on campus every day.

Joe Lawrence was a rising junior. An engineering major, who later also earned a Masters of Business Administration at UF, Lawrence was more typical of Gator players in previous programs than his own teammates during these years.

If college athletics had to construct a model for an athlete's grit and determination, it would have been Joe Lawrence. He was about two inches taller than Tom Barbee, who played in a Gator uniform during the early sixties, but in many other ways they were similar.

Both were engineering majors and burned the midnight oil. Both were a step slow on the court, but would out-think their opponents. Both were tough, hard-nosed competitors who could stick a clutch jumper. Both were hammered often by Sloan's uncomplimentary comments.

For Lawrence and his teammates, the 1986 season was a roller coaster ride unlike any season before. Sloan's staff recruited five newcomers – junior college transfers Jon Currington and Melven Jones, and freshmen Chris Capers, Reed Crafton, and Clifford Lett.

The front cover design of the media guide won a national award for originality, and Florida would be challenged to design a style of play that would be equally commanding. They were faced with accommodating the loss of a strong front line to graduation. The media had again picked Florida to finish only seventh in the conference, and most believed they would struggle to have a .500 season. But in the openers, Florida lost only to Ohio State on the road, and won the other four of its first five games.

The reason was the "M&M boys." Vernon Maxwell and Andrew Moten were the best guard tandem ever to play in the Gator back court. Maxwell was 6-foot-4, 180 pounds, and had the quickest first step of any Gator player. He could pull up and score with great range, but he was most effective slashing through the defense to score off the dribble. Moten at 6-foot, 170 pounds, could also make the 22-foot jumper with consistency and played with determination.

The M&M boys had the tools and the tenacity to make life difficult for opponents on both ends of the floor. Where other great Florida guard tandems played with surgeon-like precision, the M&M boys were performance artists. Their flair for the spectacular made for exciting nights in the O'Dome. They would start every game together for the next two years.

In the previous five seasons, Sloan had arranged to play in some very good December tournaments that were located in some very nice places. Florida had been to the Cabrillo Classic in San Diego, the Great Alaska Shootout in Anchorage, the Sugar Bowl Classic in New Orleans, and the Hoosier Classic in Indianapolis. The promise of these tournaments was not only valuable as a recruiting carrot, but also gave the Florida teams a nationally competitive perspective.

This year Florida was slated to play in the Rebel Roundup in Las Vegas. The Gators had a great time visiting this glitzy city but were embarrassingly inept, losing to lowly Iona 71-70 and San Diego State 63-62. In both games, Florida had enough talent to capture 20-point wins but gave uninspired performances which even had the cynical gamblers raising their eyebrows.

The problem had nothing to do with betting – it was coaching, plain and simple. Playing in the casinos got more attention than focusing on what would take place on the court. The coaching staff allowed slot machines to take priority over game preparation. The players just did not have a coach who made sure the team was ready to play.

As a spectator, watching Sloan coach was as frustrating as trying to compete for him as a player. Sloan would scowl and scream. He would rant and rave. He would fume and flare. But there was little method to his madness. Much of these sideline antics were one very big act.

His coaching lacked focus and consistency. There was seldom a strategy behind his substitutions. The only thing a player knew with certainty was that the "hook" was coming when he made a mistake. Most played with one eye on their opponent and the other eye on Sloan. It was a knee-jerk reaction for a player who knew he had made a mistake to look over his shoulder to see if he was coming out of the game.

The critical nature of Sloan's personality did not lend itself to constructive instruction. Because players felt defensive in their relationship, they found it difficult to comfortably focus on improving a particular skill. By force-feeding information, Sloan impaired the learning process, with the result that his teams were characterized by a one-dimensional style of play. His teams lacked fundamental preparation and relied purely on their natural allotments of talent and tenacity. Sloan's attitude was to leave them alone so as not to screw them up. Sloan once said, "At this level coaches don't win basketball games. Players win games."

Florida came back to Gainesville from the Christmas break and squeaked by an SEC tune-up with Stetson 69-66 on December 30. Three nights later, Florida was in Knoxville. Maxwell and Moten scored 24 of Florida's final 28 points. Joe Lawrence made two pressure free throws for his only two points of the night in the closing seconds of overtime to seal Florida's 77-75 victory. It was Florida's third straight win over the Volunteers and the first time ever for back-to-back victories in Knoxville.

Florida came home to beat Auburn 62-59 and then clobbered Vanderbilt 86-55 in the O'Dome by the largest margin of victory against any SEC school since the 96-63 Georgia thrashing in 1967. The Gators led by 11 at the half, and Joe and Pat Lawrence combined for 22 points. Pat Lawrence also had a career-high nine rebounds.

Joe Lawrence was having a terrific junior year even though he was playing in the shadow of the M&M boys. Lawrence came to work every day with a positive attitude that was second to none in Gator history. His personal resolve to succeed despite the circumstances that caused others to quit or withdraw made him the most valuable member of the team during his tenure. Joe had the mental toughness to focus on his role and block out distractions – a trait that would have worn well on his brother Pat.

The Lawrence brothers' parents were dedicated fans who were immersed in their sons' basketball experiences. Karen and Bill Lawrence rarely missed a Florida game on the road or at home, regularly traveling to away games or making the five-hour drive from Crestview to Gainesville. These two brothers were the first members of the same family to play together in Gator uniforms, and the proud Lawrences truly treated Florida basketball as a family affair.

The Gators need all the family they can rally together when they play the Georgia Bulldogs in Athens. No other SEC rivalry is more heated, and this year's meeting went way beyond the boiling point.

Florida, 8-4, had lost seven of its previous eight games in Athens, even though Florida teams had recorded more SEC road wins against the Bulldogs than any of their other conference rivals. The Bulldogs were coming off a stinging loss at Vanderbilt in a game which Georgia Coach Hugh Durham felt Georgia was out-fought. Their record was 9-4.

The rivalry has always been potentially explosive, and the atmosphere in the Georgia Coliseum that night was as heated as the coils in a nuclear reactor. A capacity Georgia crowd was on hand to greet the Gators.

Georgia's three seniors, Donald Hartry, Horace McMillan, and Joe Ward, were averaging double figures. The events of this night, however, would cast junior David Dunn and freshman Patrick Hamilton into the most prominent roles.

Dunn was a powerful 6-foot-8, 225-pound junior who two nights earlier played a bad game against the Commodores. Durham had challenged Dunn to get himself physically involved at the start of this game. On the first possession, Maxwell drove for a layup, and Dunn smashed him to the floor. Dunn played as if his team was storming the beaches at Normandy, and in the next 10 minutes, had eight of Georgia's first 12 points, plus five rebounds.

Georgia was physically intimidating the Gators. At the half, the Bulldogs held a 40-32 lead and were shooting 59 percent. With 7,000 partisan Georgia fans yearning for a rout of the hated Gators, Georgia ran away to a 53-40 second-half lead. With 13:01 on the clock, another in a long history of violent Florida-Georgia encounters erupted.

David Steele, who called the action, remembers the events this way:

> It was a very physical game in a highly emotional arena. A lot of pushing and shoving and trash-talk was stirring the pot pretty well. Maxwell took a length-of-the-floor pass after a Georgia basket and was hammered from behind by the freshman Patrick Hamilton.
>
> John Clougherty and Lewis Grillo were officiating, and with their attention focused on Hamilton's flagrant foul, Maxwell darted into a group of players from both teams and caught McMillan with a quick right hand. Just as quickly Maxwell backed away, and Dunn at 225 pounds and McClary at 220 went toe to toe. It was a heavyweight encounter that would rival a George Foreman – Muhammad Ali main event. McMillan quickly found Maxwell and these two were swinging away. The arena had now turned into a Wednesday night brawl, and welterweights and heavyweights were duking it out.
>
> All four players landed solid blows and McMillan was throwing punches at everyone. He even blindsided Mark Saso who was doing his best to get out of the "ring."
>
> The officials had a real donnybrook on their hands. The fans chanted "It's great to be a Gator-hater," and with so many short fuses in the stands, only a miracle kept the arena from becoming a raging inferno.

Maxwell's left hand was injured, but it would be a non-event because he and Hamilton were both tossed out of the game. McMillan, McClary, and Dunn all kept playing, and although the Gators closed to within five at the 9:15 mark, Georgia reclaimed control and cruised to an 89-69 victory.

Florida came home to shoot 38 percent and lose 72-55 to Kentucky but then upset LSU 74-65. It was only the second time Florida had beaten the Tigers in the previous 17 meetings. Pat Lawrence had his best game to date. The sophomore had six offensive rebounds and finished with 12 rebounds and 13 points for the night.

LSU brought a 17-2 record to Gainesville and a sophomore sensation, John Williams. Unknown to anyone at the time, they also brought the chicken pox. Williams and teammate Bernard Woodside, who spent most of the game on the bench, infected two young spectators seated directly behind the LSU bench. Luke Steele, son of Florida's broadcasting voice David Steele, and Ben Blevins, son of Gator golf Coach Lynn Blevins, both came down with the childhood disease.

With the LSU win, Florida began to play some very good basketball, winning eight of its final 13 games. The Gators took a 16-11 record to Lexington for the SEC Tournament, but barely had time to unpack their bags before LSU handed them a first-round 72-66 defeat.

But with another winning record, Florida received its third consecutive shot at the NIT. This time, Florida was the host. For the first time, the O'Connell Center became a site for a postseason tournament encounter. Southern Mississippi was the first-round foe.

It was a reunion for the Lawrence brothers and their former high school teammate Kenny Siler who led the Golden Eagles. A sparse crowd of 6,200 showed up and were rewarded with a Florida victory. The Gators overcame a 13-point first-half deficit and beat the Golden Eagles 81-71. Ronnie Montgomery recorded a career-high 22 points, knocking down 10 of 11 free throws in the win.

Florida's victory earned the team a second-round opponent in Gainesville – Texas Christian University. More than 7,000 fans witnessed a game-ending moment that will live forever in their memories.

TCU tied the game at 75 with under a minute to play, and Florida held the ball for the last shot. Montgomery missed a free-throw-line jumper, and Joe Lawrence outfought everyone for the loose ball. With time running out, Lawrence passed it to Montgomery who gave it back to Lawrence deep in the left corner. Joe Lawrence put up a shot. For a split second, no one moved. As the high arching jumper hung, as if suspended in midair above the rim, there was a moment of deadly silence. All of the years when the Gators' hopes were dashed by the failure to win "the big one" seemed to cast an invisible barrier across the time line of the present.

But this time the shot went in. As the clock expired, the ball tickled the twine for the 77-75 game-winner. It was the most dramatic finish in O'Connell Center history, and the explosion of fan appreciation could be heard two blocks away. That basket was the defining moment for the career of Joe Lawrence – a ticket to a lifetime of special memories in the theater of a Florida basketball fan's mind.

Lawrence's shot released all the emotion felt for so many years by loyal Gator fans. When it came down to crunch time in a big game, fans had become accustomed to withholding their hearts. They had been broken so many times before. But on this night, in this situation, something magical happened. Lawrence's shot made everyone feel like winners. The Gators didn't fold. They took everything the opponent offered and struck when it counted most. Joe Lawrence was a hero.

The emotion of that night seemed to make believers out of everyone. The NIT sent Southwest Missouri State to Gainesville, giving the Gators their third straight chance to win at home. A victory would put Florida in New York City for the championship round.

This time it was Vernon Maxwell's turn to take the team where it had never been before. With 22 points and pressure free throws in the closing seconds, Maxwell gave Florida its finest winning moment and its first-ever trip to a national final four. The Gators beat Southwest Missouri State 54-53.

FIGHTING FOR RESPECT

After the game, the Florida pep band blasted "New York, New York." Ronnie Montgomery donned a sportcoat over his Gator uniform and, with a top hat on his head, sat proudly on the rim of the basket holding a sign stating simply "Apple Time."

The celebration was one of the most penetrating emotional moments in the history of Florida basketball. All of the years when the Gators got close but never smoked the cigar were for a brief moment extinguished. This team would play for a national title.

In basketball, a conference tournament championship or a trip to one of two national final fours is the opportunity for a team to truly be winners even if they weren't the conference champion. It wasn't the Big Dance that is thrown by the NCAA, but the NIT had always been special to basketball people. For teams that didn't receive one of the NCAA's 64 invitations, it was a chance to keep playing. As Norm Sloan was fond of saying, "Winning is good, and losing is bad."

The only sad note to the occasion was that senior Mark Saso wouldn't be making the trip with the team. He had worked hard for three years to make himself and his teammates better each day. At 6-foot-11, he was far from gifted but genuinely gave his best effort. Driving back to his dorm the night before the team left for the Big Apple, he was in an automobile accident near the Florida law school, and sustained a career-ending broken ankle.

Florida lost to Wyoming 67-58 and also lost the consolation game to Louisiana Tech 67-62. But for the record, it didn't matter because getting to New York was a huge step for the Florida program.

The Art of Survival

With everyone but Saso coming back for the next season, there was a revitalization of Gator hoops. The Joe Lawrence jump shot and Vernon Maxwell's phenomenal junior season had propelled Florida basketball to the next level. The best was yet to come.

Perhaps, more than anything, the year proved beyond the shadow of any doubt that Sloan was a survivor and knew how to win. A year earlier, there had been speculation about the renewal of his contract which would come to an end after the '87 season.

Following a 1986 road loss in Nashville, the media began questioning Sloan's future and whether his contract would be renewed. Sloan challenged athletic director Bill Carr the Sunday after he returned from Nashville and demanded a contract extension. He told Carr any rumors about his departure would kill recruiting and ruin his efforts to resurrect the Gator program. Carr agreed to a three-year extension.

Soon after the season ended, Andrew Moten launched a press attack on Sloan. Moten unleashed strong personal feelings about what he described as Sloan's "communication inconsistencies."

In Bill King's *Orlando Sentinel* interview, Moten said, "Sloan lied to the media, and lied to his players." Moten announced he was leaving the program. It wasn't the first time Moten had said he was leaving, but it was the most outspoken he had been on the subject.

Sloan's reply was, "Communication is a two-way street," but this time Sloan waved a white flag and patched things up. Once again, Sloan had dodged a bullet aimed at him by one of his disenchanted players. But with the departure of Gresham the previous season and rumors of a drug problem in the program, the artillery was getting closer.

Sloan liked to remind anyone who would listen that when he was in the Armed Services they were shooting real bullets. He felt players in this era lacked his personal toughness and were being coddled by other college coaches. It was one of his old songs, but the lyrics were losing their appeal.

By Norm Sloan's seventh season, it seemed time to expect more. Some schools have the luxury of sustaining championship programs year after year. But most go through cycles with change bringing lean years. In the past Florida had been at the doorstep, but it seemed the timing was always off. It was often someone else's year. In 1967 it was ninth-ranked Tennessee that dominated the SEC. In 1977 Alabama,

Kentucky, and Tennessee were all ranked in the top 20. Florida had teams those years that easily could have won a title in a different season.

At 60 years of age, Sloan still had the fire in his belly to win. He desperately wanted that first SEC championship and thought this was finally the team that could do it. "I think this is a team that could develop into the kind of team that could challenge for the championship," he said.

There were plenty of reasons to be excited. All five Florida starters were returning, and the Gators landed a prize recruit – 7-foot-2 high school *Parade* All-American Dwayne Schintzius from Brandon, Florida.

The '87 season began with an 80-76 loss at Florida State before 13,303 fans, the largest crowd ever to watch a basketball game in the state. The Gators had a one-point lead at the half but could not overcome a 41 percent shooting night and FSU's 22 of 31 free throws, 14 more attempts than Florida.

The Gators then won eight straight. They scored 116 points to beat Western Carolina, 110 points in a win over SMU, and their first SEC win of the season 96-75 at home against LSU. The string of wins included the Gator Bowl championship when they scored 82 points on successive nights to beat both Virginia Tech and Ohio State.

After the holidays, the team traveled to Hawaii for the Rainbow Classic. In Honolulu Florida lost the tournament opener to California when a freshman scored 28 points. Kevin Johnson made two crucial free throws with time running out to ice California's 83-80 win. He later achieved years of NBA fame.

Florida's Joe Lawrence was "pure" as he made his first five three-pointers and finished with nine out of 10 three's for the game. Lawrence established a three-point field goal record which should stay in the books for a long, long time. The one he missed, however, made the difference in the California winning margin.

Ohio State then turned the tables on the Gators 88-84, paying them back for a defeat two weeks earlier. Maxwell was the leading scorer in eight of the first nine games, averaging 23 points a game. His 33 points in the Gator Bowl final against Ohio State was a career high and earned him the tournament's MVP award. He set a new high of 34 points in the final game of the Rainbow Classic against the University of Hawaii, and Florida left the island with a 115-83 win.

After three games in four days, Florida made the grueling 11-hour trip back across five time zones to land in Athens, Georgia, on New Year's Day to begin the rest of its conference schedule. The flight had been exhausting, and when the travelers got to Athens, they took the extra day of rest to get back on Eastern time and prepare for the SEC game against the Bulldogs on January 3.

Showing no ill effect from the trip, the Gators grabbed a commanding 13-point halftime lead and got their second SEC win of the season 87-80. Chris Capers gave Florida a career-high performance, scoring 18 points and snagging 17 rebounds. Joe Lawrence made all five of his three-point attempts.

The Gators then won six of their next seven conference games, falling only to the Wildcats in Lexington in a five-point loss. They beat Mississippi State in Gainesville 100-56, the biggest margin of victory ever in an SEC game. Moten and Maxwell each scored 24 against the Bulldogs, and the team shot 58 percent from the field.

The Gators drew capacity crowds in beating both Tennessee and Vanderbilt and then set an arena record with a standing-room-only official crowd of 12,087 as they took their 19th-ranked team on the floor to play Alabama. With Vernon Maxwell in foul trouble, Andrew Moten played brilliantly to score 25 points and answer big second-half baskets by Alabama's Jim Farmer and Derrick McKey. Joe Lawrence banged in two three-point baskets in overtime, and Melven Jones had 17 rebounds for Florida's 90-80 upset victory.

The Gators now had their best start ever in SEC play and shared the conference lead with Kentucky at 8-1. Never had a Florida team been at the top of the conference halfway through the conference season. Sellout crowds in the O'Connell Center were adding the exclamation point on what was shaping up to be a tremendous basketball season. Sloan had now constructed a Gator program in which every starter was a Florida high school product, and the program was back to its status as the premier college basketball program in the state of Florida.

The capacity crowds in the O'Connell Center were charged with expectations. They were confident this would finally be the year. With the M&M boys in the back court, Joe Lawrence lighting it up on the perimeter, and an All-American high school 7-footer in the post, the Gators seemed ready to pour on the voltage.

McClary and Montgomery had been starters the year before and were not accustomed to coming off the bench. But they gave the team exceptional depth. Florida also received marvelous play from the 6-foot-5 senior Melven Jones, who transferred to Florida a year earlier from Cisco Junior College in Texas.

Jones played in just four games as a junior, but started five times and played in 31 contests his senior year. In his first career start, he had a career-high 17 rebounds in the overtime win against Alabama. Jones had double-figure scoring nights against Auburn and Georgia. His athleticism gave the Gators a front-line player who was versatile enough to play any of the three front-court spots in the lineup.

The Gators had won 16 of their first 20 games, and with 11 remaining games, were well on their way to a 20-win season. They were poised to compete for an SEC championship, but they were well aware of the jeopardy that five of their next nine conference games on the road could pose.

It was beginning to become a nightmare for Sloan's teams to travel to the "loveliest village on the plain." Once again Auburn, Alabama, was a thorn in the Alligator's side. The War Eagles ignited a tailspin, popping Florida's SEC championship balloon with an 81-68 trouncing. The 16th-ranked Gators then proceeded to lose five of their next 10 games. Florida had been averaging 89 points a game through the first 20 games but managed only 75 points a game in the season's final seven SEC contests. The Gators lost a second time to Auburn and also suffered road losses to Tennessee, Vanderbilt, and Alabama.

The Alabama loss was another overtime contest, as again the ghosts in Memorial Coliseum appeared. It was the 17th straight loss on the road to the Crimson Tide, but this one was more haunting than the others. Andrew Moten was at the free-throw line with four seconds to play. The Gators were ahead by three. Moten missed, and Alabama's James Jackson threw up a desperation three-pointer which somehow connected to tie the score at the buzzer. In overtime Alabama prevailed and handed Florida a season-ending 86-85 defeat.

The Crimson Tide went on to win the conference with a 16-2 mark. Florida was a distant second in the SEC with six conference defeats. But the Gators' late-season win over Kentucky gave the program a 20-win season for the first time since 1967.

The SEC Tournament in Atlanta provided another chance for redemption. LSU was the first-round opponent, and Florida had beaten them twice by 24- and 21-point margins. But this time the Tigers controlled the overconfident Gators and stunned Florida 72-66. A year earlier, LSU had eliminated the Gators by the exact same score.

This was by far Florida's poorest showing of the season. The stinging loss made for an agonizing drive back down I-75. Many loyal Gators were very upset. They knew, with a 20-win season and a second-place conference finish, that this team would none the less get an NCAA bid. But the poor showing down the stretch, including the opening-round loss to LSU, made this season a bittersweet experience.

Winning is Everything

With a 21-10 record, Florida received its first-ever NCAA bid. The Gators were sent to bitter cold Syracuse, New York, ironically to play Sloan's former coaching venue North Carolina State in the first round. Few believed in this Gator team having the ability to beat the Wolfpack, and to make matters worse, there was a great deal of internal grumbling. As the Gators arrived at the tournament site in upstate New York, it was not a pretty picture for Florida basketball.

Sloan, however, was the most excited he had been since his return to Gainesville. This was the atmosphere he had relished with his N.C. State teams 10 years before. He felt immense pride in giving Florida its first NCAA Tournament appearance. It seemed almost too good to be true. Florida's first-ever trip on the road to the Final Four, and its first hurdle would be against his alma mater North Carolina State. Sloan's competitive juices were flowing.

The NCAA controls the hotel sites for each team. Florida was assigned the worst of the available choices – a circular high-rise Holiday Inn on the edge of downtown Syracuse. The hotel was filled with a large contingent of weekend skiers who were there to have a good time. Sloan was staying in a suite on the upper floor and that first morning waited impatiently for what seemed like an eternity for the elevator to arrive so he could go downstairs for his usual 6 a.m. breakfast.

When the elevator door finally opened, a guy was standing there in a swimming suit, a baseball cap, and a pair of half-skis on his feet. When Sloan got on the elevator, he realized that the guy was "stoned" and had pushed every single button for every floor all the way to the lobby. The granite-faced skier never said a word and just stared straight ahead as the elevator agonizingly descended floor by floor. When Sloan finally arrived on the first floor, he was livid. He went straight to the registration desk and checked the team out of the hotel.

To make matters worse, Sloan had been up late the previous night dealing with another "situation." Assistant Coach Phil Weber heard some commotion on the players' floor and thought the noise was coming from Maxwell and Moten's room. He speculated that the players might have girls in their room and told them to let him in. The players protested, but Weber got inside and found the bathroom door closed. Weber went to open the door, and Moten got forceful in pushing him away. The two got pretty physical. Weber finally got past the Moten barricade to see what was inside, but it wasn't women. It was a bathtub full of booze – champagne, beer, wine, etc. all iced down to celebrate if the Gators won.

The coaches met to decide what to do about the issue. Sloan asked each coach what he thought. "We'll have to suspend him," Towe said. "You can't punch a coach." Weber and McCraney agreed. "It doesn't send the right message to the team if we don't suspend him," Weber said.

Sloan stared back and replied, "Right, but we need the little son of a bitch. I'm sorry, Phil, we've worked too hard to get here. There are a lot of people depending on us to win these f...... games. We'll deal with his sorry ass when we get back home."

Beating his alma mater would be almost as sweet as beating North Carolina for an ACC championship. Sloan's postseason tournament adrenaline was working overtime, and he wasn't about to let a little problem like drinking beer and shoving a coach get in the way.

Vernon Maxwell had one of the greatest games of his career. He scored 28 points and capitalized on his phenomenal talent as Florida overcame an N.C. State nine-point halftime lead. Scoring 17 straight points late in the second half, the Gators snatched the game away from State 82-70 and grabbed their first-ever NCAA Tournament victory.

Andrew Moten scored 19 points and added seven rebounds. The two roommates, who might have been sent packing by another coach, redeemed themselves in Sloan's eyes by giving Florida basketball its finest moment.

These were two big-time players and this was a big-time game. Despite their poor judgment off the court, both rose to the occasion and played wisely and decisively to produce Florida's biggest postseason win. N.C. State had Chuckie Brown, Vinny Del Negro, and Charles Schackleford, but on this night, the Gators had the M&M boys and a victory-hungry coach who would savor this win for years to come.

Two nights later, Dwayne Schintzius, with 21 points and a team-high six assists, led the Gators to a stunning 85-66 upset of Big Ten champion Purdue. Melven Jones came off the bench to make all six of his field goal attempts and scored 13 points as Florida's subs outscored the Boilermakers' bench 24-10. The Gators also out-rebounded a physically intimidating Big Ten team that couldn't keep up the pace in an 80-point game.

At last the Gators were going to the Sweet 16. Florida people had never known what it was like to play basketball with prime time national TV exposure. Fans who had bailed off what they thought was a sinking ship a week earlier were desperately trying to get themselves back on board. The Gators began to feel like the Cinderella team as national interest in the program began to swell. It was another giant step for the University of Florida. Bizarrely, Sloan used the occasion to attack the media and particularly Dick Vitale.

"Hell, I'm watching ESPN all day and games are mentioned, every game but our game," Sloan said.

"I'm not bitter. I'm just tired of hearing all of this B.S., this hype. I'm tired of that. The Italian connection.

"I've got nothing against Italians and I love Italian food. But I'm tired of hearing all that. These Italian commentators promoting Italian coaches.

"There are people out there busting their butts and doing a good job and everybody's overlooking that because we're not charismatic. I'm tired of Vitale recruiting for Massimino, Valvano, and Carnesecca. They keep mentioning those programs. That's prime time TV. That's recruiting. That isn't right."

Sloan's points had a lot of validity, and there were many who were glad the veteran Florida coach had spoken out. It was, however, hardly the time or place to get confrontational, and although Sloan later invited Vitale to a home-cooked Italian dinner, the outburst left some scars on the Florida program's public relations efforts.

Florida's quarterfinal round was in the New Jersey Meadowlands Arena. Located just outside New York City, the site added to the Sweet 16 excitement. The Florida players seemed unaffected by all the hype that was surrounding their third-round matchup with Syracuse University.

The Gators were loose and they exuded confidence. Before the game, Schintzius fired a freshman remark at Rony Seikaly. He told the veteran Syracuse center, "I'm looking forward to a lot of contact – showing how much I've matured since the beginning of the year. I think I'm a great player."

Florida led the Orangemen 71-64 with just over five minutes to play in the game. Moten got a breakaway chance to put Florida in front by nine, but out of nowhere came Derrick Coleman. The 6-foot-10 Syracuse freshman made one of those classic defensive plays that is frozen forever in Gator memories as he soared above Moten and swatted the ball away.

Syracuse scored the next seven points to take a 73-71 lead. The stunned Gator basketball team could not recover. Schintzius, who had picked up a fourth foul at the 10-minute mark, came back in and promptly fouled out with four minutes to play. His six points in 29 minutes were not what he had anticipated when he taunted Seikaly before the game.

Seikaly, on the other hand, had 33 points, and Howard Triche made crucial baskets down the stretch as Syracuse shot 56 percent from the field to win the game. The Gators got 25 points from Maxwell and 11 rebounds from Schintzius in the 87-81 loss to close out the remarkable season.

In a *Florida Times-Union* account of the game, Greg Larson said, "Last night's game was a war. It was by far the most physical game the Gators have been involved in all season." He went on to say, "It was also a game where a lot of bounces could have gone either way. Luck played a major role. And the Gators just didn't seem to get their share of the bounces."

Florida dominated the SEC statistics that year:

- Joe Lawrence led in three-point field goal percentage at 50.4 percent.
- Chris Capers was first in field goal percentage at 62.9 percent.
- Schintzius topped the league in blocked shots with 2.7 per game.
- Maxwell was the No. 2 scorer with 21.7 points a game.

Florida also led the SEC in scoring with 84.2 points and scoring margin with 12.3 points a game. It was the program's best-ever scoring margin and surpassed the 1967 team which bettered opponents by an average of 11.8 points a game. The team posted four 100-plus point games, Florida's most ever in a single season. This was truly a great team – many feel the best ever in the history of Florida basketball.

The team had four seniors – Melven Jones, Joe Lawrence, and Andrew Moten – who were major contributors and a fifth-year senior, Rollie Castineyra. Castineyra had come to Gainesville from Miami, and while only playing a total of 76 career minutes, worked hard every day in practice for five years to make his teammates better. The senior leadership was no small part of this season's success, especially when it counted most in the NCAA Tournament.

Florida's pressing, running, and high-scoring offense produced eight of the top 10 crowds in O'Connell Center history. With 27 wins in its previous 29 home games, Florida basketball was no longer being taken for granted.

Chris Cameron, who had done such an outstanding job as Florida's sports information director, had been hired before the season in a similar capacity by the Kentucky Wildcats in the part of the country where basketball is considered to be bigger than life. Even from that vantage point, it was clear to Cameron that the Gators were breathing life back into the sport he loved and were beginning to find respect all across the country.

Maxwell Lights up Broadway

The 1987-88 season began with the motto "The Sky's The Limit." In reaching for the clouds, Florida would have the phenomenal soaring and scoring ability of senior Vernon Maxwell, and the sky-high reach of 7-foot-2 sophomore sensation Dwayne Schintzius. With Moten's departure, senior Ronnie Montgomery was back in a starting role. Pat Lawrence and Kenny McClary were also seniors.

Lawrence had tremendous talent on the perimeter and McClary, at 6-foot-8, 230 pounds, had a chance to once again compete for significant playing time.

Sloan's staff also brought in two outstanding freshmen, Livingston Chatman and Dwayne Davis. Chatman was a *Parade* All-American from Kathleen High School in Lakeland. Davis was another in a long list of St. Petersburg's Dixie Hollins High School players who had the potential to succeed at the highest level.

This team would give Sloan his 600th career win. Coming off a 23-win season the year before and a Sweet 16 berth in the NCAA Tournament, the O'Connell Center was sold out before Joan Sloan ever picked up the microphone to sing the national anthem.

The Gators were invited to play in the Preseason Big Apple NIT and recorded home-court wins over Jacksonville and Georgia Tech. Florida got 25 points from the agile, powerful freshman Livingston Chatman and defeated the 18th-ranked Yellow Jackets 80-69. Bobby Cremins had his own sensational freshman Dennis Scott, who scored 28 points. The Tech coach was outspoken in his praise, declaring, "Florida has a great basketball team."

With these two wins, the Gators headed back to New York City for the third consecutive year to play in the finals of the tournament. The Big Apple once again provided great national exposure.

Florida arrived at the team headquarters, the Marriott Marquis on Times Square, the evening before Thanksgiving Day. Schintzius and Pat Lawrence were roommates, and they hustled back down from their room to get a quick glimpse of Times Square before boarding the bus for dinner. The players went walking out into Times Square where barricades were placed to manage the crowd for the next morning's Macy's Thanksgiving Day parade. This is one of the quietest evenings of the year in the Big Apple, and as the two players stood behind the barricades looking at the glitter and bright lights of the city, two street toughs came across Broadway Avenue toward them.

One guy carried a boom box on his shoulder and the other had at least a half dozen gold necklaces draped around his neck. The two men stopped in front of Schintzius and Lawrence. They looked up at the 7-foot-2 Schintzius, then at the 6-foot-5 Lawrence, and then back again at Schintzius. "How f...... tall are you, man?" they wanted to know. Schintzius, who had heard comments like this a million times before, looked straight ahead and answered, "7-foot-2." Without hesitating, one of them asked, "You play basketball, man?" Schintzius, dressed in his Gator warmup suit, nodded. The two men stood there for another split-second, and the other one said to Schintzius, "Man, are you any f...... good?" Schintzius looked him in the eye and just smiled.

No matter where he went, Dwayne Schintzius attracted attention. He was quickly discovering that a major college basketball player had few places to hide. In every public setting, he was fair game for tiresome personal abuse. Even comments like, "How's the weather up there?" felt like an insensitive slap in the face. Being young and immature, Schintzius handled most encounters badly, but he got little help from those who were in a position to support him.

Schintzius was potentially very good. But as he began his sophomore year, his play was erratic. Inside Madison Square Garden, he scored just 20 points in the two nights and had just three rebounds in the NIT final against Seton Hall.

The only player the Gators needed, however, for these two nights was Vernon Maxwell. After failing a drug test prior to the start of the season, Maxwell was suspended for the season's first two games. Vernon was starved for action. He played his two best back-to-back games of the season.

In the semifinal, he scored 28 points as Florida beat Iowa State 96-89 and gave a second consecutive prime time performance in the final. Maxwell scored 27 points and made two free throws in the closing moments to beat Seton Hall 70-68 for the championship. He scored 55 points in two nights and was named the tournament MVP.

With a perfect 4-0 beginning, the team soared into the top 10, climbing to No. 7 in the AP poll. Next up was Southern Methodist in Dallas, Texas. The Mustangs led 52-32 at the half, and the Gators almost pulled it out with a furious comeback, outscoring SMU in the second half 45-22 before running out of gas and losing 82-76.

Florida came back home and held FSU to just 48 points, the second lowest number of points ever scored by the Seminoles in a game against the Gators. Florida's tenacious full-court man-to-man defense held FSU to just 34 percent from the field. Next, Florida crushed Ohio State 102-69, the highest point total ever against a team from the Big Ten, and then beat South Florida 83-69 to keep their 7-1 arms around their No. 8 national ranking.

A holiday tournament appearance at the Fiesta Bowl Classic in Tucson, Arizona, found Florida facing Duke in the opening round. Pete Van Wieren, who rarely made a mistake, was doing televised play-by-play for SportsChannel Florida and in his pregame intro, said "... and we'll be right back with tonight's game between the

Florida Gators and the Bluke Due Devils." The Blue Devils, however, had little trouble keeping things straight and slammed the door in Florida's face 93-70.

Florida got the consolation victory over Jud Heathcote and Michigan State as the Gators placed Lawrence, Maxwell, Montgomery, and Schintzius in double figures.

The Florida players flew 3,000 miles back across the country to Pittsburgh, arriving on New Year's Day to take on the third-ranked Pitt Panthers. The game would be played in the ancient Fitzgerald Field House where the Big East power had one of the best home-court advantages in the country.

Pitt's Charles Smith scored 30 points and blocked seven shots and Jerome Lane brought down 21 rebounds to hand the eighth-ranked Gators an 80-68 defeat in the nationally televised CBS Game of the Week. Florida was never in the game, shooting only 34 percent. Schintzius, who had picked up the flu after arriving in Pittsburgh, had a season-low two points and made only one of 12 field goal attempts.

Florida came home to win its 22nd straight non-conference game, beating former Florida Assistant Coach Terry Truax and Towson State 77-55. The win was characterized as much by bad behavior as good playing. The fans stooped to booing Schintzius because of his poor play in recent games, the only time in recent memory that Florida's fans had booed their own player. Ronnie Montgomery walked off the court while the game was still in progress after a verbally abusive Sloan had berated him one too many times. Still, the whole ugly mess was Norm Sloan's 200th win as Florida's head coach.

The Gators opened the SEC with high hopes that they could be a contender for the championship. They desperately needed to finally win a game at Auburn. The Tigers were playing without their two key returning players and were depending upon rookie freshman Chris Morris. This game was also the first matchup between Dwayne Schintzius and freshman Matt Geiger from Clearwater Countryside High School who had spurned Florida for Sonny Smith's Tigers.

Schintzius had 23 points and nine rebounds, while Geiger contributed only 12 points and eight rebounds. But Morris tallied a career high of 26 as Florida once again fell to its nemesis Auburn 72-67. It was Florida's seventh straight loss to the Tigers on the road and the 11th time in the previous 12 meetings that Auburn had beaten a Norm Sloan team.

But Florida rebounded, going on to win six straight, including the first of another two regular-season victories over Kentucky. The Gators went to Lexington without Livingston Chatman who had suffered the first of several painful knee injuries. Livingston's legs were just not built to take the pounding of college basketball. He had a very strong upper body and thighs that angled into a knock-kneed alignment. Chatman endured severe pain in both knees throughout his career.

In Rupp Arena, Chris Capers grabbed 12 rebounds (seven on the offensive end) and scored eight points as Florida upset the fourth-ranked Wildcats. It was a Florida team's first victory against a top 10 opponent on its home court. Kentucky shot just 21 percent in the second half and made only 28 percent for the game. The Wildcats kept things close by making 21 of 23 free throws. Schintzius controlled the paint from the opening tip, scoring 18 points and grabbing eight rebounds as Florida silenced a capacity crowd 58-56.

Three nights later, Florida crushed Tennessee in Knoxville 76-56, handing the Volunteers their worst home loss in 26 years. It was also the first time in 10 years that Florida would win three straight conference games on the road. The team came home to whip an LSU team that held down the pace of the game, only to lose 61-50. This was a powerful basketball team. With six straight SEC wins, Florida took command of the conference at 6-1. In the first 19 games, Florida had won 15.

Costly Mistakes

Dwayne Schintzius, from Brandon, was one of three outstanding 7-footers who played high school basketball in the state of Florida at about the same time. The others were Matt Geiger of Clearwater (who later went to Auburn) and Will Purdue of Merritt Island (who later played for Vandy.)

Schintzius was clearly the best prospect of the group. He had a big frame, soft hands, ran the floor, and was exceptionally well coordinated. His potential seemed unlimited. Geiger and Purdue were thinner than Schintzius, and neither of them had the athleticism or the basketball skills that Schintzius possessed. But both of them had work ethics that saw them through college careers and make them solid NBA players today.

Anytime these players met on the court, an extra home-state competitive incentive added to the excitement of the games. So the stage was set for a matchup of "big men" when Florida took its 15-4 record and headed to Nashville.

Behind a determined Will Purdue's 19 points and 15 rebounds, Vandy smacked the Gators 92-65. The Commodores shot 61 percent in the second half and made all 23 of their free-throw attempts. Schintzius had 23 points, but he managed only three rebounds, all defensive. It was a bizarre defeat that raised many questions about the team's preparation. Vandy had a good team, but it wasn't 27 points better than Florida. Vandy had dominated the backboards.

Next up was Alabama in Tuscaloosa. It was the Tide's worst team in 18 years, which was exactly how long it had been since Florida had beaten Alabama on its court. The Gators trailed by six at the half. It looked like Coleman Coliseum would once again prevail, but Maxwell made eight consecutive free throws in a second-half run to put the Gators in command for a 74-64 win. Maxwell finished with 16 points, and Schintzius had 18 points and nine rebounds. Pat Lawrence and Ronnie Montgomery were also in double figures. Another road ghost had been busted.

More importantly, the SEC race was at the halfway point, and the Gators were in first place with a half-game lead over Kentucky and Vanderbilt. For the first time, Florida could truly dictate its destiny. Of the nine remaining SEC games, six were at home. Only Georgia, Ole Miss, and LSU were on the road, and the Gators had already put these three teams away without much trouble.

Auburn came to the O'Dome three nights after the win over 'Bama and made seven second-half three-pointers to upset the Gators 58-57. Once again, Auburn controlled the game's tempo and frustrated the Gators' effort. The Tigers broke Florida's 13-game winning streak in the O'Connell Center. Schintzius, with 12 points and 10 rebounds, managed to get the best of Matt Geiger, who had just two rebounds and finished with four points.

Joel Glass had been named Florida basketball's sports information director, and the Gators were sabotaging his public relations effort as the team bounced out of the top 20 with another 71-65 loss to a very average Georgia squad in Athens.

To make matters worse, Sloan became confrontational with a University of Georgia police officer after demanding the officer control the unruly fans targeting the team both during and after the game. As the Florida players came off the court at halftime, they were pelted with cups of ice. After the game, Sloan protested even more vehemently to officer Mike Leonard. Leonard reportedly told Sloan to go into the locker room and take care of his team. The *Gainesville Sun* reported that Sloan told Leonard he was a gutless little f...er, hassling Sloan instead of taking care of the problem.

"We went back and forth and he became extremely agitated," Sloan is quoted as saying. "He started playing John Wayne with his hand over his pistol, and I said 'Get away from me.' He screamed, 'He's mine,' and tried to put the handcuffs on me. I shoved him away and another one of those rednecks grabbed me. I pushed by those guys into the locker room."

The incident was yet another in a long history of Florida-Georgia games in Athens that seemed prone to violent endings. Even more detracting, it occurred in the middle of a Florida conference title chase. The head Gator did not seem to have a good grasp of his team's priorities.

The loss to Georgia and the two losses to Auburn had changed the momentum of this title run and once again it appeared the Gators just weren't determined enough to take home the title.

Sloan's 600th career victory had also been put on hold with the previous two losses, but Mississippi State was coming to town with its last-place record. Florida got an unimpressive tenth straight win over the Bulldogs 69-52. The Gator coach became one of only three active coaches in America to reach 600 wins. North Carolina's Dean Smith and Oregon State's Ralph Miller were the others in that prestigious group.

"Although we've been in and out of the top 20 this year, I'm pleased that we've reached the point where we are expected to be there," Sloan said. "Coaching is all I've ever done. It's all my family has ever known. I've dedicated as much of my life to this profession as anybody ever has."

Florida posted a non-conference win over Miami 83-73, and Livingston Chatman had his best game since injuring his knee, scoring 20 points.

Crunch time had arrived. The Gators needed a win on the road, which should not have been a problem – they were the clear favorite to win. But Florida's effort was agonizingly uninspired, and Ole Miss tallied one of only six SEC wins that year, upsetting Florida 82-75. With Kentucky on the horizon three nights later, this talented Florida team should have put away Ole Miss with its bench. It was just another Florida flop.

But on Saturday night, it seemed like a different Florida team that showed up at the O'Connell Center. For the second time in Sloan's return visit to Gainesville, Florida beat the ninth-ranked Wildcats twice in a regular season. Chatman, Davis, Maxwell, and Schintzius controlled things from start to finish, and all had double figures.

Maxwell was incredible, scoring 32 points and breaking down the Wildcats defensively with his awesome talent. The win put Florida just a half game off Kentucky's conference-leading 9-4 mark, and a nationally televised NBC audience saw a dominating Florida team win its 19th game of the year.

With four straight SEC home games, the league championship chase took on the character of a Kentucky Derby horse race and Florida was now just a half length behind. Next up was a visit from Tennessee. Florida had previously dominated the Volunteers, beating them in Knoxville by 20.

Never to be underestimated, Tennessee Coach Don DeVoe had a knack for putting together a game plan that could upset a superior opponent. But the biggest contribution to the Volunteers' cause was an inadvertent one – a couple of quarts of malt liquor in Florida's Maxwell. A "spaced out" Vernon Maxwell had prepared a potent pregame meal and missed 12 of 16 shots in 35 minutes of action. Tennessee made each possession a nerve-wracking experience, and 9,500 Florida fans felt emotionally betrayed by a 65-63 Volunteer victory.

The Gators won two of the remaining three SEC games, losing by 17 to LSU on the road. With seven SEC losses, Florida had beaten Kentucky twice but finished a distant second to Kentucky and shared that spot with Auburn. The two defeats by the Tigers, the loss at Mississippi, and the inexcusable home loss to Tennessee once again sealed the coffin in Florida's quest for its first-ever conference championship. It was beginning to seem as if Florida was indeed snake-bitten and was destined never to obtain a conference ring.

Florida had fought the SEC wars the past four years with the most talented teams in the school's history. They were quick, athletic, physically strong, high scoring, and deep. But something was missing.

Some felt it was character, and there were plenty of incidents that pointed in that direction. Some believed it was coaching. The failure to get so much talent focused to win big games, especially the games they were highly favored to win, seemed to indicate that Sloan's staff just couldn't deliver when it counted.

For whatever reasons hindsight and second guessing can muster, 55 years of not quite being able to grasp the gold ring is a lot of inertia to overcome. More than anything else, this team, like many others in the recent past, just didn't believe enough in themselves or have the toughness to pull together when it really counted.

COSTLY MISTAKES

For one thing, the team lacked discernible leadership. Maxwell and Schintzius were the two most talented players Florida ever had on one team at the same time. But they were as opposite as two players could be and had little respect for one another. Their immaturity became a team liability. Maxwell fought everyone, including his own teammates, and created an environment that kept everyone on edge. Schintzius was immature and vulnerable to criticism. It made for a very confusing situation.

And coaching issues compromised the team's spirit. Ronnie Montgomery walked off the court after enduring one too many of Sloan's demeaning verbal attacks. Chris Capers quit the team and transferred to Jacksonville, throwing in the towel from the frustrating experience of trying to find his spot in the program.

With 21 regular-season wins, Florida got a first-round bye and beat Tennessee 67-60 in the second round of the conference tournament. Next was Georgia which had advanced to the semifinals with two tournament wins.

In another fiercely contested Florida-Georgia rivalry, Ronnie Montgomery and Georgia's Alec Kessler were tossed out for fighting in the game's early minutes. Florida held on to a slim lead until the Bulldogs' reserve guard Jody Patton made a four-point play to put Georgia ahead 65-63.

With 19 seconds to play, Patrick Hamilton, who was a perpetrator in a Florida-Georgia fight two years earlier, nailed a three-pointer to give Georgia a 72-70 victory. In the closing seconds, Sloan wanted Schintzius to re-enter the game to potentially rebound a missed free throw. Schintzius refused. The loss offset Maxwell's magnificent 28-point effort and stopped Florida short of the tournament final once again.

The NCAA gave Florida its second straight postseason bid. The opponent would be St. Johns – the site Salt Lake City. The Redmen were clearly overmatched and shouldn't have been a formidable opponent. But the Orange and Blue needed a big-time three-pointer from Maxwell, who drove the length of the floor and buried a 25-footer with seven seconds to play, to clinch a 62-59 victory. Maxwell again led Florida with 18 points and seven rebounds.

The worst was just around the corner, and it wasn't having to play Michigan in the second round. Players knew they would be drug-tested if they won a first-round game in the NCAA Tournament. A year earlier, while still sweating profusely, all five Florida starters had been led out of the Carrier Dome (after defeating N.C. State) on a frigid Syracuse night to a testing lab.

It has been conjectured that some Florida players were afraid a positive drug test from after the St. Johns victory would become public information if they then won the Michigan game, so they folded their tents against the Wolverines. All speculation aside, on this night the drug test was a non-event because Florida was never in the game.

Michigan's Glen Rice had 39 points and Loy Vaught had 22 points and 15 rebounds to gun down Florida 108-85. It was the most points scored against a Gator team since LSU's 112-81 win in 1979.

It was another example of the frustration many felt with the fortunes of Florida basketball. Here was a team that had the best individual player in school history and a supporting cast that in its own right had the talent to go up against anyone in the country. They had achieved another 23-win season, a trip to the NCAA Tournament, and two wins over 10th-ranked SEC champion Kentucky. Florida was the Preseason Big Apple NIT champion and held a No. 7 national ranking. Still there was no ring. Florida again came away from the round-robin conference chase with nothing for the jewel box.

Maxwell became the all-time leading scorer in the history of University of Florida basketball with 2,450 career points. Only Pete Maravich and Allan Houston have scored more in the history of the SEC. A hometown star, he was earning all of his records less than three miles away from the neighborhood where he grew up. All four of Maxwell's Florida teams finished in the league's top five, and twice they were the conference runner-up. The teams' 42 conference wins were the most ever in four consecutive seasons, and these teams averaged 20 overall wins a year. Maxwell scored in double figures in his final 108 straight games and set 15 career and single-season records.

As the most talented player in school history, Maxwell had the potential to become a true hero in his hometown and a legend in Florida basketball. The 1988 season concluded his four years of eligibility, and he was drafted by the NBA's Denver Nuggets in the 2nd round. By summer's end, he had been traded to the San Antonio Spurs, and with his admitted drug use, left Gainesville under a cloud of shame and humiliation.

In an earlier interview with the *Orlando Sentinel*, Maxwell had admitted that he used cocaine in a Gainesville bar before the team traveled to Salt Lake City to play St. Johns in the NCAA Regional. The April 13, 1988, article quoted Maxwell as saying, "I fess up. I was caught. I did get caught." He went on to say, "I'm sorry this happened. Everybody makes mistakes. I made a big one. I don't have a problem. I'm not a user. I did (use drugs) and got caught that time at the St. Johns game."

In high school, Maxwell was a likable young man. He was polite. He was friendly. He was also good at conning people to get what he wanted, but what he wanted most was to play ball. And plenty of others used Maxwell to get what they wanted – wins. The whole scenario is a familiar story – the end result justifies the means. Maxwell's problems with substance abuse were certainly a symptom of his irresponsible behavior. But irresponsibility is a factor on both sides of the equation – Maxwell's ability to deliver blinded many to his problems.

Norm Sloan knew Maxwell had a drug problem. Florida knew Maxwell had a drug problem. Maxwell certainly knew Maxwell had a drug problem. Some would argue that it's a cop-out to say that administrators' hands are tied by the Buckley Amendment and bureaucratic regulations which are so sterile that human beings are forgotten.

Perhaps someone could have grabbed Maxwell by the collar in high school or in college and said, "Vernon baby, it's over. You can go to school, but until you're done with drugs, you're done playing basketball." Given the choice, maybe he would have gone the drug route. But maybe he would have taken the other road, and would today be counseling others like himself.

The Gators forfeited NCAA wins as a result of penalties handed down for Maxwell's indiscretions, and his final two seasons have been removed from Florida's official records. He is the only player in any sport to be singled out in this way by the University of Florida. Some feel the record book on Florida basketball is incomplete without all of Maxwell's accomplishments. Today, Maxwell is one of the most effective performers in the NBA. He possesses every physical tool necessary to succeed at the sport's highest level.

One day several years after he'd left UF, Maxwell was having a sandwich in Joe's Deli across the street from the university. Across the room were Craig Brown and a table full of his Gator basketball teammates. According to Brown, Maxwell approached the group and said, "I'm Vernon Maxwell, and I want you guys to know that I made a lot of mistakes when I played at Florida. I did things that I'm not proud of. I hurt people that gave me a chance. Whatever you do, don't make my mistakes. Stay in school and get a degree. I'm pulling for you guys."

Talent Personified

Strong basketball programs are noted for losing talented players, and then simply reloading for the next season's wars. Florida had finally reached that stage of development, and although they lost a great player in Maxwell, there was a recruiting class arriving which had earned national credentials.

But the patience of Florida's faithful was running out. They had tasted unprecedented success. It was a bittersweet experience. With a new no-nonsense athletic director in Bill Arnsparger, the Sloan program was coming under some heavy scrutiny.

Livingston Chatman had been one of the top freshmen in the country the previous season. He was the only Florida basketball player to be named an Associated Press First-Team Freshman All-American. His 25-point debut against Georgia Tech demonstrated Chatman's ability to be an impact player, but when injuries took him out at midseason, it appeared he might never play again. Chatman underwent arthroscopic knee surgery three times his freshman year but characteristically missed only five games.

Chatman was one tough young man. He was physically strong at 230 pounds, and his 6-foot-7 frame was well coordinated. "Liv" could face up, put a rocker step on the defense, and power to the basket with surprising quickness. He could also back a defender down low with a good pump fake and use his upper body to finesse a wedge in the defense to score.

As Florida basketball looked to a new year, Chatman would be the rock upon which Sloan hoped to finally build a championship season. With two consecutive runner-up finishes, the program had been baptized in stretch runs. This group had ability complemented by experience.

Three straight 20-win seasons and six straight postseason appearances legitimized Florida as one of the nation's most competitive programs. Florida fans had responded with record numbers pushing through the turnstiles of the O'Connell Center, and statewide interest in Gator basketball was at an all-time high.

Recruiting had gone well. Sloan signed seven players: Jose Ramos, Johnny Walker, Cesare Portillo, Stacey Poole, Brian Hogan, Kelly McKinnon, and Tim Turner.

Ramos was a high school teammate of Portillo. Both had played for Shaky Rodriquez, coach of the Miami Senior High "Stingray" teams that had earned enormous respect as a state power. Ramos was regarded as the state's fifth best player.

TALENT PERSONIFIED

Sloan said he liked Ramos because he was a tough-minded competitor who had exceptional passing skills. Sloan was normally a great judge of talent, but in this case he was trying to sell ice boxes to Eskimos.

Ramos was a step slow, and his hard-headed selfishness reflected an immaturity that made him incapable of running a point-guard spot for a contender. Ironically, though, he would become the catalyst to the events that inspired a championship season.

This recruiting class was considered one of the best yet. Johnny Walker, from Quincy, Florida, was named Mr. Basketball, just as Vernon Maxwell had been years before. Once again, Sloan had nabbed the state's top player. Walker played at the same Quincy high school that produced Andrew Moten and gave the Gators another powerful 6-foot-8, 230-pound body to battle in the SEC wars.

Cesare Portillo had been named one of the top 50 prospects in the nation. At 6-foot-9, 240 pounds, Portillo appeared to have the potential to be a major force on Florida's front line for the coming season.

Another headliner in this group was Stacey Poole, 6-foot-6, one of the most athletic players ever to come out of Jacksonville. Poole had an explosive leaping ability that mirrored David Thompson's when he led Sloan's North Carolina State team to a national championship. Sloan knew Poole lacked some fundamental basketball skills but believed his exceptional athleticism would make him a great player.

Brian Hogan, Kelly McKinnon, and Tim Turner rounded out a class that *USA Today* rated the fourth best in the nation. Also suiting up for his first season of competition was Renaldo Garcia, a 6-foot-2 guard from Tampa who was academically ineligible for his freshman year but possessed a good outside shot and played solid defense.

Clifford Lett was the lone senior. The Pensacola native had experienced three tortuous years of catching every abuse Vernon Maxwell and Andrew Moten could throw at him. Lett never permitted his personal frustration to affect his attitude. In three full seasons, Lett had only started two games, and he had averaged just 11.5 minutes of playing time per game. His career high had been the 16 points he scored as a freshman in the dramatic NIT win over Texas Christian. At 6-foot-3, he could dunk with two hands and could also pull up from 20 feet and nail jumpers. He had been dubbed a role player – this was the year he would get his chance to show just how big that role would be.

Lett was mature beyond his years. He had the character and integrity to focus on the constructive aspects of the team's challenges. He refused to be drawn into behavior that was contrary to the principles which had been instilled in him by a loving family and a strong religious faith.

Lett earned his teammates' respect, which would pay huge dividends as the season went along. *Sport* magazine said Lett was one of the five most underrated players in the nation. The publication couldn't have been more accurate in profiling him.

The championship season began in a bizarre manner. As much attention was being garnered by what was happening off the court as most championship teams would have commanded by their performance on the court.

Dwayne Schintzius was center stage in the O'Connell Center "big top" atmosphere, drawing national media attention for a forehand smash with a tennis racquet. In November of 1988, Schintzius was outside a late-night spot in downtown Gainesville when he was confronted by another student. He was charged with hitting the student with a tennis racquet.

Athletic director Bill Arnsparger put the incident in the hands of the university's Student Conduct Committee. An incensed Sloan felt it was a disciplinary issue to be resolved by his coaching staff. The committee handed down a four-game suspension for Florida's 7-foot-2 center.

The Great Alaska Shootout attracted a nationwide audience, tuning in to college basketball's winter-season debut. Florida's athletic director was on hand to defend the university's decision which had become nationally controversial.

The Gators took the floor in Anchorage, Alaska, with six players who had never seen a minute's action in Florida uniforms. Michael Kerr, a 6-foot-6 redshirted football linebacker was among the six. Kerr had two weeks of basketball practice before starting in his first regular-season Florida game.

The Gators got thumped by California in the opener but received solid play from Chatman, Davis, Lett, and Kerr in a win over Division II Alaska-Anchorage 83-72. In the consolation bracket, they beat Utah 77-68 to come home with a 2-1 record.

The Gators' home opener was against lightly regarded Siena, but the upset-minded Indians led 42-33 at the half. Siena set an O'Connell Center record 13 three-pointers with 35 attempts and held a 14-point lead in the second half before Dwayne Davis took over with two blocked shots, 16 rebounds, and a game-high 20 points. Davis carried his teammates across the finish line for a 71-67 victory.

With Schintzius back in uniform, the 19th-ranked Gators traveled to Tallahassee to take on the 14th-ranked Seminoles. It was the first time in 20 years that two in-state teams ranked in the top 20 would meet on a basketball court. FSU scored 56 first-half points and had Florida down by 12 at intermission. Schintzius scored 22 points and pulled down 12 rebounds in his season debut, but the Seminoles ended the evening with 104 points, beating the Gators by 18.

The Gators flew to Champaign, Illinois, where another nationally televised appearance in Illinois' Assembly Hall found Florida gasping for air. Illinois forced 26 Florida turnovers and took 35 more shots to rout the Gators 97-67. Jose Ramos was trying to perform as a point guard, but the freshman was in way over his head. Florida was unable to move the ball into its own front court on eight first-half possessions.

Four nights later, LSU freshman Chris Jackson made 16 of 29 field goal attempts including five three-pointers to set an O'Connell Center record 53 points. The Tigers took a pound of alligator meat 111-101.

It was the most points ever scored by two teams in a Florida game. Ricky Blanton, one of the state of Florida's prized high school players, had escaped UF's recruiting grasp and contributed 25 points and 13 rebounds for LSU. Livingston Chatman scored 28 points, and Schintzius had 25 points and 13 rebounds, but the Gators could not overcome another 17-point halftime deficit and lost again on national TV. The Gators had lost three straight, and their opponents had averaged 106 points.

More than 7,500 people showed up in the O'Dome to see the Gators break the losing streak by routing Miami 101-81. It was the 11th consecutive victory over the Hurricanes. Clifford Lett got a career-high 22 points, and Davis grabbed a career-high 18 rebounds and also scored 18 points. Florida placed four other players in double figures: Chatman with 20, Schintzius with 17, Hogan 10, and Ramos 10.

Two nights later, with less than a handful of days before Christmas, Clifford Lett set a new career high of 25 points in a game against Pittsburgh. The Panthers, however, took control in the second half. With yet another national television audience and 8,000 in the O'Connell Center watching, the Panthers beat Florida 90-87.

The players went home for the Christmas break confused and tormented by their fourth defeat in the past five games. Fingers of blame were pointing in every direction. Discussion about the prior year's drug problems was discrediting the program, and the national television exposure had worn out the incident with Schintzius and the tennis racquet.

Opposing fans had taken to greeting the Gator center with streams of tennis balls during the pregame warmups. The 7-foot-2 junior had brought undesirable attention on himself that compounded the pressure on him to perform successfully. Everywhere Schintzius went, his character was assassinated. His problems made him public enemy number one in opposing arenas.

Florida also lost the anticipated services of three talented newcomers, Walker, Poole, and Portillo. As the team counted heads during the Christmas break, Walker was an academic casualty, Poole had ripped an Achilles' tendon, and Portillo had broken his hand. The program was finding a lot of sticks and coal under this year's Christmas tree.

Still, there was a tremendous front line – Chatman, Davis, and Schintzius were the most talented inside contingent ever to line up at one time in Florida uniforms. There weren't three better front-line players in any lineup in the country, and Clifford Lett was averaging 17 points a game at the shooting guard.

The problem was at the point. Ramos was at the wrong place at the wrong time. His selfish nature had made for violent confrontations with his teammates. More importantly, he couldn't run the offense and he couldn't play a lick of defense.

The Florida team went to New York for the fifth consecutive year, this time to play in the ECAC Holiday Festival. Its opponent was 15th-ranked Ohio State, the fourth nationally ranked team Florida met in its first 10 games. Ohio State led by 18 at the half and embarrassed Florida 93-68. In the consolation game, the Gators barely slipped by lightly regarded Fordham 59-52.

It was not a pretty picture heading into the start of another conference season. This talented Gator team was stubbing its long nose and getting its tail caught in too many embarrassing televised ringers.

Little Yellow Balls

Sloan was becoming very distraught. The normally tough-minded, veteran Florida coach was experiencing personal stress as never before in his 37 years of coaching. None of the pieces would fit into place. Academic woes, athletic injuries, and player indiscretions tormented Sloan. He was gaining weight, drinking more than his share of hard liquor, and really questioning his own commitment to continuing in the coaching profession.

As the team took the floor to play Ole Miss on January 5, 1989, Sloan was introduced as the head coach of a major college for the 1,000th time. He had logged his first win December 4, 1951, at Presbyterian College, and his 611 career wins ranked second only to North Carolina's Dean Smith, who in 28 seasons had counted 656 victories.

It was a Thursday night ESPN double-header, and with the game being played in the Central time zone, had a 6 p.m. tip-off. It was a miserable night in Oxford. A passing cold front was dumping torrential rains on this tiny northern Mississippi college town, and only 3,500 people showed up in the 8,100-seat Tad Smith Coliseum.

Florida did not get a field goal until the game was four minutes old and they trailed 14-2. At the half, Florida was behind 44-30 and, for the eighth time in 12 games, faced climbing a huge mountain in the second half. With Chatman, Davis, and Schintzius all fouling out and Mississippi's Gerald Glass and Tim Jumper combining for 40 points, the Rebels humiliated the Gators 80-71.

As Florida boarded the team plane the next morning to head to Athens for a Saturday night encounter with Georgia, there was a death pall hanging over the Florida coaching staff. The assistants were in shock, and Sloan was struggling with his own feelings of depression. He confided in others that it might be time to hang things up. Sloan was tired, angry, and embarrassed by the performance of his team through the first 12 games of this season. He questioned his own ability to communicate with 19-year-old egos who showed no tangible evidence of relating to this 62-year-old's coaching style. Sloan would often say in the face of adversity that "this too shall pass." However, it did not appear likely that this situation would get much better.

As the Captain Jack sailed along with a tailwind and clear blue skies, the mood inside the cabin was somber. In the front of the plane, Sloan had shared with some of the team's traveling party a newspaper article which described many of the symptoms he was feeling at the time. The article suggested that the only way to reverse frustration and find professional satisfaction was to be consistent in your behavior and true to your deeply held convictions. Sloan speculated that perhaps in trying to accommodate the many conflicting personalities of these immature young people, he had lost his sense of purpose. He proposed the thought that only a radical change in his own behavior could give these remaining months of his coaching career a chance to end with satisfaction.

In recent years, Sloan had mellowed considerably. He still swore and his words could bite, but players no longer responded in fear. They saw him as an old man. He rarely ate with them at pregame meals, and he made little attempt at forming personal relationships. Towe had taken a more visible coaching role, and McCraney and Weber maintained the direct link with the players.

Some who knew the situation believed the end of Sloan's career might come that weekend. Athletic director Bill Arnsparger had confronted Sloan over a number of issues in recent months, and Arnsparger seemed close to resorting to radical surgery on the program. The Schintzius affair had again tainted the athletic program with negative attention. And Arnsparger continually challenged Sloan to debate the standards of athletic department integrity.

Would Sloan resign? For those who knew Norm best, it was out of the question. Would Arnsparger fly to Athens and announce Sloan would be taking early retirement? It seemed unlikely. Would players revolt? Chatman was visibly dejected. His painful knees were like a mild headache compared to his own frustration with his teammates' attitudes. Chatman, Davis, Garcia, and Lett had bonded, but they felt estranged from the rest of the team. It was an atmosphere filled with anxiety.

At practice in the Georgia Coliseum that afternoon, it felt like a pressure cooker was about to blow. Sure enough, as practice began to unfold, the volcanic Sloan erupted.

Jose Ramos had been given every opportunity to succeed in the Gator back court. From the first day of fall practice, Sloan had handed the freshman the starting point-guard position and truly tried to put a positive spin on each Ramos performance. Ramos was supposed to be a high-percentage shooter, but he just couldn't get the ball to go in. He'd made only 21 of 58 field goal attempts, shooting just 36 percent.

Ramos' bigger shortcoming on the court, however, was his decision-making. A point guard's most important attribute is court awareness and the ability to make the right decision. Ramos did neither well, and his selfishness prevented him from improving in these areas.

He and Portillo were also in trouble with Tigert Hall. Their SAT scores had been challenged, and neither could get a passing score even with intense additional preparation. Sloan had become increasingly displeased with every aspect of the behavior of these two freshmen.

As Ramos dogged his way through a nightmare practice, Sloan spared no amount of personal criticism. Sloan spoke directly to Ramos, and Jose dropped his head. Sloan challenged him, "Look at me." Ramos continued staring straight down at the floor. Sloan grabbed him to force him to raise his head, and Ramos fired back, "Take your hands off of me, old man, or I'll knock you out."

With a hushed and stunned Florida team looking on and writers from around the Southeast in attendance, Sloan tossed Ramos back to the South Florida Everglades, and his career with the University of Florida was finished.

"Clifford take the one, Renaldo play two," Sloan ordered, and the championship season began.

In his first career start at the point-guard position, senior Clifford Lett took the controls like a veteran Air Force fighter pilot. Lett had nerves of steel and the self-confidence to direct the Gators' march to the conference title. Georgia was in trouble from the opening tip, and the Gators had a commanding 38-18 halftime lead. It was the biggest advantage at the midway point in three years. Lett had 15 points, a career-high nine rebounds, eight assists, and eight steals.

Where had Clifford Lett been? Buried, but now he was risen from the dead. Actually, Lett was averaging 13 points a game, but his leadership potential had been in a locked box. His teammates seemed to be reincarnated, too. Chatman had 21 points on five of seven from the field, and Davis made six of seven field goals and finished with 12 points. Schintzius had 22 points and nine rebounds. With the 80-66 victory, Florida headed back to Gainesville with a new spirit and an altogether new focus.

Two nights later, the Gators met a very good South Florida team in the Sun Dome for their third road game in five days. Florida made nine of 10 free throws in overtime to win 87-82. Chatman was spectacular. He went six for six from the line and finished with 22 points. Davis and Schintzius combined for 37.

Kentucky came to town three nights later, and another national television audience watched Florida fall to a Wildcat zone that forced Florida into a perimeter game and a 38 percent shooting night. Chatman and Davis were completely shut down and combined for just 11 points. If not for Schintzius' 20 points and 13 rebounds, the game would have been a blowout. Kentucky won 69-56.

With the loss to the Wildcats, Florida dropped below .500 to 7-8. But more importantly, Florida was now 1-3 in conference play. Kentucky remained unbeaten in the league 3-0 but was just 8-7 overall. It was a long way to the SEC finish line, and Florida did not appear likely to become a contender.

The Gators headed to Auburn, Alabama, the site of 10 Florida losses in the last 11 starts. Auburn was the last place Florida would ever look to for relief from a disappointing season. But the Tigers were also struggling.

Auburn had started the season with 14 players, but six were gone. A seventh, Derrick Dennison, had recently quit but was returning to suit up for the Florida game. The Tigers had their worst start in 38 years and were 0-4 in conference play.

NORM SLOAN: 1981-1989

The Gators led 64-46 with less than five minutes to play, but somehow Auburn cut the lead to 78-75 with 21 seconds on the clock. Clifford Lett made a free throw to put a desperation Auburn three-pointer out of reach as Florida won 79-75. Florida had an SEC road win that would become huge in the next few weeks.

Florida next headed to Thompson-Boling Arena in Knoxville, Tennessee. The Volunteers were enjoying their best start since 1944 as Tennessee had won 11 of its first 12 games and was 4-0 in the conference.

This would be a matchup between Schintzius and Tennessee's 7-foot center Doug Roth. It would also showcase two of the league's best forwards, Dyron Nix and Livingston Chatman. Schintzius had a great night, scoring a career-high 28 points and 12 rebounds to categorically outplay Roth, who finished with only 11 points. But it wasn't enough as Tennessee won the game 83-76 and remained undefeated in the conference.

The Gators now had four defeats in their first six conference games – not exactly the stuff that makes a championship season. Still, there was a different atmosphere inside the locker room. Ramos was out of the picture. Portillo had retaken the SAT, had come up short, so he was gone. The remaining players had begun to settle into their respective roles, and the team had stabilized.

Chatman, Davis, Garcia, Lett, and Schintzius were the starting five, and there was no one on the bench to push these guys for playing time. Sloan was forced to let the season sink or swim on their shoulders.

The players on the bench were all supportive. There were no bench jockeys complaining about their lack of playing time. If anything, it was quite the opposite. These were guys who genuinely pulled for their teammates.

Everyone knows you must have talent to win, and Florida had a starting five who were the best in the conference. The Gators had boatfuls of talent in previous years, but they never pulled the oars together. Brian Hogan, Kelly McKinnon, and Michael Kerr would briefly spell the starters. Mike Ramirez, Tim Turner, and Todd Zehner held up the end of the most supportive bench in the SEC. All of these guys had great attitudes and appreciated the chance to wear the Gator uniform. There was no bickering in the dining hall or on the team plane, and everyone was sold on the team's objectives.

Lett was a natural leader, and every player identified with the Pensacola senior. Even Schintzius was beginning to enjoy the experience, and with tennis balls greeting him at away games, he seemed more relaxed as he toyed playfully with the opposing fans.

Florida came home to blow Mississippi State out of the O'Connell Center 81-57. The Gators led by 28 at the half and posted a record 11 blocked shots in the game. And the players gained some confidence from the experience of winning by a big margin.

What happened next seemed like a story line out of a movie. As Florida arrived in Nashville, the news of the day in this famous country music town had nothing to do with an SEC title chase. Commodore Coach C.M. Newton had just announced that he had taken the position of athletic director at the University of Kentucky.

Newton brought Vanderbilt unprecedented success and he did it with class. His competitive and statesman-like conduct stood in stark contrast to Sloan's. Vandy's head man was going back home to Lexington where he had played on the Wildcats' 1951 national championship team and had coached for 12 years at tiny Transylvania College. A basketball man would now be the athletic director at the conference's premier basketball school.

The Vandy game was Florida's eighth road game in the last 10 contests, and with four wins in the last six games, the chemistry was finally at the right mix. Schintzius was playing his best basketball as a Gator. He had scored 20-plus points in four straight games and was averaging 22 points and 11 rebounds a game. Since Lett took over at the point-guard spot, Schintzius was getting more and better chances to score.

The first half was a typical Memorial Gymnasium tussle as 15,498 fans booed Schintzius loudly. Vanderbilt played a sticky zone with some full-court traps, and Florida shot only 31 percent. Vanderbilt, however, didn't get much done either as both teams slugged it out until halftime with Florida holding a 25-24 edge.

The second half began as a gun-slinging shootout. Both teams were spectacular. They battled through 13 second-half lead changes, and the game was tied nine times. With time running out, Florida trailed 72-70. The Gators gained possession of the ball and scrambled to get to their front court. But they lost the ball out of bounds. The ball crossed the sideline at about midcourt with :01 on the Memorial Gym clock.

SEC officials John Clougherty, Don Ferguson, and Danny Hooker comprised a veteran crew who knew both teams well. The game had been a powder keg all night long, and there were plenty of short fuses to go around. As Hooker signaled Vandy's ball, the crowd spontaneously realized the game's fortunes rested with the Commodores. Like a giant popcorn machine, the stands erupted with dozens of yellow tennis balls cascading down onto the court. Clougherty never even flinched. He threw up both hands to display the most beautiful "T" that a Gator basketball fan had ever seen. The crowd deflated into a stunned split-second silence.

Vandy's fans had been holding those little yellow balls all night long. They were clutching them in their sweaty palms as the game moved and swayed. When someone put the first tennis ball airborne, the spontaneity of the moment overtook the entire crowd of Vandy faithful. A two-shot technical was called on the crowd. They had been warned. Before each Florida road game, an announcement warned fans that objects thrown on the court would result in a crowd technical.

This turn of events was too good to be true. First the clock operator had stopped the clock with just :01 showing. Second, Clougherty, the crew chief, had the guts to blow his whistle. He made the correct, if controversial, call. And third, Florida had the perfect candidate to step to the line and put the contest into overtime. There was only one choice for the person who would go to the line in the bizarre drama that had unfolded, and he happened to be a 70 percent free-throw shooter. Sloan never hesitated.

The "dork," the Ivan Drago look-alike from the film *Rocky*, the biggest, at times the goofiest, and certainly the most controversial Florida basketball player ever, stepped to the line. With a raucous and highly emotional Vanderbilt crowd breaking decibel records, Dwayne Schintzius calmly drained both free throws without even a brush stroke of the rim.

Schintzius sank the two most pressure-packed free throws in Florida basketball history, and he never flinched. Then he literally destroyed Vanderbilt in overtime. He scored the first seven overtime points, finishing with 24 points and 12 rebounds for the game. Commentator David Steele closed his broadcast aptly: "The final score in overtime Florida 81, Vandy 78. Game, set, and match Florida."

There was a celebration in the Florida dressing room to rival any NCAA victory. No Gator team had ever bonded through a shared experience as this team did on that night. The Georgia game provided the welding rod, Clifford Lett. The Vanderbilt game was the torch. Now Florida was coming together like a piece of welded steel.

A Red LETTer Run

With the first half of the conference schedule behind them, the Gators were 5-4 in the conference and 10-9 overall. There was a seven-day break, and Florida came back home to get some rest and reload for the stretch run of the conference season. Five of Florida's next seven games were at home.

Alabama came to town February 1. The Tide had a much improved 14-4 overall record and were in second place in the conference behind LSU. The Gators came out of the blocks and had Alabama down 41-24 at the half. With all five starters in double figures, the Gators shot 56 percent from the field and put the Tide back in the soapbox 85-76.

Three days later, the Gators rode the bus to Orlando for the nationally televised game which would inaugurate the Orlando Arena. The largest crowd ever to attend a basketball game in the Sunshine State – 14,684 – packed the new arena. The opponent was the 20th-ranked Stanford Cardinal who had never before appeared in a nationally televised contest.

Stanford's Todd Lichti gave an awesome prime time performance, scoring 27 points as the Gators fell 84-69. It was beginning to appear that the Florida players were camera shy. "It's a jinx, I tell you," said Dwayne Schintzius. "TV games haven't been good to us." They were now 0-6 in nationally televised games this season.

The Gators came back to Gainesville the next day to play their third game in five days, this time against Ole Miss. The Rebels were whistled for 30 personal fouls, and Florida made 30 of 44 free throws to only six of eight for Ole Miss. The 78-67 win was Florida's fourth straight in the conference and moved the Gators to within a game of first-place LSU. Florida was 6-4, LSU 7-3, and Alabama was right in the hunt at 7-4.

More than 9,000 fans showed up three nights later as Georgia came to town hoping to get revenge for the earlier Gator victory. Trailing 29-20 at the half, Florida was sparked by a flurry of scoring by Clifford Lett and Renaldo Garcia early in the second half. They scored 11 of the team's first 13 points, and a 14-2 run was climaxed by a "Double D" Dwayne Davis jam that put Florida ahead 41-38.

"We looked at the stat board at halftime and saw that only two or three guys had two or three rebounds," Chatman said. "It was just a bad first half and we knew we had to do better." Florida's fans roared and rocked the O'Connell Center as Florida went on to beat the hated Bulldogs 65-60. The fans wouldn't go home, cheering long after the buzzer for the Gator players to come back to the court.

Florida had now won five straight SEC games, approaching its record of six in a row. To tie the long-standing mark, Florida would have to win on one of the most formidable basketball courts in America – Rupp Arena.

"Of all the teams I've coached at Florida, this one cares more about the conference race than any of them," Sloan said. "They really want to win it. The conference is generally the No. 1 goal every year. But with the past teams, we could be in front of the conference and it didn't seem that it was that important to them."

Lexington, Kentucky, is recognized for its thoroughbreds – the ones with four legs and a saddle as well as the ones with two legs and short pants. Just as Calumet Farms is the Bethlehem of the horse-racing industry, Rupp Arena is the Churchill Downs of college basketball.

But these were difficult times for the bluebloods. Their horse-racing industry was struggling, and the Wildcats were faltering. The Kentucky basketball program had not experienced a losing season in 62 years. The most defeats Kentucky had suffered in a season was 13, and Rupp Arena, the Roman Coliseum for the Wildcats' Christian opposition, had seen only 22 losses in the previous 197 games.

Once again Florida was under the lights of a nationally televised game. The national press, however, wasn't focused on the Gators. The NBA had stolen the Wildcats' "Crown Prince of Basketball," Rex Chapman, and the Big Blue were being measured by their shortcomings.

The big story could be a Kentucky record, but not the kind that would be rewarded with roses. A Gator victory would hand Kentucky its 13th defeat and its fifth that season in Rupp Arena. Kentucky had never lost more than four games in one season at Rupp.

There were two very opposite streaks on the line, and Florida desperately needed a victory to stay in the championship chase. Florida had given the Wildcats two of their 22 Rupp Arena defeats and had beaten Kentucky nine of the 14 times the teams played on the tube.

Chris Mills was able to "Federal Express" 17 points, and Kentucky had Florida down 35-28 at the half. "We went into the locker room at halftime thinking we should have built a double-figure lead," said Kentucky Coach Eddie Sutton after the game. "Then there would have been a lot less pressure on us."

Once again Clifford Lett and Renaldo Garcia came out of the locker room at halftime to ignite a Gator surge. The guards forced two consecutive steals to open the second stanza. Florida's vise-grip of a defense held Kentucky to just 14.3 percent shooting in the second half. Brian Hogan nailed his only three-pointer of the night to give the Gators a 42-40 lead.

"We hung in and hung in until our shots started falling," Lett said. "We did what we had to do to win. Isn't that what it's all about?" Florida's five starters averaged 36 minutes of playing time in the dramatic 59-53 win.

"Neither team played very well today," Sloan said. "But we played hard, very hard, and that made up for not playing well. We opened the door to the conference race a little wider."

The Gators were on a roll and came back home where another 9,300 fans watched them sweep the season's series with Auburn for the first time in eight years. The win tied a school record of seven straight SEC victories. Florida trailed by two at the half and the score was 62-53 with under 15 minutes to play in the game. The Gators then went on a 15-0 run in the next five minutes. Brian Hogan nailed a pair of three's, and Clifford Lett made his only three-pointer of the night as Florida spurted out to a 68-62 lead.

"What those three-pointers did more than anything was get the crowd into the game," Auburn Coach Sonny Smith said. "This is one of the great crowds in the league and we had tried to keep them out of it. The three-pointers put points on the board and put the crowd in the game so it was a double kicker." Schintzius had his first 20-point night since the Vandy game and finished with 24. Lett and Davis both added 18 as Florida cruised to the finish line 90-79.

"I'm really proud to be part of the record," Hogan said. "They've had a lot of success here the last four or five years. So to be part of a record like that means a lot. But we need to just take each game one at a time and understand that the one we are playing is the most important one."

The season began with Florida as the consensus pick to win the championship. Then the bets were off as Stacey Poole came up injured and Portillo, Ramos, and Walker bit the dust. But now the chase was back on, and no one was living a fantasy. This was the real deal. It had been 22 years since a Gator team had been in a stretch run with an honest-to-goodness shot at bringing home the glory. Of the five remaining SEC games, only two were at home. Florida would have to start by beating Tennessee.

In 1967 Tennessee broke a seven-game Florida winning streak and beat the Gators in back-to-back games that squeezed Florida out of an SEC title. As Yogi Berra would say, "It was déjà vu all over again" – the Gators' seven-game SEC win streak would again be tested by the Volunteers. Equally as unnerving was the fact that Tennessee had handed the Gators one of their four conference defeats earlier in Knoxville.

The drama and the dynamics inspired an emotionally charged 11,644 Gator fans to witness Florida's 99-81 drumming of the Volunteers. Florida locked in its eighth straight SEC victory. Schintzius had 27 points, Chatman scored 19, and Renaldo Garcia played 34 minutes and finished with 17 points.

"We're playing with a lot of confidence and it feels great," Schintzius said. "I don't think anyone could beat us the way we played today. We did an exceptional job, no flaws. We know if we lose we're pretty much out of the race. It's just a matter of going out and getting it done."

Lett had 16 points and Davis had 12. This time Florida's version of the Fabulous Five played an average of 37 minutes. Dwayne Davis was spectacular on the defensive side, holding the Volunteers' prolific scorer Dyron Nix to only eight points. "He's always played well here," Davis said, "and he got 29 against us in our first game (a Vol victory). Today I was just determined he wasn't going to kill us. We stayed after him as hard as we could."

The UF basketball program was now poised to capture its first conference crown. Since Joe Lawrence's last-second basket against TCU for an NIT victory three years earlier, the program had become established as a conference contender.

Florida headed to Starkville, Mississippi. Mississippi State was just 5-8 in the league, but oddsmakers knew the difficulty of a Humphrey Coliseum assignment. This game was rated a toss-up.

The Gators had the Bulldogs beaten in the first six minutes as they ran off to a 19-2 lead and went to the locker room 49-31. Davis had 19 points and 13 rebounds to support Chatman's 20 points and Schintzius' 21. In the 78-69 win, Florida shot 38 free throws and made 20 to State's six of 11 from the charity stripe.

Florida was in a first-place tie with its next opponent Vanderbilt. LSU had fallen a half-game off the two leaders with a Wednesday night loss to Alabama.

Vanderbilt's entire athletic program is centered around the success of basketball. Through the years, the Commodores have produced some of the SEC's most successful teams. In the prior 10 years, the Gators had fought Vanderbilt to a virtual standoff.

In head-to-head battles, the Commodores had won 11 and Florida had won 10. A win this time would not only deadlock the 10 years of competition, but it would put Florida in sole possession of first place.

The Gators had never been in first place this late in the season, and after the earlier Academy Award performance in Nashville, this game would be the biggest sporting event in Gainesville's history.

Forget the football. If the O'Connell Center could have held 80,000 fans, they would have been there. This was Florida basketball's biggest night, and a regional television audience had basketball fans across the Southeast tuned in.

It was also Senior Night, and the lone senior on the team must have decided that meant it belonged to him. For the record, February 25, 1989, is Clifford Lett night. Every February 25 in all the years to come, the Pensacola native should be commemorated for his contributions to the Gator program.

Others have distinguished themselves, and many have made Florida's basketball faithful proud, but no one had done it more dramatically and at a time when it counted as much as Clifford Lett.

Go back a moment to the practice court where in previous years Lett endured knees in the groin from Maxwell. Go back to the locker room where insulting language and attitude were often dished out. Go back to the dormitory on an early Sunday morning where some hung-over, drugged-out teammates were sleeping off a Saturday night high, and Lett was headed for church.

Look back for an ever so fleeting glance at a coaching staff which chose to ignore his character, his compassion, his conscientious desire to contribute everything he had in him. Then remember just for a second the many others, those who arrived like Lett, but left crushed and rejected.

When the public address announcer brought him to center court with his parents before the start of this most monumental Gator game, everyone was on their feet. A near-record crowd of thousands cheered and some were blinded by tears of emotion. Clifford Lett was hailed as a Florida hero.

This game rained emotion and excitement, not tennis balls. It took a Dwayne Davis dunk on a pass from Garcia inside five seconds to give the game an extra period. "There wasn't any real set play," Davis said. "Coach Sloan told us to take the three if it was open and if not to take it inside. We could either go for the win or the tie."

The Gators beat Vandy for the season's second time 83-80 in overtime, and Lett went out in high style. He played 44 of the 45 minutes and had only one turnover. He dished out eight assists, he grabbed six rebounds, and he scored 21 points. Clifford Lett scored seven of Florida's nine overtime points and nailed a 22-foot three-pointer in the final minute of overtime to seal the victory. Since Clifford Lett had taken the point-guard position on January 7, the Gators had won 13 of 16 games.

"This was a real nice way to go out," Lett said. "But I'll let you know how it really feels in a week when we are the conference champions. We want to be the first team from Florida to win the conference and not just share it. This game is right up there with any I've been in. We had a big game here my freshman year against TCU (in the NIT) but this one was more exciting."

"This was probably Clifford's finest performance of all," Schintzius said. "And he couldn't have picked a better time for it. He carried us down the stretch."

Officially it was Florida's third largest crowd ever in the O'Connell Center – 12,042 – and Florida's head coach knew this team had put it all together.

"We're starting to feel like maybe it's destiny, maybe it's meant to be," Sloan said. "This is the biggest win I've ever had here. This game was everything all those people coming here thought it would be."

Clifford Lett received the Lt. Fred Koss Award which recognizes leadership, character, sportsmanship, and personal sacrifice during a four-year career. Lett truly inspired excellence in the University of Florida basketball program.

In the years to come, February 25 should belong to a former 6-foot-3 guard from Pensacola, Florida – Clifford Lett.

Championship Rings

Florida was now in sole possession of first place. A win on the road against LSU would make the Gators conference champions. Regardless of the outcome of the season's final game at Alabama, if the Gators beat LSU in the Pete Maravich Assembly Center, they were assured a piece of the championship pie.

LSU had beaten Florida in the first SEC game of the season 111-101.

The Tigers were 20-12 and had an 11-5 conference season. If LSU won, it would possibly be a three-way tie for the championship. If LSU lost, the Tigers were out of the picture, and Florida had its first-ever conference crown.

Despite the Gators' dramatic late-season run, they still weren't getting much respect. Even LSU's head coach decided to contribute some bulletin board material for the Gator locker room.

"A week ago I thought the teams with the best chance to win the league were Alabama and LSU," Tiger Coach Dale Brown said. "Now that Alabama lost, I think the team with the best chance to win the SEC is LSU."

It was Wednesday night, March 1, 1989. A regional telecast and 14,417 ragin' Cajun fans revved up the Maravich arena. The team's Bengal tiger mascot was fired up and sweating so profusely that people could smell him three rows into the stands. Florida's starters were averaging 37 minutes a game, and they would be asked to lace up their Converse shoes and take everything they had to the court just one more time.

Let's go to courtside on the LSU campus and pick up the pregame radio comments:

> Welcome back to the Maravich Assembly Center as Florida prepares to take on LSU in what has become the biggest game in the history of University of Florida basketball. You've got to go back through the years to feel the agony of seasons past to sense the magnitude of the present.
>
> From Brady Cowell, the coach of Florida's first SEC team, to Sam McAllister, Johnny Mauer, and then a blond, square-jawed, steely blue-eyed Norman Sloan, who stormed the state of Florida for six years in the early sixties trying to lay a foundation for basketball pride. Who sensed the potential and evangelized the promise of what

might be accomplished in the program at the University of Florida.

And then came Tommy Bartlett and John Lotz with teams that produced winning moments but never quite enough to complete the assignment. Then back again came Stormin' Norman, back to complete a job he started so many years before, and like Dorothy in *The Wizard of Oz*, he brought with him a dream and a mission to take Florida basketball where it had never been before. But like the cowardly lion, the program lacked courage, and the people had lost heart, and so he believed in them and he fought for them, and with back-to-back trips to the NCAA and consecutive twenty-win seasons, one job remains. And one final hurdle to cross. And the cowardly lion asks, "But is it a real heart, and do I have real courage?" Can the dream become reality?

And so the fantasy was about to be played out. LSU had a great ballclub. They were led by one of the school's most prolific scorers Chris Jackson (Mahmoud Abdul-Rauf). Jackson had scored 53 in the O'Connell Center in December and averaged 30 points a game during the season. Ricky Blanton was a senior, and the Miami native had made Gator teams pay for failing to land him on the North Florida campus. Lyle Mouton, Wayne Sims, and Vernel Singleton rounded out the starting lineup which had won the previous 10 straight home games, adding flavor to the night's contest.

LSU and Florida lit up the building in the first half. Each team shot over 50 percent from the field. Florida made nine of 13 first-half free throws to only four of seven for LSU, but the Tigers controlled the offensive backboard and led 50-44 at the half.

In the second half, Florida grabbed the lead and then hung on down the stretch. Renaldo Garcia had his greatest game as a Gator. Garcia had only turned the ball over 40 times in the previous 18 games since the changing of the guards in January. Prior to that, he had committed 42 errors in the previous 12 games. Furthermore, he had just one turnover in the last three games, and his contribution was significant on the defensive side of the ledger.

Garcia had become a forgotten man in the shadow of his Gator teammates' accomplishments. But on this most important night, he had what at the time was a career-high 20 points in 29 minutes of action. Playing with four personal fouls, he made key defensive plays against the Tigers' Chris Jackson.

"There is no answer to stopping Chris Jackson one-on-one," said Garcia. "I was lucky he went cold in the second half. On offense I got a couple of transition baskets toward the end. We are a pretty good team when it's close at the end." Garcia also made all six free-throw attempts. Lett made 11 of 15 free-throw attempts, had nine defensive rebounds, and tied a career-high 10 assists in 40 minutes. Florida was awarded 34 free-throw attempts and made 27 to LSU's eight of 12.

Florida players got to the free-throw line because they initiated the action, whereas LSU was comfortable firing away from the perimeter. Chatman had a team-high 26 points, and Schintzius had 24 as both Gators played 39 minutes. Double D added 18 points and five rebounds.

The Gators played a nearly flawless game. They scored 104 points and had just 12 turnovers. No one fouled out. They made 79.4 percent of their 34 free-throw attempts and shot 55.2 percent for the game. In the second half, Florida made 58.8 percent of its 34 field goal attempts. The final score was 104-95.

The team celebrated its school's first SEC championship by winning on the road and in a contending enemy's territory. It was the culmination of the dream Norm Sloan had when he arrived in Florida in 1960.

"I can't express how I feel. I'm just as happy as I can be," Sloan said after the victory. "This is more gratifying than 1974 when we won the national title (at North Carolina State). That team was expected to win. This team just reached down and won it."

Perhaps Livingston Chatman said it best, "When you see this team, you see a Gator team with a lot of heart. We didn't win any of these games with a 45-foot last-second shot. It's been heart. And desire, defense, hustle and love for your team and not letting each other down." This team was welded together like a solid piece of steel. Never before had Florida basketball excited so many.

What happened next can only happen at a football school. Florida played LSU on the road with a chance to win the school's first-ever conference title. Some had been waiting since 1933 for this night, but no light bulbs had gone off inside the brains of the university administration to speculate on how to handle a possible celebration. Maybe they didn't think many people would notice.

The Gators were greeted at the airport's fixed-base terminal on the opposite side of the runway from the main terminal by an estimated 5,000 people. They climbed the roof of the old airport terminal building and hung off the top of security fences to let their heroes know how they felt.

Larry Vettel was covering the event live for WRUF radio and people kept asking, "Larry, are the players and coaches going to make comments?" Vettel said, "Why, of course they are. Can't you see all of these microphones? When they get here, there will be a mini-news conference."

Sorry, Larry. When the team arrived, the players and coaches were put in vans and driven around the back side of the terminal and away from the throngs of Gator faithful. The one night, after 56 years of waiting, that Florida fans had a chance to put their arms around Florida basketball and someone decided to keep the team from celebrating with them.

Former Gator players also shared in the pride of seeing Florida finally achieve this milestone goal. Curt Cunkle was on the Florida team that finished third in 1953 and reminisced with the *Gainesville Sun*'s Pat Dooley: "Kentucky was so powerful then," said Cunkle. "You thought about winning the SEC a little, but it was a faraway dream. Nothing, as far as I'm concerned, compares with this in the school's athletic history."

There was one game left, but it was anticlimactic for the worn and weary Gators. They trailed Alabama in Coleman Coliseum by 16 at the half and lost 83-63. The clincher came that same night in Tennessee as the Volunteers whacked Vanderbilt 78-61. Florida claimed sole possession of the SEC trophy.

The team came home from that Saturday afternoon game and this time had a police-escorted caravan to – where else – Florida Field, the football stadium, where 5,000 people showed up to honor Florida as the SEC Champs. The public address system played the song "We Are The Champions," and for the first time in either of the Gators' major sports, *the University of Florida owned an SEC Championship trophy.* Just for the record, some suggested the O'Connell Center might have been a more appropriate place to celebrate.

Florida went to the SEC Tournament as the first seed, and it was once again the team's best chance to date to claim a tournament championship. Georgia was the opening-round foe, and the Bulldogs had an 11-point halftime lead. With five seconds left in regulation, Dwayne Davis followed up a Dwayne Schintzius miss and gave Florida its only lead of the game in the 62-61 quarterfinal victory. It was Florida's 20th win of the season and the first time since 1969 that Florida had swept Georgia three times in one year. It was also Florida's third straight 20-win season.

Tennessee was the Gators' semifinal opponent, and the tournament was being played in Knoxville's Thompson-Boling Arena. Tennessee had a one-point lead with just over four minutes left in the game, but the Gators scored the next 11 points to take a 71-61 lead with under a minute and a half to play. Livingston Chatman carried Florida with 25 points, and Clifford Lett added 17. But Renaldo Garcia made eight free throws in the final two minutes to ice the 76-71 victory.

The win, however, was dampened by an injury to Dwayne Davis. Double-D was the tournament's leading rebounder, and with 42 seconds left in the Tennessee game, he suffered a partially torn tendon in his left knee. He would be lost to the tournament's final game the next day.

Alabama had beaten Vanderbilt to face the Gators in the title game. The last time Florida had been to a SEC Tournament final was in 1934, and their opponent, Alabama, beat the Gators 41-25.

This time it was a severely short-handed Gator team that faced the Tide for the tournament championship. Freshman Michael Kerr stepped into the starting lineup for Davis and delivered a career-high 15 points. The Gators' five starters played 195 out of a possible 200 minutes in the game. Alabama, however, with Keith Askins knocking in five three-pointers and Michael Ansley adding 14, was just too deep for this worn-out Gator squad. Alabama walked away with it 72-60.

Livingston Chatman was named the tournament's most valuable player after leading all scorers with 70 points in three games. Schintzius was also named to the first-team all-tournament squad, and for the first time ever, Florida basketball had two players in the first five all-tournament selections.

The Gators received their third consecutive invitation to the NCAA Tournament and were sent to Reunion Arena in Dallas, Texas. Their first-round opponent, Colorado State, had won the Western Athletic Conference championship and played with exceptional patience on offense and a sagging zone defense to gun down the Gators.

"This one is going to haunt us for quite some time," Schintzius said. "That was not the Florida team that has brought us so far this year. We were bickering out there and throwing the ball away. It was very frustrating. That's not us."

Florida shot just 39 percent for the game, and the 68-46 defeat was the lowest point total for Florida that year. "I'm sorry about our last two games because people remember the way you finish," Sloan said. "We had a fine season. I hope Colorado State goes a long way in this thing. They're a good basketball team."

Dwayne Davis hit 72.7 percent of his shots during the regular season to lead the nation in field goal percentage. Also impressive was the fact that 32 percent of the "human pogo stick's" field goals were slam dunks. It was the second-best field goal percentage mark in Division I history for a single season. Davis had 58 dunks, which was unofficially the record for jams in a single season by a Gator player.

Schintzius, Chatman, and Lett averaged 37-plus minutes throughout Florida's 34 games. These three, along with Dwayne Davis (33.3 minutes per game) and Renaldo Garcia (27.7 minutes per game), were the "Iron Men" of Florida basketball during the 1988-89 season.

Florida won an all-time school record 11 consecutive SEC games, and it was the first time since 1969 that Florida had defeated every SEC team during the league's round-robin schedule. Florida had won 44 conference games over the last two seasons which was more than any other SEC team. Four Florida players were selected for the Associated Press All-SEC team – Schintzius, Chatman, Davis, and Lett.

From Penthouse to Outhouse

During the next six months, the Florida basketball program went from its finest hour to its most disheartening moments. Seldom has the University of Florida been so challenged. An NCAA investigation had the university facing a major sport death penalty. The DEA and a federal grand jury were looking into allegations that had implicated Norman Sloan. Although Sloan was ultimately cleared of any criminal activity, his 37-year coaching career had come to an explosive conclusion.

The University of Florida was determined to have Sloan leave. Although there seemed to be little tangible evidence to support NCAA accusations concerning inconsistencies within the basketball program, the university was forced onto the defensive.

Some players had given sworn testimony that Sloan had given them money which they may have then used to purchase drugs. Maxwell told the grand jury that Assistant Coach Monte Towe paid him $800 when he was a senior in high school. He said he received another $1,000 after he signed with Florida. "Any time I asked for money, I could get it from them – $200, $50, – whatever I asked for I could get," Maxwell testified.

Players and people close to Sloan in those years have said that Sloan did give players money. There is no evidence, only rumors. If Sloan broke NCAA rules, he was wise enough to do so with cash. The one tangible public NCAA disclosure was an airline ticket purchased on a University Athletic Association account to send Vernon Maxwell to a basketball camp in Boston. At the time, Sloan reasoned that he was giving Maxwell a potential link through the Boston Celtics to the NBA.

The university administration was dealing with an individual who believed he had done nothing wrong. Sloan would fight to the bitter end to defend his honor. After days of negotiations, Sloan agreed to a settlement for the remaining one and a half years of his contract.

Anyone who knew Sloan couldn't help but be impressed by his confidence. His personal strength came from a sense of righteousness which he constructed to attack or defend every issue he confronted. "Truth" was his interpretation of any set of circumstances, and he could passionately persuade people to feel that his perspective was correct.

Socially, Sloan was magnetic. Among adults, he projected warmth and compassion. He was a humorous and vivid storyteller whose strong convictions won him affection from those who enjoyed his friendship.

Sloan's stories often exposed another person's weakness in an embarrassing moment, which delighted his audience. Rarely did one of his anecdotes pay tribute to someone's strengths. Sloan was masterful in giving lip service to the idea of helping players who fit his definition of disadvantaged. But in reality, he never demonstrated true caring in a way that might help someone achieve personal growth.

There may have been exceptions, but those who observed his interaction with players at Florida during both coaching eras were dismayed to see him sabotage the personal development of so many young men who genuinely tried to be successful in his program.

In the early years at Florida, he was misguided in his approach to working with young people and developing team-related goals. By his second stint in Gainesville, he had lost touch with even the ability to communicate with players. The players in the sixties feared him. The players in the eighties mocked him.

Sloan was passionate in all his beliefs, and he believed in recruiting the most talented players. He thought the x's and o's of a game plan were overrated. You won with talent. In the eighties Sloan recruited a number of talented players, some of questionable character. Sloan would not distinguish between players who were disruptive to the team and those who were constructive to the team. By his own failure to deal consistently with principles that he seemed to genuinely believe, Sloan created an environment where others learned to distrust both his motives and his judgment.

Norm Sloan made mistakes and he paid dearly for them. Sloan left Gainesville accusing the school of failing to give him support. He talked about trust. He complained about being a scapegoat. He lashed out at those in charge. Once Sloan told me that the difference between the two of us was simple. He said, "Bill, you trust everyone and are disappointed a lot. I don't trust anyone and I'm never disappointed."

If you don't trust others, it will be impossible for others to trust you. Young people can't develop respect for each other in an environment where there is a complete lack of trust. Florida basketball's failure to capitalize on its immense athletic potential in the eighties may have come down to the lack of one fundamental element – trust.

The players were not, as some would want you to believe, all bad kids. After all, the coaches recruited them to one of the most attractive Division I campuses in America. Surely in the recruiting process there were opportunities to discover a player's personal strengths and weaknesses.

Those players who displayed behavior that embarrassed the university, their own teammates, and every former University of Florida player who represented the program with pride are fully accountable for their actions. It is, however, an enormous injustice to focus on the bizarre behavior of some players and the unfortunate events that took place without holding the people in charge also accountable.

This is exactly what motivated interim UF President Robert Bryan and athletic director Bill Arnsparger to undertake a purging and cleansing of an athletic program that had become a national mockery.

FROM PENTHOUSE TO OUTHOUSE

Arnsparger knew very little about basketball. He was hired by President Marshall Criser in January of 1987 to restore credibility to the university's athletic program. Criser knew there were some serious problems, and he believed Arnsparger had the maturity to assess the damage and understand the dynamics.

Criser learned first-hand that he could not trust Sloan because Criser had been manipulated through one of Sloan's indiscretions. Sloan had given money to Vernon Maxwell to take care of a personal problem concerning his girlfriend. Knowing at the time that Criser and athletic director Bill Carr were less than enamored with his coaching profile, Sloan contrived a way to protect his job. He knew that if he told Carr what he had done for Maxwell, Carr would inform Criser.

It is the responsibility of all university presidents to annually affirm to the NCAA that they are not aware of any improprieties in their athletic program. Carr was in a very difficult situation because he had accepted the athletic director's job underpaid and underprepared. He was thrust into a role where others were dictating circumstances that paralyzed his own ethical management philosophy.

Carr was hired after football Coach Charlie Pell had been appointed, and he found himself taking the heat for the football program's violations. One of his first acts as Florida's A.D. was to fire John Lotz and hire Sloan, so he was totally compromised by Sloan's admitted rules violation. He knew he must go straight to Criser.

At that point, Sloan had everyone where he wanted them because the school was vulnerable to an NCAA death penalty. If something this outrageous was disclosed, what remained of the university's already damaged reputation would hang in the balance.

It appears that Criser never acknowledged the information he had been given by Carr. It did, however, make him painfully aware that this serious violation was perhaps only the tip of the iceberg. Criser might have shuddered to think what could be revealed under closer inspection.

Sloan knew from the moment Arnsparger was hired in 1987 that he was in trouble. Arnsparger had been tough and demanding as a football coach, and this trait carried over into his decision-making as an athletic director. He immediately began to question Sloan's management of the basketball program.

Some feel Arnsparger was a difficult man to know. He was not always comfortable in the visible, social roles required of an athletic director, and Sloan tried to take advantage of this. He tried to leverage his own personality and alumni friendships to fracture Arnsparger's armor. But it didn't work – too much damage had been done. Criser resigned in the spring of 1989, citing his own need to get back into private law practice. But one has to wonder if he was not jumping off the same sinking ship which had previously tossed Bill Carr. The university's athletic reputation was now totally in the hands of interim President Robert Bryan and his athletic director, Bill Arnsparger. There would be some very trying moments in the months ahead.

Agony and Ecstasy

It was October, and the good news was Norman Sloan had resigned. The bad news was Arnsparger had hired Don DeVoe. Arnsparger felt the program needed a strict disciplinarian for a caretaker. DeVoe, as a former University of Tennessee basketball coach, was a strict disciplinarian who needed a job. Arnsparger figured Florida needed someone to pull in the reins, tighten the noose, take names, and kick ass.

If Arnsparger understood basketball, he would have inquired about the past and realized that the first time Sloan left Florida, it was a Tennessee man who took the job. Tommy Bartlett had let the players out of straitjackets, released all the steam from the boiling kettle, and showed compassion for the turmoil of 20-year-old student-athletes. That coach was rewarded with Florida's best season ever.

Don DeVoe was a disciplinarian who never coddled an athlete's tender ego. He prided himself on a coaching philosophy that treated players fairly, rewarded hard work, and functioned with consistency of purpose. When you think of DeVoe, you must go back to Ohio State's Fred Taylor, his college coach, who provided the framework for both DeVoe and another former Ohio State player, Bobby Knight.

Fred Taylor had great integrity and taught fundamental basketball. Knight and DeVoe tried to incorporate the Taylor philosophy into their individual personalities. As different as day and night, DeVoe and Knight did share two basic coaching traits. Both were unwavering fundamentalists and absolute disciplinarians. The success of these two coaches through the years can be credited to consistency in these two qualities.

Florida's players had no idea what was wrong with the program. They just knew the symptoms – irresponsible behavior by some, discontent in others, bad attitudes in a few, confusion in all. But plenty of talent – talent good enough to win an SEC championship the previous year. In the past three seasons, Florida was the winningest basketball team in the SEC. Florida had achieved three straight 20-win seasons and had made three trips to the NCAA Tournament.

The 1989-90 team returned four starters from the championship year: Schintzius, Chatman, Davis, and Garcia. Except for the four games for which he was suspended, Schintzius had started every game from the first one of his freshman year. He had scored 1,414 total points. He had blocked 244 shots, a school record. He was Florida's 10th all-time leading rebounder. Schintzius had elected not to go hardship and returned to play his senior season. His basketball future had a lot riding on a successful year.

Chatman was a confused young man who had played in agonizing pain with knees that would have looked bad on an 85-year-old man. His finest credential was courage. Sure he had scored 936 career points in two seasons. Yes, he was the most valuable player in the SEC Tournament. Of course, he was a first-team freshman All-American. But most impressively, he was a bright, sensitive, and compassionate athlete. He had played hurt. He played sick. He was burdened with the psychological challenge of uncertainty. How in the world could such a 20-year-old kid make sense of what was going on?

On the outside, a federal grand jury was investigating his coach. Former teammates were in court testifying. His friends and fellow students were quizzing him daily. His mother was trying to support and encourage him.

With his own eyes he had witnessed things the last two years that had confused him. He couldn't help but wonder – who could be trusted? What should he believe? How should he act? On top of all this, he could see his one greatest hope fading away. An NBA career was vanishing in front of his eyes because his knees were more broken than his spirit.

And then there was Dwayne Davis. For two years he came to practice every day with a big smile. Davis wasn't a great scholar, but he went to class. He was on time for his appointments. He played with emotion. He competed with a good-natured determination. Davis tried hard and he trusted. And he got results.

Davis led the nation in field goal shooting percentage. He was considered one of the top five college rebounders in America. Intensity was his middle name. He was the quickest leaper ever to wear orange and blue. The Dwayne Davis dunk – a "3-D" – brought fans in droves to Gator games.

Don't forget Renaldo Garcia. At first it was feared he might not be able to do the schoolwork (he eventually earned his University of Florida degree). Next he was gathering splinters on the bench while a Miami hot-shot was running his mouth and ruining his team. Garcia quietly, patiently waited, and when given the chance, made a substantial contribution to the championship season.

Clifford was gone. Lett had graduated, but Hogan was back, and so was Turner. Stacey Poole was finally on the court after spending two years in the physical rehabilitation center with two torn Achilles' tendons. And, there were some new faces – B.J. Carter, Hosie Grimsley, Scott Stewart, and Travis Schintzius, Dwayne's younger brother.

This was a very good team. Granted they didn't have the foggiest notion of why things seemed to have grown so bizarre. After all, it was all they had ever known. These players related well to each other and met the personal challenges of the circumstances of the times.

"Trust me," Bill Arnsparger said. "I know what's best for you young men." And with the blink of an eye, it wasn't Monte Towe, a coach they respected, a coach they knew, a coach who had earned their trust. It wasn't Kenny McCraney, a man who lived with them every day and spoke their language.

Presto-chango. Florida's new head coach – interim head coach – was Don DeVoe. Now don't get this wrong. Don DeVoe is a good coach. He is a good man. He had proven his ability to succeed at this level. He was just the wrong guy in the wrong place at the wrong time.

Bill Arnsparger wasn't going to give the job to Towe or McCraney because there were some unconfirmed issues which had implicated these two coaches in the program's troubles. But perhaps he should have. They were two of the greatest casualties in this travesty. Many believe Towe and McCraney were capable of coaching the team and keeping the program afloat. Both were respected by the players, and they might have moderated the turmoil of Sloan's departure. Towe and McCraney genuinely cared about the players. Towe and Schintzius had a strong personal relationship.

Sloan's indiscretions had been damaging enough. In hiring interim coach Don DeVoe, Arnsparger inflicted more hurt on the basketball program. Arnsparger could have invested some time being constructive himself. He might have assessed the damage and given Towe a caretaker's role. Instead of leadership, Arnsparger demonstrated marksmanship. The people caught in the crossfire saw their futures unfairly destroyed. There appeared to be sufficient justification for Arnsparger to replace Sloan, but the strength of Arnsparger's convictions about the former coach seemed to have desensitized him to the feelings of everyone else.

Although his career ended sooner than he'd planned, Sloan had been able to negotiate a financial settlement and was already near retirement. Towe and McCraney, however, were in the prime years of their coaching lives and were suddenly out of work. Moreover, because the nature of their dismissal put a black mark on their coaching careers, both have been disadvantaged in their career aspirations.

When DeVoe arrived in Gainesville, he said, "Fellows, I don't care what has happened in the past, all I care about is what you do for me in the future." It didn't take him long to come down hard on this vulnerable team. He called the team together and said, "Listen, I've watched you guys for years. You're undisciplined and out of shape. You guys never push yourselves. You Florida guys are an embarrassment." He singled out Dwayne Davis and accused him of being lazy.

You can picture the wheels turning in the players' minds. Let's see now, coach. You got fired last year at Tennessee. Let's check something a minute. The last 12 times Florida played Tennessee, Florida won nine. Florida beat your team two out of the last three and won the SEC. Florida beat your team two out of three the year before and went to the NCAA. Florida beat your team in Knoxville three out of the last five times.

We're an embarrassment? We can trust you? You have our best interest at heart? Cut what hair? Put in whose shirttail? Shave what facial hair? For you? Man, you're "Saddam" DeVoe.

Chatman started the first 10 games before he said, "See you later." He had scored a season-high 22 points in an O'Connell Center win over Georgia. But after an 89-81 loss in Lexington, Chatman hurt his knee and lost his cool. He told DeVoe to shove it and packed it in.

It was sad. Very sad.

Dwayne Schintzius started the first 11 games. He broke an all-time record for career starts – 107 – and then bailed out of DeVoe's sinking ship.

"No one had greater dreams for this season than I did," Schintzius said. "No one can argue that Coach Sloan and Coach Towe were easy to play for. With them you had to accept the coach as the absolute authority and their word as final. But that does not mean I must sail under the authority of Captain Ahab ...If you can play for Coach Sloan, you can play for almost anyone, *almost* anyone." It was one of the most appropriate statements on the subject that anyone had made.

Dwayne Davis never quit. Like a semi-tractor trailer that goes down into low gear to get over the mountain, he swallowed his pride and kept playing. He finished the season with 1,003 career points and made second-team All-SEC. The number crunchers said Davis now had one dunk every 21.3 minutes. He had a new career-high 29 against Georgia and led the team in scoring with 12.3 points a game.

Garcia started every game and had his career-high 22 points in a 62-59 loss to Miami. In the win over LSU, Garcia scored 17 points and for the second straight year played a key role in a classic kind of win over the Tigers.

Hogan, Grimsley, Stewart, and Turner did everything that was asked of them. They kept their mouths shut and played hard. The late-season win over LSU is a tribute to this group's character. It reflects the personal pride of young men who weathered the most violent public storm in the history of Florida's basketball program.

Hogan played in all 28 games. He made 41 percent of his 66 three-point attempts and sank six straight free throws in the last three minutes to ice an 85-77 win over James Madison.

Poole started 20 of 28 games and averaged 10 points and four rebounds a game. When his team-leading 22 points helped upset 15th-ranked LSU, he was named the team's MVP.

Turner played in 23 games, but his most prominent role was in being an encouraging influence on the practice court and in the locker room. He had been in the company of Schintzius at the ATO fraternity house the night Dwayne got mad and reportedly tore a mirror off the side of a parked vehicle. After Turner served a one-game suspension for being in the wrong place at the wrong time at the fraternity house, the incident rapidly matured his focus. He became visibly an inspiration on the team.

With Schintzius and Chatman in the troubled lineup, Florida won six of its first 11 games and two of its first four SEC games. A crushing 82-69 win over FSU in the season's first game and a stunning late-season upset of 15th-ranked LSU were the highlights on the court.

The LSU game was broadcast by ESPN, and Dick Vitale predicted there was no way

Florida could win. But the Gators' Hosie Grimsley throttled Chris Jackson by keeping him off-balance all night. Jackson had a career-low 15 points against Florida. The Gators played like "Jack the giant killers" and held the massive Shaquille O'Neal to just nine points. Shaq only had seven field goal attempts. The 76-63 victory was the one piece of positive news in a year that was one of Florida basketball's worst nightmares. The win-loss record for the '90 season was 7-21.

Behind the scenes, the wheels were turning. Earlier in 1989, Marshall Criser had resigned as president. Dr. Robert Bryan was second in command and took the reins on an interim basis. Unlike interim coach DeVoe, who had little perspective on the University of Florida, Bob Bryan was a deeply-respected university administrator with a lot of savvy.

Dr. Bryan had been on the inside at Florida for 32 years. He understood the dynamics of a complex university environment, and he was respected for his decisiveness. Dr. Bryan knew things were a mess in the athletic department, and it was going to require his best management skills to get them back on track. No single individual has more profoundly impacted the University of Florida basketball program.

Dr. Bryan peeled back the layers of issues that had confronted University of Florida basketball throughout the years and made his own assessment of what needed to be done. He knew Arnsparger had a limited perspective on Florida's basketball potential and would find it difficult to give the program its best chance to be successful. He also respected Arnsparger's position in the matter and, while not wanting to cause Arnsparger embarrassment, quietly managed the process of finding a new coach.

On one occasion, I asked Dr. Bryan if he thought this university truly wanted to have a great basketball program. He said he wanted a basketball program that reflected the greatness of the university.

Dr. Bryan employed a coaching headhunter, Richard Giannini, to search for a new coach. Giannini was a Florida graduate who had been the school's associate athletic director. He left Florida to start a sports marketing venture in Charlotte, North Carolina. Giannini was chosen because he knew the University of Florida's athletic challenge and understood what it would take to hire one of the nation's best prospective coaches.

Giannini had Florida in the hunt for the best coaching prospect in America because Dr. Bryan had also given him some valuable ammunition – enough money. Dr. Bryan told Giannini, "We will provide the basketball coach the same dollars we are paying the football coach. We want both sports to be equally successful. You find us someone who can reflect the greatness of this university."

Giannini's reaction? "Hey Lon! Can I talk to you about something?"

Lon Kruger

Family Time
1991-1996

ors outlast ... les, 74-66

Once-troubled Gators now big trouble for foes

Free throws lift Florida over UConn

real Lon Kruger ...s to emerge

Gators enjoy a feat that cries out for its greatne...

DeClercq graces ... with effort on def...

ors: A super season for a team without a supers...

...mbarrasses UGA 100-78

UF's Hill ...

...ainesville, high time for high fives

NCAA EXTRA

The Healing Touch

Lonnie Duane Kruger became Florida's 15th head basketball coach on April 1, 1990. He was hired on April Fool's Day, but this Florida coach never tried to fool anyone. He faced issues head on and by example demonstrated to others a daily approach to life's challenges that was inspiring.

"You coach at a major school," Kruger said, "and you've got a platform from which to teach. The time they will spend playing basketball for you is insignificant. But what you can give them beyond basketball will stay with them for 40 or 50 years.

"You have to get them to care about each other, and you will find that they wind up caring about all the other people they will meet long after they leave you."

Norm Sloan spun words with similar connotations, but his actions belied those words. Kruger was for real, and everyone he met came away excited.

"Coach told us he wanted to be a family," Stacey Poole said. "That's something we haven't had around here in a long time. To tell you the truth, it feels pretty good when you know someone cares about you. He is close to his players and is an outright winner. When he came to Florida, he brought a whole new atmosphere."

Kruger is a truly selfless individual. Those who know him well say Kruger's interest in others is genuine. It's rare to find anyone as accomplished in the sports world who reaches out to others with more grace.

Raised in Silver Lake, Kansas – population 1,450 – Kruger was the oldest of Don and Betty's six children. His values are the legacy of parents who provided a living example of doing the right things for the right reasons.

In 1994 Chris Harry wrote about the early years of Kruger's life in a *Tampa Tribune* profile: "The only time I can remember Lonnie getting into any trouble was when one of his teachers complained that he wasn't playing with the other kids," said his father Don Kruger. "The others would be swinging on swings and playing in sand boxes, and Lonnie would be watching the big kids playing ball across the street. That's where he wanted to be."

Kruger's childhood revolved around family and sports. His father coached a little league baseball team, helped raise the money, and drove the bus so the team could play against better competition outside the immediate area.

"It wasn't like he was a born player," Ellis Dahl, his high school basketball coach, said. "He would go home after baseball practice and shoot baskets for hours. He'd dribble the ball for miles. His was a tremendous work ethic."

And if Lon said something, you knew it was true. "If I looked out the window and said it was snowing, the whole family would run to the window to see if I was right," Don Kruger said. "If Lonnie said it was snowing, nobody had to look. Whatever Lonnie said was fact. It was the same at school. Whenever there was some trouble, the teachers would ask him what happened. That's how they settled it."

Kruger was twice named the Big Eight Player of the Year while at Kansas State and was the team's captain both his junior and senior seasons. He was an academic All-American in 1974.

His coaching career began as an assistant at Pittsburg (Kansas) State University in 1977, and his first head coaching job was at Pan American University in 1982. After four seasons at Pan American, his former Kansas State coach Jack Hartman retired, and Kruger returned to coach his alma mater.

When Kruger made the move to Florida, he brought most of his staff from Kansas State, where his teams had made it to the NCAA Tournament each year during his four-year tenure. Ron Stewart, Robert McCullum, and Mike Shepherd knew what Kruger expected. Each had helped cement the framework for his accomplishments.

Kruger also hired a new associate, Kirk Speraw, who had been named the 1990 National Junior College Coach of the Year at Pensacola Junior College. These four individuals uniquely melded their personal strengths with Kruger's effective hands-off leadership style and found avenues to quickly reshape the direction of Florida basketball.

Kruger, dubbed the "daddy" of the team by player Tim Turner, began by reaching out to the returning players. Stacey Poole was having knee surgery, and Kruger stood in the operating room beside orthopedic surgeon, Pete Indelicato. "He didn't have to come, but he cared enough to be there," said Poole.

Then Livingston Chatman had arthroscopic surgery, and Kruger looked on. When it was Craig Brown's turn to get "scoped," Kruger stood by.

Kruger made everyone who enjoyed Florida basketball feel like they were part of a great Gator family. From Tom Williams, the players' academic counselor to Marty Stone, the public address announcer, to his first athletic trainer, Tony Sutton, to his first head manager, Tim Klein. Dawnette Lauramore and Sharon Sullivan were so energized by Kruger's genuine interest in everyone that they put more than they ever dreamed was possible into an already over-extended secretarial work day in the Gator basketball office.

One of Kruger's first big changes was to make daily contact with the players. Players were encouraged to come into the office to talk about any problems and share their concerns. The coaches made sure that each player knew the staff was equally interested in each one of them. Every player was important, and Kruger was genuinely committed to finding ways to help each one reach his full potential.

"We want our players, when they leave Florida, to have a respect and concern for others, and a sincerity about them," Kruger said. "Sincerity is extremely important – living something as well as talking about it. It's true in life and true on the court. In every ballgame there are three or four minutes where the game is decided. You must have that sincerity to be willing to do anything, to lay it on the line and do whatever it takes to win the game."

The media quickly discovered that Kruger was for real and praised Florida's selection. "He's not a good choice – he's a great choice," Dick Vitale said.

Hubert Mizell of the *St. Petersburg Times* had followed Florida basketball for 25 years and wrote, "They couldn't have done better. Kruger is one of the country's best ten or fifteen floor coaches. Better yet, he's a youthful talent whose reputation borders on the angelic."

The *Gainesville Sun*'s publisher, John Fitzwater, had refocused the sports section's coverage of Gator hoops when he came to the *Sun* in 1987. In covering Kruger's new leadership style, the newspaper gave the program even more extensive coverage. Everyone was eager to learn more about this new approach to Florida basketball.

In Kruger's first season, Florida earned immediate respect on the court. With Kruger's encouragement, the team demonstrated an unprecedented togetherness as well as the ability to capitalize on individual strengths.

"If a player makes a mistake during the game, it's my fault because most likely I permitted him to be in a position on the floor where he had a high probability of failure," Kruger once said. "My job is to learn what players do well and give them the best chance to use those skills effectively."

Players realized Kruger was their kind of coach. While many coaches would yank a player who made a mistake from the game, Kruger would wait until the player had done even the smallest thing well before bringing him out of the game to work out his instructions. For example, when the player came to the bench, Kruger might compliment him for keeping his man from receiving a pass and then tell him why moments earlier he had thrown a pass away.

Kruger respected seniority and believed if a player gave the program everything the coach asked, then the player should be given opportunities to find rewards. Playing time went to seniors Livingston Chatman, B. J. Carter, Dwayne Davis, and Renaldo Garcia, who finished their careers under Kruger. Each of them played in at least 23 of the team's 28 games.

Chatman became the program's 11th all-time scorer despite being overweight and limited by his crippled knees. Junior college transfer B.J. Carter played in 39 games during his two-year career, scoring a career-high 10 points against Florida State.

Davis led the team in scoring at 15 points per game and had the best career field goal percentage in Florida history – 64.1 percent. The *Sporting News* described Davis' leaping ability as the "greatest show off earth." His 168 3-Ds (Dwayne Davis dunks) set a school record.

Renaldo Garcia became the glue that held Kruger's first Florida team together. Garcia finished a three-year career starting 79 of 88 games. He led the team in minutes played and averaged just under three assists per game. Garcia's career high was 20 in Florida's SEC-clinching win over LSU.

"It was a great experience to play for Coach Kruger," Garcia said. "I learned a lot about basketball and life in just one year with him."

The highlight of this first season on the court was the presence of team unity and unselfish effort. Players again dove for loose balls. They were coached on how to set good screens. They began talking to each other on defense. And, most of all, they pulled for their teammates when they were on the bench. The sulking of the past was replaced with a sense of unity for the future.

Three freshmen appeared in uniform for the first time and two of them would markedly impact the program. Craig Brown from Steelton, Pennsylvania, was a welcomed addition to Kruger's first recruiting class which included Martti Kuisma, Louis Rowe, and junior college transfer, Jeremy Ulmer.

In the first home game of his freshman season, Brown was called to the free-throw line with Texas leading 75-74 and :04 on the clock. Brown shot and missed his first two free-throw attempts ever as a Gator, and his pain and dejection were felt throughout the O'Connell Center.

Many worried that these failed free throws and the eventual 76-74 Texas victory would be a devastating blow to the young player's career. But Brown went on to give Florida one of the season's best wins. He scored 13 points in the second overtime period and set an NCAA record for points by an individual in overtime as Florida beat Ole Miss on the road 91-81. Brown was the first freshman in 10 years to score 28 points in a Gator game. Unfortunately, Brown also tore cartilage in his knee and missed the season's last four games.

Martti Kuisma came from Helsinki, Finland, and the 6-foot-11 freshman became the Gators' first European player. Broadcast journalist Larry Vettel has been around the Gator program since the late seventies, and has witnessed much of Florida's basketball history. Vettel delights in telling the story of Kuisma's introduction to Gator hoops.

"Everything Florida learned about Kuisma had come over the phone lines between Florida and Finland," Vettel recalls. "Kuisma's coach had highly recommended the big forward, but the Florida staff was still trying to get comfortable with bringing him to America. In a conversation they asked Martti, 'Do you like to play down low, fight for the rebounds, mix things up?' Kuisma replied, 'Oh no coach, I don't rebound. I shoot.'"

And Florida fans discovered that Martti Kuisma could really shoot the basketball. In a four-year career, he made 34 percent of 221 three-point attempts. Florida took full advantage of this unique skill in a player his size. Florida finished that first year 11-17 overall. The 7-11 SEC mark was good for seventh place in league play.

THE HEALING TOUCH

In 1992 Florida's returning players had experienced a full season with Kruger and were beginning to grasp the coaching staff's expectations both on and off the court. In these first transition years of the Florida program, Kruger's staff was challenged to help players who had been recruited to a different coaching philosophy adjust to a new way of basketball life. The newcomer coaches were surprised to find players who just didn't enjoy working on personal improvement.

Back at Kansas State, the players had lived on the gym floor, playing pickup games, shooting around, and working on their skills. At Florida, Kruger had to persuade his players to practice. He gave them specific summer assignments prior to the start of the '92 year.

"Obviously, during the summer you always like to think that you are working hard," senior Brian Hogan said at the beginning of the season. "But this year there is no doubt — everyone is putting forth the effort we need to be the kind of team I've wanted to play on all four years."

One of the players who benefited most from the focused teaching was Stacey Poole. He was a McDonald's High School All-American selection and overcame three potential career-ending injuries to have one of the most celebrated careers in a Gator uniform. The Jacksonville native, who wore number 22, had the greatest vertical leaping ability of any Florida player ever before he suffered Achilles' tendon tears of both ankles. Still, Poole managed to complete a four-year career in which he started 104 of 116 games.

Poole's first injury was on his fourth day of practice in 1988, and he was granted a medical redshirt season that year. The next summer he tore a left knee ligament, and Dr. Pete Indelicato transplanted a cadaver's patellar tendon to once again give him new basketball life. Poole became an honorable mention All-American and first-team All-SEC player his senior year. He scored 1,678 career points and averaged 14.4 points a game during his four-year career. Poole missed out on the SEC championship season in 1989 and graduated a year too soon for the Final Four run in 1994. He was perhaps Florida basketball's most courageous player. In a *Gainesville Sun* article, Paul Jenkins said of Poole, "We hear all about the bad things in athletics, but once in awhile we are given an example of why athletes are a special breed." Stacey Poole earned the respect of everyone for his personal courage.

With Poole averaging 18.6 points a game, Florida was 5-0 before South Florida got 29 points from Radenko Dobras and left Gainesville with a 73-71 win. Florida took a 7-3 record into conference play and slipped by South Carolina 53-52. At the halfway point of the SEC schedule, Florida was 3-5 and then won six of its last eight SEC games during the regular season.

One of the most dramatic wins in the early Kruger years came in the next to last regular-season game of the 1992 season against 10th-ranked Kentucky. Yet, just before the Kentucky game, Kruger was on Perry Field outside the O'Connell Center working with his son Kevin's Little League team. Three hours later, 11,000 fans watched Florida overcome a six-point halftime deficit and make 15 of 20 second-half shots to upset the Wildcats 79-62. Stacey Poole had 19 points and 12 rebounds playing 37 minutes. Brian Hogan, in his final home game as a Gator senior, scored 12 points.

In the SEC Tournament, Florida was eliminated by Alabama 62-60 in the first round. But with a 16-12 record, the Gators were invited to the NIT. The team was playing on all cylinders as Kruger had ten players involved in each game's outcome.

Florida became a first-round NIT host and defeated Richmond 66-52. The Gators were then sent to Pittsburgh, Pennsylvania, for their next game. The game was played in Fitzgerald Field House, a building that is on the national register of historic sites. Pitt fans numbering 6,541 crammed into every open space, but the Gators played with poise and upset Pitt 77-74. It was the Panthers' first non-conference loss in Fitzgerald in four years.

Craig Brown was in his home state and scored 17 points. With ice in his veins, Brown dropped four free throws inside the one-minute mark. Stacey Poole had 17 points. "There was no way in the world we were going to crack," Poole said.

The "Find a Way" slogan that became identified with Florida's 1994 march to the Final Four was actually adopted first by this group of determined Florida players. "We want the other team to walk away saying they've never been blocked out like that, they've never been out-hustled like that and they've never had to work as hard as that," Kruger said. Kruger's motto: Find a way.

Kruger took a talented Stacey Poole and found a way to weave nine other players in and out of the lineup to develop one of Florida's most competitive basketball teams. This group resembled the 1967, 1969, 1974, 1977, 1989, and 1994 teams that played with exceptional heart, toughness, and team chemistry. Of these seven teams, only the 1974 team was less talented. Kruger squeezed every drop of useful talent from his roster. The players were heavy on the floorburns and flat out expected to win.

After beating Pitt, Florida waited up until after midnight and learned the team's next game would also be on the road. Brian Hogan had a premonition. He told Kruger the team would play Purdue in his home state of Indiana. Hogan must have been tied into a bigger source than anyone realized at the time because the transplanted Hoosier was indeed going to be back home in Indiana to play Purdue.

Hogan was born and raised in Kokomo, just about an hour's drive from Market Square Arena in Indianapolis. He came to Florida in 1988 and camped just outside the three-point line during his four-year career. Hogan and Florida's Tony Miller were two Indiana natives who demonstrated to Florida fans the art form of shooting a basketball. Hogan was also a dynamically motivated and inspirational player who left absolutely every ounce of his personal energy on the court.

Florida basketball had its own version of the basketball film *Hoosiers* when the team met powerful Purdue in the NIT. Hogan had grown up with Purdue's Matt

Waddell and played on the outdoor courts with the Boilermakers' Woody Austin, who was the state's high school Mr. Basketball. Hundreds of Hogan's high school friends and family tailgated their way to the big city to see their hometown hero. Hogan had left the comfort zone of his Indiana nest; this would be his first and last chance to play a basketball game in the place he had sharpened his skills.

The Gator team gave its second straight flawless performance, shooting 50 percent from the field and committing just 10 team turnovers. In 23 minutes of action, Hogan came off the bench and buried crucial long-range jumpers to stop each of Purdue's attempts to change the momentum. Hogan had saved his best for this special night. The 6-foot-2, 174-pound Florida senior scored a career-high 18 points, making five of nine field goals and all five free-throw attempts. He took charges, made steals, slid his teammates easy passes, and all the time with a fire in his eyes that said Florida has come here to win. Nine Florida players put points on the scoreboard, and it was another magnificent team effort as Florida headed to the NIT's Big Apple final with a 74-67 victory.

When the game ended, Hogan carried his personal celebration up into the stands where he embraced his mother and father and high-fived his friends. It was a dramatic finish to one of Florida basketball's most celebrated nights.

"We like players who are enthusiastic and unselfish," Kruger said when the season began, "people who put their teammates first and do whatever it takes." Kruger was talking about players in general, but his definition most appropriately fit Brian Hogan. Hogan certainly wasn't the most gifted, and he is a footnote in many of his career box scores. But on this night and on this stage, he gave an Academy Award performance.

Florida went to New York for the NIT final for the second time, but lost to Virginia 62-56 in the semifinal game and to Utah 81-78 in the consolation game. For the team, beating Pitt and Purdue was their season's final four, and the program began to walk with more dignity in the national limelight.

Everyone Contributes

As Kruger and his staff worked on and off the court to rebuild and reshape Florida's basketball future, they were inspired by individuals who also gave the program their best efforts.

With all due respect to Lon's caring, enthusiastic, and loving wife Barbara, if Kruger was dad, Sharon Sullivan was "mom." Everyone who has interacted with Sullivan through the years will attest that she, as much as anyone, has provided continuity for Gator basketball in her capacity as the basketball program's executive secretary. Nothing has ever been too much trouble for Sharon Sullivan. When Mark White led the Gator Tip-Off Club for two years through the Sloan to DeVoe to Kruger transition, Sullivan provided a shoulder to lean on and the extra hours to help make Tip-Off Club activities successful.

"The one person who most encouraged me that we could keep our club going was Sharon," White said. Ron Marks, Mac McGregor, and Bill Perusek, all past Tip-Off Club captains, say that Sullivan reassured them in their most trying moments that things would work out." Sharon does not have a mean bone in her body," Marks said. "She is Florida basketball's most dedicated ambassador."

Florida basketball was also fortunate to have a sports information director who was such a basketball enthusiast that he would have liked nothing better than to be reincarnated some day as Larry Bird. Joel Glass spent as much time in the gym shooting baskets as he did at a keyboard writing releases.

Glass had some big shoes to fill starting with those of Florida's first notable basketball SID, George Solomon, who became the sports editor of the *Washington Post*. Others like Richard Giannini, Dwight Johnson, Pete Kynion, Bert Lacey, Lee Tobin, and Chris Cameron have provided basketball with a dedicated touch. But Glass set new standards and became the best yet. He took his job to another level.

Behind the scenes, Glass was the hardest-working person that Florida basketball had ever known. With genuine credibility, Glass built meaningful relationships with the media. He made the program come alive in print. Glass's media guides won national awards. During Florida's 1994 Final Four year, he earned immense respect from broadcast and print journalists across the country. CBS's Bill Raftery said of Glass, "He's the most thorough and accessible college basketball SID in the country."

Glass captured the essence of the new Florida basketball program and was tireless in projecting it to the media. In 1992 as Florida first found a way to the NIT finals, Glass probably sent 3,000 faxes to print and broadcast media to promote players' accomplishments. With the success of the NIT experience, he was able to land space for Stacey Poole in *Sports Illustrated*.

As the '93 season began to unfold, there was an altogether new look to the program's personality. Andrew DeClercq, Dan Cross, and Svein Dyrkolbotn were sophomores, and six new faces appeared for the first time on the practice court. Kruger had signed Jason Anderson, John Griffiths, Dametri Hill, Brian Thompson, and junior college transfer Jermaine Carlton. They were joined by walk-on Clayton Bates.

Day by day, Kruger was now on the inside building the values that would soon become evident to others outside the program. His patience for the most seemingly insignificant detail characterized his personal drive to do everything in a first-class way. He was masterful at teaching young people about life. The players came to realize he was a coach in the truest sense of the word.

Craig Brown got an early dose of Kruger's values. "Early in my freshman year, I picked up one of those credit card applications you see all over campus," Brown said. "I got the card and got into trouble with it. My parents helped me out and paid it off for me.

"But Coach Kruger didn't think that was right. He told me I should take responsibility for my own actions. He would take my [extra] meal money for road trips and send it home to my parents for the credit card bill."

On the practice court, the emphasis was on team values. Players had to be reminded over and over again to talk. "I've got your man – take mine." "Watch the screen on your left." "Get down! Get down!" "Touch the floor!" "Switch." These were fundamental concepts, but people who had watched Florida practice over the years were delighted to finally see players encouraging each other and helping their teammates succeed.

Kruger rarely swore, but if he said "damn" or "hell," a player was quick to take notice. "You have a lot more respect for him because he doesn't have to use those tactics," said Jason Anderson. "He's not going to yell and cuss you out. But if you make him mad, he'll give you a look you don't want to see. That right side of his lip kind of curls up and you can tell right away that he's mad. But the thing with Coach Kruger is that even when he's mad at you, he doesn't treat you any differently. A lot of coaches might not want anything to do with you in those situations. Coach Kruger might get mad at you and let you know what he expects from you, but he always treats you the same way."

Florida's players for the first time in over a decade were being taught both the game of basketball and the game of life. Attitudes were changing. Confidence had been restored. Character was built. But great programs are built one day at a time, and the real tough work of teaching the game still had a lot of days to go.

The '93 season was not one for the faint of heart. Fifteen of Florida's 28 games were decided in the final three minutes, and 13 contests were determined by five points or less. Of those 13 games, the Gators won seven and lost six. The highlight of the season was the program's second straight NIT appearance even though the Gators came up short, losing 74-66 in Minneapolis to the eventual NIT champion Minnesota Golden Gophers.

The Gators were 4-0 against in-state rivals Florida State, Jacksonville, South Florida, and Stetson and won nine of their first 12 games. Florida's three seniors, Hosie Grimsley, Stacey Poole, and Scott Stewart, were tri-captains and gave an otherwise young Gator contingent good veteran leadership.

Poole finished his career third on the all-time scoring chart with 1,678 career points. Stewart made a career second-best 119 three-pointers and had the fourth best career free-throw percentage, 82.8 percent. Grimsley played the small forward, big guard, and point-guard positions over the course of his career and is remembered for having one of the program's best-ever vertical leaps of 38.5 inches. Dick Vitale named Grimsley to his five-man national all-defensive team.

The Gators went 16-12 with Poole as the go-to guy down the stretch, and Stacey became a consensus first-team all-conference player. He averaged 16.4 points a game and played 31 minutes. A late season 94-47 win over Ole Miss was the largest margin of victory ever against an SEC team. But unbelievably, Ole Miss came back to upset an uncharacteristically less than motivated Kruger team in the first round of the SEC Tournament.

Martti Kuisma had 50 three-pointers, after scoring just one three in the previous two seasons, and Florida drew a school-record 9,191 fans per home game. The Gators 9-7 SEC record was good for fourth place in the overall standings.

As the season concluded, the coaching staff was busy recruiting and making plans for an international opportunity to play basketball in Australia. When Kruger took the Florida job, he arranged to take the Gators to Australia in the off-season before the 1994 year. Always two steps ahead in his planning, Kruger knew this would be a critical time period in which to solidify his early recruiting classes and build some team cohesion.

When Tommy Bartlett took a Gator team to South America prior to the '67 season, Florida gained a valuable chance to enhance its team's potential. When the Gators embarked on this journey to the far side of the globe, they had no way of knowing they would accomplish even more than they dreamed possible. It seemed like a fairy tale had come true. But the Gators' long road to the Final Four in 1994 actually began with that journey in the spring of 1993.

The Florida contingent left Gainesville on May 5 for a 17-day, eight-game exhibition tour of Australia, playing in Sydney, Melbourne, Canberra, and some less familiar sites like Wollongong, Newcastle, Albury, and Bendigo. It was an adventure that was unique in all of University of Florida sports and thrust the Florida team members into

EVERYONE CONTRIBUTES

roles of goodwill ambassadors in a country with a reputation for outstanding hospitality.

It was kangaroos and bungee-jumping, surfboards and koala bears, the bright lights of Melbourne and Sydney and the "g'day mate" hospitality of Wollongong and Albury. Far from home, players bonded, and Florida basketball poured concrete into the foundation of a team that would come to portray the very best of intercollegiate athletics.

Basketball-wise, it was the fuel for the championship season. Kruger and his players had a chance to live together minute by minute and day by day as they traveled by bus across the Australian countryside in a barnstorming atmosphere. They went sightseeing together, ate pizza together, had soul-searching team discussions about issues like black and white relationships, and most of all, competed in an environment where there was no external pressure. Florida won six of the eight games and scored more than 100 points four times. The biggest win was 136-100 over the Albury Bandits.

"I think we accomplished what we wanted to accomplish on the trip," Kruger said later. "Off the court, the guys got to spend a lot of time together and experience another part of the world. On the floor, there was a lot of playing time for everyone. Getting to play 48-minute games was exactly what we'd hoped for to give everyone a good chance to play.

"I think all the players will enter next fall with a different attitude. They all know their roles better, and they can all feel that they are a significant part of what is happening. We will go into next season with a little better idea of what to expect instead of just hoping some things are going to happen."

Craig Brown and Martti Kuisma would be Florida's only seniors that season. It was now their turn to step forward and provide the leadership for a cast of players that was, for the first time, all Kruger recruits. Both had paid their dues and both uniquely influenced the potential of this team. Kuisma's outside jumper was a potent weapon which kept teams honest in a zone. Brown earned the respect of his teammates for his ability to positively influence the outcome of every game. He was the team's acknowledged leader.

In 1991 Brown had been named to a 12-man junior national team that Lon Kruger coached to a junior world championship gold medal. Brown had rehabilitated his injured knee in time to work his way into a supporting role of this cast of the nation's best rising sophomores. The basketball experience that summer was one which began to shape his playing future.

More than any player who ever wore a Florida uniform, Craig Brown was the leader. From the moment he arrived his freshman year, Brown brought a northeastern basketball mentality. He was competitively unselfish and confidently competent. He always gave the ball to someone with a better chance to score, but he never hesitated to pull up and let it go.

In 1993 he started 30 of 33 games, and each day his leadership became more and more evident. Brown scored in double figures 16 times and was second to Stacey

Poole in scoring, averaging 10.6 points per game. He had a team-leading 51 three-pointers and made five three-pointers against Texas A&M. Brown also led the team in minutes played, 33.3 per game. He hit game-sealing baskets to help Florida beat South Florida, Auburn, and Georgia.

Brown shouted encouragement and was quick to express displeasure. He did more than was required and made sure others did, too. As practice unfolded in the fall of 1993, he ran the sprints and took the charges and made every shuffle cut just right. He arrived early on the practice court and was the last one to leave. Brown ran to every huddle and was the first to pick up a teammate who had hit the deck. He knew when to take the shot and when to make the pass. Craig Brown had emerged to lead Florida as no player had ever done before. Later, Kruger would say, "Craig Brown has absolutely set a standard that is still going to mean something to players in this program two decades from now."

A team can have its marquee player at small forward, and it can have its game-stopper in the middle. But for a team to be successful, the leader must have the rock in his hand. It's the guards who set the table. It's the guards who establish the tempo. It's the guards who dictate the defense. And it's at guard where a team must have its leader.

The Pennsylvania native gave the coaching staff a keystone to the program's future, and the Australian trip helped to more prominently solidify this role in the eyes of his teammates. But another player who was expected to fill some big shoes on the court became a major setback for the program.

In the fall of 1992, Kruger announced that 6-foot-8 Ben Davis, a former state of Florida Mr. Basketball from Bradenton Southeast High School, was transferring after one season as a Kansas Jayhawk to be closer to home. NCAA rules precluded the All Big Eight freshman from practicing that year or making the trip to Australia. But he would be eligible for the '94 season.

Ben Davis appeared to be Kruger's first recruiting breakthrough and the blue chip player they needed to go to war in the SEC. He had a Gentle Ben personality coupled with a Rambo-style body, but unknown to most at the time, Davis had a problem with marijuana. Before long he tested positive on two occasions at Florida. Even with extensive professional counseling and hours of personal attention, Davis failed his third drug test and was forced to leave the program. He transferred to Hutchinson Junior College in Kansas.

The media guide for the '93-94 year featured Kruger and four players on the cover, posed around a large-size Reebok shoe. It was another of Joel Glass's award-winning creations, but unnoticed by most was a bare spot on the toe of the shoe in the carefully choreographed picture – it was the missing piece of Florida's potential starting five. With Davis' departure, many thought Florida's '94 season had also vanished into thin air.

Finding A Way

In 1989 David Steele, one of basketball's best play-by-play broadcasters, left Florida to become the first play-by-play voice of the Orlando Magic. When he departed, he passed the microphone to Mick Hubert and "Oh My!" became as popular as any two words ever spoken about Florida sports. When Hubert began creatively nicknaming the players, everyone around the program was having fun again.

There was "the Norwegian Collegian," a 6-foot-8, 244-pound Norway native, Svein Dyrkolbotn (Dear-kol-botin). Needless to say, everybody knew the bright, good-looking Gator as Svein (Svain). Martti Kuisma (Mar-tee Kwees-ma) was "The Thin Fin" from Helsinki, Finland. There was Brian "Bee-trey" Thompson and Dametri "Da Meat Hook" Hill. Clayton Bates was C.B. and Andrew DeClercq was A.D.

In the summer of 1993, Assistant Coach Kirk Speraw left to become the head coach at the University of Central Florida. Kruger hired a veteran NBA and collegiate assistant coach to fill an important instructional role. R.C. Buford had worked for Larry Brown at both the University of Kansas and the San Antonio Spurs. He brought a strong teaching background to the program.

Florida emerged from the fall's preseason workouts well conditioned, and the coaching staff was excited to begin laying the groundwork for a challenging 29-game schedule. Little did anyone suspect at the time that this club would play more games than any Florida team in the past. Fifteen games would be played against teams which were in postseason play the year before, and 11 were against opponents who had been in the '93 NCAA Tournament.

After a 6-1 start, the 1993-94 Florida team got one of its early confidence-building wins when senior Craig Brown went back home to Pennsylvania to lead Florida to an 85-77 upset of Villanova in Philadelphia. Brown scored 16 of his team-high 20 points in the second half, and Florida put four players in double figures.

The December 22 game was scheduled as a homecoming for the Florida senior captain, and he gave his family a night to remember. Before a capacity crowd, Brown answered several key Villanova baskets and made nine of 10 pressure free throws. The victory gave Florida a 7-1 start.

Kruger sent the team home for Christmas with their families for a much-needed break before they traveled to Hawaii to play in the Rainbow Classic on December 28.

LON KRUGER: 1991-1996

In Honolulu, Florida was tested by 20th-ranked Oklahoma State, a preseason Big Eight favorite who showcased a massive front-line talent in Bryant "Big Country" Reeves.

Scoring a career-high 23 points, Florida's own mountain man, Dametri Hill, with a soft, little right-hand jump hook, muscled the 7-foot, 280-pound Reeves in the paint to dominate the Sooner center. Reeves was the 1993 Big Eight Player of the Year but managed only four points and four rebounds as the Gators held on to a six-point halftime lead for the 74-69 first-round win.

The next night, 11th-ranked Louisville failed to contain Hill, who broke his previous night's high with 28 points. But Florida made just five of 17 three-pointers and shot a miserable 35 percent to lose 83-68. The final night of the three-day event saw Florida outscore Evansville 19-9 during the first nine minutes of the second half to overcome a three-point halftime deficit and leave the Hawaiian island with a hard-earned 66-63 win.

Cross and Brown both were averaging double figures and each had three-plus assists per game. In the Evansville game, they combined for 33 of the team's 66 points, and on Evansville's final possession, Cross stole the ball to seal the victory. If it wasn't DeClercq blocking a shot or delivering a fast-break basket, it was Hill freezing the defense and dropping one off the backboard. When the opponent kept the ball out of the middle, Cross would nail a 19-foot jumper. If Cross was covered, Brown would answer. This team was really together and anxious to play.

The three pivotal games in Hawaii closed out the 11-game preconference schedule. The Gators were ready to head down the dusty southern roads of the Southeastern Conference. The players had confidence, they had chemistry, and they were committed.

With only 8,300 fans in the O'Connell Center, Florida opened the SEC season with a 74-73 win over LSU. In the final seconds of the game, Cross drove for the layup and miraculously scored the go-ahead basket. LSU had the last shot, but Jason Anderson, who scored 12 second-half points, grabbed the rebound, and Florida recorded its 10th win of the season.

The Gators then set a school- and SEC-record 27 for 27 from the free-throw line and won their sixth straight 86-71 over Tennessee. It was also the fourth straight win in Knoxville. Florida beat South Florida in St. Petersburg's ThunderDome 69-64 with Cross and Brown making big baskets inside the one-minute mark.

Four days later the scene was Columbia, South Carolina, where Florida went from nine down to nine up in the second half and then dodged a final-second Gamecock bullet to escape with a 77-75 win. Brown made a career-high six three-pointers and refused to let his teammates down before 8,000 raucous Gamecock fans.

At 13-2 Florida had its best start in the 53 years since 1941. Things were starting to get pretty interesting. If this was Lexington or Chapel Hill, people would be talking Final Four. But this was Gainesville, where fans had always been afraid to hope for too much. But, could this be the year? There was incredible excitement in the air.

Florida's first five home games had drawn an average of only 6,176 fans, but a frenzied O'Connell Center record 12,221 spectators were in their places as Kentucky came to town. In the past, the Big Blue faithful who lived in the Sunshine State had had little trouble getting tickets in Gainesville to watch their Wildcats. But this time they were paying $100 scalpers' prices, probably thinking they were outside Rupp Arena.

Dan Cross had a career-high 20 points, and an ESPN nationally televised audience saw Andrew DeClercq grab a career-high 20 rebounds. Kentucky's powerful offense that was averaging 95.6 points a game was throttled by the Gators' tenacious defense and made only four of 22 three-pointers to shoot a paltry 35 percent overall in the game. Brown, Cross, DeClercq, Hill, and Brian Thompson all scored crucial points in the final two minutes to secure the 59-57 victory.

The Gators *were* for real at 14-2 overall and 4-0 in the SEC. Ten of their first 16 games had been played away from the O'Dome, so going on the road was no longer the program's insurmountable obstacle.

This team was rewriting the record books. In Tuscaloosa, however, Alabama had a different agenda. Florida had one of its worst performances in recent memory as the Tide gave Florida a lesson in second-half toughness, winning 69-61.

Florida went to Georgia and, for the first time in five seasons, scored 100 points. The last 100-plus point game had been the SEC championship win over LSU 104-95. This time Georgia was never in the game, and 7,100 normally vocal Bulldog fans were uncharacteristically silent as Florida shot 62 percent from the field in the 22-point victory.

"We were really pumped up for this game because we hadn't played well against Alabama," said Dan Cross. "We knew this was a big game for us." It was Florida's largest conference road win since beating Mississippi State by 28 points in 1987. It was the first time in Georgia head Coach Hugh Durham's 28-year career that his team had lost back-to-back games with the opponents scoring over 100 points.

Cross finished with 24 points, and Martti Kuisma had his best night of the year with 16 points. "Martti looked like himself tonight," Kruger said. "No one on our team works harder than Martti, and it's really good to see him play like this again."

Fans once again crammed into the Gators' home dome, and 12,021 saw five Gators score double figures as Florida downed Vanderbilt 75-66. Brown led the way with 17 points and DeClercq and Hill combined for 17 rebounds. Vandy shot 46 percent but Florida dominated the backboards 42-30. Kentucky and Vanderbilt were the first back-to-back O'Connell Center sellouts since the 1987 season.

Surprisingly, only 9,000 fans showed up to witness a pivotal 68-67 victory over Auburn. This time the War Eagles would not be the spoilers for Florida. Jason Anderson came off the bench to score eight points and forced the talented future NBA pick Wesley Person to work for his shots all night.

"I thought Jason did a nice job on Wesley," said Coach Kruger. "Jason can cover very good players and he needs to develop that talent." The game ended with a 15-foot jumper by Person that rimmed out at the buzzer. "I thought it was in," said Auburn Coach Tommy Joe Eagles. "It was exactly the way we drew it up and exactly what we wanted to happen."

At 17-3 Florida owned its best start in the school's 75-year basketball history. Once again, this magical group of Gators found a way to win.

Florida was now a serious contender in the conference race. The Gators won five of their next six games. The preseason prognosis was for Florida to finish fourth in the SEC's Eastern Division and eighth overall, but writers had already begun to burn any trace of those earlier predictions. Dan Cross was the SEC Player of the Week and scored another career-high 26 to beat Mississippi State 84-75. Craig Brown had his first career double-double, and Florida crushed Ole Miss 74-55 in Oxford.

With a 9-2 record, Florida traveled to Arkansas to take on the third-ranked Razorbacks who were noted for wearing teams down with "forty minutes of hell."

"If you don't think it is forty minutes of hell," said an exhausted Dan Cross after the Arkansas victory, "then you need to get out there on the court with them." Florida lost to Arkansas 99-87, which broke a five-game conference win streak. But Florida held on to first place in the league.

"I think the Razorbacks (eventual NCAA champions that year) are the best team in the country," Kruger said prophetically. "They've got an impressive group of athletes and they've got all the pieces. It was a pretty good basketball game, but we just couldn't cut into that margin enough." Kruger, who picked up his second technical as a Gator coach, went on to say, "I'm disappointed for our guys, but I'm not disappointed with our effort or with the way some of our guys played."

Florida came back home where only 9,000 fans showed up *again* for the normally inspired visit of Georgia. The Gators had their highest second-half point total – 55 – and Cross and Brown combined for 42 points to whip the Bulldogs 91-79.

"Dan and I were joking on the plane ride home from Arkansas," said senior Craig Brown, "that sooner or later we've got to have a game where we're both playing well at the same time." It was Florida's 20th win of the season and one of the noteworthy numbers in the world of sports that commands respect for a successful year in college basketball.

To help target twenty wins early in the season, Sloan Hemmer, the fiancee of Florida Assistant Coach Mike Shepherd, had constructed a big homemade jigsaw puzzle with 20 pieces. When completed, the puzzle would show an NCAA Tournament ticket. It was most likely that a 20-win season would earn a bid to college basketball's biggest event. With the Georgia victory, the puzzle was now complete.

The season's second victory over South Carolina by a score of 88-64 boosted Florida's record to 21-4, matching the school's record for regular season wins. It was the identical record with which the '67 team had finished its season. Two nights later, Florida broke that mark with a 72-61 victory in Gainesville over Florida State.

Florida was now the 16th-ranked team in the nation, and in the previous two years had won 11 of 12 games against in-state schools. There was little doubt that Florida basketball was the most prominent college basketball program in the Sunshine State.

Vanderbilt and Kentucky took some shine off the Gators' Reebok shoes and handed the team its only back-to-back defeats during the season. Vandy won 82-78 and got 52 points from Billy McCaffrey and Ronnie McMahan. Kentucky knocked Florida off its first-place perch in the Eastern Division with an emotional come-from-behind 80-77 win in Rupp Arena. Florida led 44-34 at the half and had a 19-point lead, but Kentucky's full-court press and home-court crowd were too much for the Gator players.

The Gators concluded their regular season with an emotional Senior Night tribute to Craig Brown and Martti Kuisma and then, right before tip-off, learned that South Carolina had just upset Kentucky in Columbia. A win over Tennessee that night would earn the Gators a tie-breaking top seed in the SEC Tournament.

With 11,212 fans in the O'Connell Center chanting "SEC! SEC!" Florida overcame a 50-45 deficit and completed a perfect 13-0 home season by beating Tennessee 82-71. It was just the fifth Florida team in history to go undefeated at home and was the first perfect home record since the 1961 season.

"Even before we heard that Kentucky had lost, this game still meant a lot to us," said Andrew DeClercq. "We wanted to finish the season with a perfect record at home, and we wanted to send the seniors out on a good note." Martti Kuisma had his sixth double-figure night of the year with 10 points, but senior Craig Brown scored just seven points in 35 minutes, although he pulled down 10 rebounds.

With a cushion to the score's final margin, Kruger was able to take Brown and Kuisma, one by one, from the game to thunderous crowd ovations. Cross greeted Brown at midcourt and the two embraced as Brown bid farewell to the O'Connell Center crowd.

"I kind of wanted to be out there until the very end," said Brown. "Especially if I could have gotten one more shot to fall. It kind of hit me coming out that this was my last time in front of the home fans. It felt good." As the 19th-ranked team in the nation, Florida could celebrate a truly remarkable season.

"Nothing has come easy for us," Cross said after the win over Tennessee. "We had to work from the bottom and now we're at the top. We're starting to get the recognition and the respect we deserve. It took some people a while to believe in us, and it may take other people a while longer."

The Florida players had achieved this success during a year in which the country viewed their two conference rivals – Arkansas and Kentucky – as possibly the two best teams in America. Mike Bianchi wrote in a *Gainesville Sun* column after the Tennessee victory, "As of right now. Today. At this very moment. At the end of the regular season, the Florida Gators are better than the tradition-drenched Kentucky Wildcats."

It was Florida's first-ever first-place finish in the league's Eastern Division since the East and West brackets were established in 1992 when Arkansas and South Carolina joined the Southeastern Conference.

"Obviously, Kentucky sets the standard for basketball in this league," said Kruger prior to the SEC Tournament. "All that tradition and those championships Kentucky won – to be up there challenging them for the East title is something the players on this team can feel good about." Never before had the SEC been this strong. Basketball gurus were beginning to realize that SEC basketball might be the best in the nation.

The site of the conference tournament was the Pyramid in Memphis, Tennessee. The Gator players waited out a 24-minute midgame delay, as the lights went out in the building, before beating South Carolina for the third time 84-57. With the victory, this Florida team recorded the winningest season in Gator basketball history, 24-6.

The next night Craig Brown tied an SEC Tournament record with a perfect five for five three-pointers, and Florida beat nemesis Alabama 68-52 to advance to the tournament finals for only the third time ever. Beating the Tide was a true hurdle. Both of the previous championship game appearances – in 1934 and 1989 – had resulted in losses to the Crimson Tide.

In the Memphis, Tennessee SEC Tournament final, 10th-ranked Kentucky was just too much to handle. With 12 of 28 three-pointers from what sometimes seemed as far away as Graceland, the Wildcats won the tournament championship 73-60.

When Kruger arrived in 1990, he established traditions and reference points to help focus the team on its objectives. One of those was to gather the team together in the locker room on the Sunday afternoon of the NCAA Tournament selection to watch the pairings. This year in Memphis, the Gators literally walked off the court, showered, and were escorted into a private room inside the Pyramid. Crowded together with family, friends, coaches' wives, etc., the team eagerly anticipated its first trip to the NCAA Tournament.

Kruger had been there before. Four straight times prior to arriving in Gainesville, he had taken his Kansas State alma mater to the Big Dance. But this year he had to feel especially proud when Florida popped up in the East as a third seed to face first-round opponent James Madison in Uniondale (Long Island), New York. St. Petersburg, Florida, was also a first-round site, and with such a high seed, it was conceivable that Florida would be sent closer to home.

"We would have liked to have gone to St. Pete for our fans," Kruger said. "Yet we look forward to the challenge of playing in the NCAA Tournament. We're certainly very pleased to be a three seed and it is indicative of the fact that this group has done a good job throughout the year."

For basketball people, the 64-team NCAA Tournament is the biggest event of the year. Programs are measured by their trips to the tournament. The Gators had been invited only three times in the previous 56 years of postseason competition. The bid was particularly meaningful this year because Kruger's staff had overcome the program's thorny past to emerge in the national spotlight.

In an interview with Paul Jenkins of the *Gainesville Sun*, DeClercq said, "We've gone out and done the things we needed to do this year to make sure our name would pop up there today. We knew we were in, but we were extremely happy to see it, and we're extremely happy with the draw."

Florida's season had drawn rave reviews from the media and other coaches. "Lon Kruger is an outstanding leader and a great teacher. He's done a great job with the Florida program and has it moving in a positive direction," ESPN and ABC's Dick Vitale said.

Kentucky's Coach Rick Pitino said, "They didn't come into this season with much hype, but they've gotten respect the old-fashioned way; they've earned it."

"Make no mistake, this is a Lon Kruger-type squad," Brian Schmitz said in the *Orlando Sentinel*. "Unselfish. Undaunted. This is team intangible. You sacrifice. You scrap. You succeed. You find a way."

Final Four Fever

Again and again throughout the season, Florida's players found a way. But as they embarked on their chartered plane for New York City, there was more than a four-leaf clover in their back pocket.

Between them, Dan Cross and Craig Brown were averaging almost nine three-point attempts a game and were making 43 percent of them. Andrew DeClercq had eight rebounds and at least one blocked shot every game. Hill's stature made him tough to match defensively, and the 300-pound center averaged 13 points a game. Florida's opponents shot just 41 percent against the Gators, and Florida claimed an impressive six rebounds a game margin against other teams. The Gators were unselfish, they were scrappy, and perhaps most of all, they believed that they would find a way to win.

In the NCAA Tournament, it just takes six wins to be the national champion. Each weekend of the three-week tournament, half the field goes home. Florida was a favorite to beat 14th-seeded James Madison, but Lefty Driesell had the Dukes ahead 60-59 with 48 seconds to play. Florida, looking to get Brown or Cross open, found Greg Williams who never blinked and dropped a 23-foot jumper. It was his first three-pointer in the previous five games and gave the Gators a 62-60 lead.

"As well as Greg has played during the year, that shot kind of solidified his contributions to this team as a freshman," Kruger said. "He has not played as many minutes as he's earned because Dan and Craig have played so well this year. That shot says a lot about Greg and the type of player he's going to be for us. He's got that air about him that he can play against the best and step up and deliver."

"He's my roomie," Brown said of Williams. "Last time he went to take a three like that, he hesitated. I pulled him aside and said, 'Next time you have the opportunity to shoot one like that, just step up and hit it.' That's exactly what he did." James Madison tied the game with two free throws, and Dan Cross dropped a game-winning shot for the 64-62 margin.

"Ideally, we'd have liked to have run the clock down a little more," Lon Kruger said. "But in that situation you also don't want to pass up a good shot. The opening was there, and Dan took it aggressively."

It was touch and go, but the Gators survived the first round to meet the Ivy

League's representative – Penn. The Quakers were buoyed by a 16-game winning streak, and they had beaten Big Eight Tournament champion Nebraska. Cross led Florida in scoring with 22 points, making all 10 of his free-throw attempts. Hill added 16 points in 27 minutes of action. The Ivy League champs shot just 31 percent from the field despite a heroic 23-point effort from a future NBA selection, Jerome Allen. Florida coasted to the 70-58 finish line and got a game-ending three-pointer from former walk-on, Clayton Bates.

The Gators were going to the Sweet 16 for the first time since 1987 when they lost to Syracuse in the Meadowlands. This time, the selection committee put them a little closer to home. The headline in the *Miami Herald* on March 25 read, "No Fear; Underdog's Here."

Indiana and Connecticut were favored to beat Boston College and Florida. The overachieving Eagles from Boston College had unexpectedly earned a trip to Miami by sending top-ranked North Carolina home in the sectional round. With Connecticut and B.C. both out of the Big East, it was Boston College that was expected to soon be headed back home. But the real upstart was the home-state favorite – the Florida Gators. They had become the darlings of Dixie.

"It's almost amusing to think back to the perceptions people had of this team in November and December," Kruger said. "Now it's to the point where people are wondering why we didn't beat Kentucky in the SEC Tournament championship game.

"As a coach you enjoy this like you enjoy watching your kids open their packages at Christmas. You get a lot more from watching them open their presents than you do from opening your own. As a staff, that's the kind of enjoyment we're getting."

Florida's players were having the most fun ever, but in many respects they were handling things as if they had all been in this position many times before. "We kind of got used to people doubting us, and we were able to feed off that doubt," said Dan Cross. "Even when people didn't believe in us, we still believed in one another."

Andrew DeClercq had been relatively quiet in the tournament's first two rounds, scoring a total of only eight points. "Right now we're having a lot of fun," DeClercq said. "We're one of sixteen teams still playing and we're thrilled to be here and have a chance to keep playing."

And keep playing they did. Connecticut was the nation's No. 4 team and the No. 2 seed in the East Regional bracket. At 29-4 the Huskies were led by Donyell Marshall, the Big East Player of the Year, but they didn't have a senior in their starting lineup.

Dick Vitale made his pregame predictions. "I would give a slight edge to Connecticut because they have a superstar in Donyell Marshall, an absolutely dominating player," he said. "Florida has very underrated guards in Dan Cross and Craig Brown ... and Lon Kruger should get a lot of votes for coach of the year."

In a *Miami Herald* interview with Linda Robertson, Connecticut Coach Jim Calhoun was asked if he was taking Florida seriously. "I don't know if there are any pure underdogs," he said. "Most of the teams today are separated by two, three points, and that's a traveling call or a three-pointer."

How about two free throws, coach? With 3.4 seconds to play, Florida had come back from a 44-34 deficit to tie the game at 57-57. But standing at the line was Connecticut's Donyell Marshall – the difference according to Vitale. Marshall had two shots.

"I was praying he would miss them," said Dan Cross. "And he did." Florida had held the U-Conn star to just five of 13 from the field and 16 total points. But with the game in his hands, Marshall dropped the ball. He missed both free throws, and Florida went into an overtime in which Jason Anderson hit a pair of charity tosses to take a 59-58 lead. Craig Brown drilled a three-pointer, and Florida took command 62-58. The Huskies were finished. Florida celebrated with a 69-60 win.

"That was definitely the biggest shot of my career," Brown said at the time. "I came off a good screen, Dan got me the ball, and I was able to get a good jump shot."

Well, it was 56 teams down and eight teams to go. On the other side of the East Regional bracket, Boston College upset Indiana and sent Bobby Knight's team home 77-68. It was an all-underdog final. B.C. was coached by Jim O'Brien. Kruger and O'Brien were good friends and shared a common relationship through their Reebok shoe contracts. Of O'Brien, Kruger had said, "Jim O'Brien is a good coach and a good man. It's hard to pull against him even when he's playing us."

The Miami Arena was becoming the O'Dome South. South Floridians were gladly giving up the sand and surf to head inside to cheer for the Gators. "It's amusing. It's wild!" Florida senior Craig Brown said. "But that's just how people are."

More than 15,000 fans watched a basketball game they will always remember. It was 35-33 at the half, and the Gators had the lead. But the Eagles hung tough and led 56-53 with five minutes to play.

It was crunch time, and Florida called upon "Captain Crunch," Craig Brown. He dropped a three-pointer, and the score was 56-56. Brown blocked his fourth shot of the season as he rejected Boston College's Bill Curley and then hit another three-pointer with Howard Eisley's hand in his face. Eisley missed a three-pointer, and Florida called timeout. Brown got open again and buried his third straight three-pointer as Florida took a 62-56 lead with 3:50 to play. "I was feeling the shot at the time," Brown said later, "and my teammates were looking for me."

Brian Thompson had seen Brown do it before and was thrilled he did it again against Boston College. "I was like, 'Thank you, God. Craig did it again,'" Thompson said. "He stepped up big. The first two three's, I knew those were good. When he took the last one, the guy was in his face and he had to shake him a little bit. He didn't even take a dribble. He just pulled up, BAM. That's Craig."

Another player who "stepped up big" was DeClercq. He recorded his first double-figure game in the NCAA Tournament and for emphasis made it a double-double. His 16 points and 13 rebounds were his most in over two months, but what people will always remember most was his defense in the last three minutes.

With 2:30 to play, Eisley stole a Florida pass and seemed to have an easy basket to cut a 64-59 Gator lead. But DeClercq changed ends and rejected the shot off the glass backboard. Television replays showed it was a clean block, and the tape sequence played over and over during the next week to reflect the big man's hustle.

"I really don't know if it was goaltending or not," said B.C. Coach O'Brien. "He deserves credit because he didn't give up on it. His ability to run was big when he caught Howard (Eisley) from behind."

Then, with less than a minute to play and Florida leading 65-61, B.C.'s Curley tried to power two more of his team-high 20 points. DeClercq stood his ground, and the burly Boston College center was called for charging.

"It was a very important point in the game," Kruger said. "Andrew's a smart player. He got good position and did a nice job drawing that charge."

Finally, with 38 seconds to play, DeClercq slapped the ball away on the Eagles' next possession. Brown retrieved it and gave Cross a pretty feed for a breakaway basket. "I think without a doubt that was probably the best I've played all year," DeClercq said. "I was just going after it more aggressively."

With an incredible 74-66 victory, this team was headed to the Final Four!

The Miami Arena fans were engaging in a lovefest with the Gator team, and Florida's victory at this time in this place couldn't have been better scripted. Players embraced each other. Coaches' wives cried. Fans continued to cheer in a thunderous rhythm that would have left goose bumps on even the most disinterested observer.

"Everything was a blur," DeClercq said. "You don't see anything but a blur. You hear everything, and you hear nothing. You hear little snippets. You can't remember things. It feels like ... ecstasy."

The next stop was Charlotte, North Carolina. Years ago, CBS scripted the phrase, "The Road to the Final Four," and to basketball fans it might as well have been called the stairway to heaven. It somehow seemed fitting that Tobacco Road, where ACC basketball added flavor to the sport's southern roots, would be the final stop of the trip. The "Queen City" was preparing to be a fabulous host.

Florida had now rallied a huge contingent of fans who journeyed north for the big event. Some felt Florida's biggest challenge would be dealing with the aura of the event itself, but Kruger was determined to let his players soak up all of the excitement. Some coaches are so overly protective of their teams that the players never get to enjoy what others are finding so special in their success. But not Kruger. He set some basic guidelines and for the most part told the players to use their own good judgment.

Mike Shepherd, Kruger's assistant, was asked by David Stirt of the popular Florida sports publication *Gator Bait* how Florida would prepare: "Coach Kruger is having fun," Shepherd said. "I think he acts like he did when he was a player. This is what it's all about for him ... the close games, the big games, he enjoys it. When he gets to this situation, he's not going to do anything different. We do the same things we've done over and over all season."

As Kruger observed the moment, taking pleasure in the joy others were experiencing, his wife Barbara struggled to put words to her deep respect for the accomplishment. In an interview with Mitch Stacy of the *Gainesville Sun*, the energetic Mrs. Kruger said, "It's the most fascinating, interesting, exciting, frightening ... You can't describe what you feel. You can't describe what is happening. It's just tremendous."

Her voice still raspy from screaming in Miami, she went on to say, "You see the flashes on ESPN or CNN and they're talking about the final four teams left in the country, and Florida is one of them."

For all that has been written about Lon Kruger, an equal amount of space could be allotted to Barb. Her devotion to the Kruger family and her tireless energy to the Gainesville community won many admirers. A coach's wife knows this is what every coaching family works toward, but Barb wasn't one to want the spotlight. "It's been interesting. It's been fun," she said. "I've been surprised by it. It's been flattering. But the story is the players. The story is the guys who work on the court. We're flattered to be involved, but it's those guys."

Four teams lined up in the Charlotte Coliseum on April 2, 1994. Two of them were from the SEC. Arkansas faced Arizona in the first game at 5:42 p.m., and Duke and Florida squared up in the nightcap at approximately 8:30.

"We're definitely pulling for Florida," said Arkansas All-American Scotty Thurman. "The SEC doesn't get enough respect and is always overlooked. So we're hoping to take care of ourselves and hope Florida will do the same."

Arkansas took care of business and eventually won the national championship game, but the nation's eyes were focused on Cinderella Florida as the school went to its first ball. "We never thought of ourselves as a Cinderella team," said Dan Cross. "Others may think of us that way. That's their opinion."

Eleven times in the previous 14 years, an ACC school had been in the Final Four. It was Duke's seventh trip in the past nine years, and some people were calling it the "Duke Invitational." But the Blue Devil coach wasn't about to take Florida for granted.

"We kind of mirror each other," said Coach Mike Krzyzewski. "We both play tough, hard-nosed defense and make good decisions on offense. They're experienced and they take care of the ball well. Cross is the guard who can run a team, but he can create his own shot. With no five-second closely guarded call, that's a very dangerous player. Brown is a big time three-point shooter. Half of his shots are three-point shots."

As Krzyzewski voiced respect for Florida, the Gators expressed being equally impressed with Duke. "Duke is one of the best teams in the country," said Dametri Hill. "They set the standard by winning so many national championships and being in so many Final Fours. When you talk about college basketball, Duke is a team you talk about."

These two teams took a workman-like approach to the game and displayed striking similarities. Duke's Jeff Capel and Chris Collins had the back-court savvy of Brown and Cross. Grant Hill, Antonio Lang, and Cherokee Parks were a formidable match for DeClercq, Hill, and Thompson along the front line.

On the bench, both teams had "Coach K's" who held the highest respect for one another and were viewed by their peers as two of the nation's best. No two NCAA teams could more accurately reflect the ideals of intercollegiate athletics, and they were playing each other on the nation's most visible stage.

The game itself was a masterpiece of college basketball artistry. The Gators led by seven at the half and pushed their advantage out to 13 early in the second stanza. But Duke was tournament tough and had the Player of the Year as well as the player of the moment, Grant Hill. The 6-8, 225-pound Hill sparked an 18-8 Blue Devil run with two three-pointers and closed the Florida margin to 53-50 with 12:49 to play.

"Grant took over in this game," Krzyzewski said later. "He was the difference. I'm glad I have Grant Hill. I'm glad I've had him for four years."

The lead changed hands 19 times in the contest, and with 4:42 to play, Hill canned an 11-foot jumper as Duke took a 61-60 lead. Craig Brown got Florida on top again with a jumper at the 2:52 mark 63-62. But Jeff Capel made a big trifecta, and Cherokee Parks rebounded his own miss with 14 seconds to play to seal the Gators' fate. Grant Hill finished with a game-high 25 points, but perhaps more importantly, held Brown to just eight. Dametri Hill with 16 led Florida's scoring. DeClercq had 14 and Cross 10.

The final score – Duke 70, Florida 65.

"We gave it our all and we had chances to win," said Cross. "Nobody expected us to get this far and we have a lot to be proud of."

"It was an awfully good college basketball game," said Kruger. "I couldn't be any more proud of these guys. I feel awfully, awfully sad that these guys won't be playing Monday night."

Florida's theme for the year was to Find a Way to win. More than any other team in the program's history, these Florida players did just that. They were a perfect 13-0 at home. They were 9-3 in games decided by five points or less. Their record 29-8 was the winningest season in Florida's 75 seasons of competition.

This was a team with very good players, but not great players. It was, most of all, a team. There are many ways to achieve success in life, but Kruger believed the rewards came through a shared experience with people you trusted. The most valuable treasures from this mountain-top experience were found inside the hearts of each participant. These players liked each other, cared for each other, and were willing to sacrifice personally for each other. What was being lived each day off the court became the way of life when the Gator team took the floor.

"You always wonder how teams are going to be remembered," Kruger said later. "This one will be remembered as a team filled with unselfish players who trusted one another completely; players who have a complete lack of ego. In terms of being special, this group goes off the scale."

Just about everyone participated in the baking and took home a piece of the pie. June Stewart had the Dazzlers dancing. Mary Jane McGregor had the Gator Gals cheering. Chris Koenig was taping ankles, Bill Holloway was shuffling tickets, and Jim Sproull was praying. Mick Hubert and Steve Babik captured on air each sneaker-squeaking, rim-rattling, gym-jamming moment. And with UF President John Lombardi leading cheers, the Gator fans raised their voices to a decibel level never heard before.

From Greg Williams' three-pointer with 48 seconds to play against James Madison to Craig Brown's three consecutive three-pointers against Boston College. From Andrew DeClercq's momentum-slaying swat of Boston College's Howard Eisley's apparent breakaway layup to Da Meat Hook's 15 points in 39 minutes against Connecticut. From Sloan Hemmer's 20 puzzle pieces that formed an NCAA ticket to Ron Marks' organizing a Tip-Off Club bus trip. From 10-year-old Kevin Kruger's prime time talk with CBS's Pat O'Brien to Barb Kruger and Beth Buford holding the Find a Way sign. Andrew DeClercq summed up the season best when he said, "It's indescribable. Just picture your biggest dream coming true."

Before every game, the players reminded each other of how they had gotten where they were – the running, the weight lifting, the early morning practices, the off-season training. They never forgot their priorities.

Most of all, Lon Kruger's teams took care of business every day. The players went to class, and they went into Gainesville classrooms to tell kids to stay in school. They played punishing team defense to stop an opponent on the court, and they appeared at YMCAs and boys' clubs to tell kids to say no to drugs. They set screens for their teammates in games, and they became surrogate fathers for disadvantaged youths at Kruger's parent-child camp. Florida's basketball program climbed to the top of college basketball's most respected ladder, and the players came back down to share with others the lessons they learned on each rung of the climb.

This was senior Craig Brown's team. Yes, it was also Andrew DeClercq's. And it belonged to Dan Cross. Dametri owned a big piece. Anderson, Bates, Dyrkolbotn, Griffiths, Kuisma, Mickens, Greg and Dan Williams, and the trivia question stumper 20 years from now – Joel Reinhart – they all owned stock. But it was still Brown's team.

"Craig Brown put this team on his shoulders and said, 'Give me the ball and I'll take you to the Final Four,'" said Jason Anderson. "And then he did it."

Brown was Kruger's first recruit in 1990 and he is the model most Florida basketball players would like to measure up to. But while his dedication was his alone, his success was possible because of the encouragement he got from others.

Brown came to Florida with a dream. The dream became a reality because others shared the vision right along with him. Brown did everything you might expect, but his teammates also shared his high expectations. Craig Brown was a very talented basketball player who was lucky enough to be the beneficiary of basketball philosophies that enhanced his chances to succeed.

When the University of Florida hired Lon Kruger, the school found a coach who would establish standards by which others would measure a program's success. Kruger proved that in athletics you can take seemingly ordinary young men and help them discover the extraordinary in their lives.

There may well be a lot of people who, like Joel Glass, would like to be Larry Bird in another life. But it is certain that there are many former University of Florida basketball players who would have traded places with Craig Brown in a heartbeat for the chance to reincarnate their Florida basketball lives with Coach Lon Kruger.

Sailing Uncharted Seas

Since replacing Bill Arnsparger as Florida's director of athletics in 1992, Jeremy Foley has been a tireless worker for University of Florida sports. His UF career began in the ticket office in 1976. After 20 years, Foley is an encyclopedia of Florida sports history. He told Mike Dame of the *Orlando Sentinel*, "Everybody knows we have a great football program, but Florida basketball has been an afterthought. This is the beginning where we don't think of it as an afterthought anymore."

It was apparent from this Final Four moment that Florida basketball would be changed forever. Tuesday morning after returning from Charlotte, Kruger arrived in his office about 9 a.m. after visiting an elementary school classroom. I met him there, we exchanged pleasantries, and I asked him what he was feeling.

"Bill," he said, "I'm so appreciative of the opportunities we have now for basketball at Florida, but I just finished a prayer in which I said, 'Dear Lord, you have given us all an even bigger assignment. I hope you know what you're doing.'"

Throughout the summer, Florida basketball's new status became increasingly apparent. Around the nation, young people were wearing hats and shirts that identified with Gator basketball. The national networks were negotiating with Florida to arrange the broadcast of key matchups. Sponsors wanted to project Gator hoops in their commercials. And the basketball players were hard at work preparing for the next season.

By fall, Florida returned an experienced team to face unprecedented media attention and the most challenging schedule ever. The first taste of what was coming occurred on the night of October 14, 1994, when Florida opened its first official day of practice with Midnight Madness. Over 10,000 fans rocked the O'Dome that night, and millions more tuned in around the country to watch ESPN's live coverage. The Gators were featured on CBS and ABC and appeared on ESPN six times that season. But while the program's image received a tremendous boost, the team was facing a schedule of tough competition.

Florida opened the year beating Boston College in the inaugural game of The Great Eight. Held in Auburn Hills, Michigan, the event featured seven of the 1994 NCAA Tournament's Elite Eight teams. The ESPN broadcast was a rematch of the previous year's East Regional final. The eighth-ranked Gators easily handled Boston College, this time 91-65.

SAILING UNCHARTED SEAS

Next up, the Gators beat Wake Forest in Greensboro Coliseum 81-70 and played what many felt was their best game of the season. Wake's Tim Duncan had 21 points and nine rebounds, but the Deacons could not control Cross, who finished with 27 points. Hill added 17 points and seven rebounds. Florida shot 50 percent for the game, and Wake made only four of 18 three-pointers. It was Florida's fourth win against the ACC school in the previous five meetings, dating back to 1962. With the victory, Florida emerged as the nation's No. 6 team – its highest ranking ever.

Next were the fourth-ranked Kansas Jayhawks, and the site was historic Allen Fieldhouse in Lawrence, Kansas. The game marked the return of head Coach Lon Kruger to his home state. From the moment of arrival at the Kansas City terminal, it was evident that Kruger was a statewide hero. As the team gathered around the baggage claim area, Kansans greeted the Gator coach to speak and exchange pleasantries. Kansas was a serious basketball environment, and it was clear that people felt the Florida-Kansas game would be special.

Allen Fieldhouse on the University of Kansas campus is the Mecca for modern-day college basketball. It's a shrine of memorabilia from James Naismith, who first nailed up peach baskets in Massachusetts for the sport's beginnings, and who later became the Jayhawks' first basketball coach. The atmosphere surrounding Allen Fieldhouse is electric. Students in sleeping bags camp out all night, studying by battery-powered lights, to vie for the spartan allotment of remaining game-day tickets.

Inside, the building overflows with evidence of Kansas basketball traditions including the building's namesake, Dr. F.C. "Phog" Allen. The former Kansas coach is the winningest in Kansas basketball history. Allen won 746 games, an NCAA record eventually broken by one of his former Kansas players, Kentucky's Adolph Rupp. Another former Allen player, Dean Smith, is still setting winning records as the head coach at North Carolina. Talk about a penetrating basketball experience. Florida basketball was now in the national spotlight right in the midst of the sport's heritage.

Kansas hospitality ended, however, when 16,300 rock-chop Jayhawk fans provided the backdrop for the third straight nationally televised Gator contest. Defensively, Kansas held Florida to a 34 percent shooting night and for the first time exposed weaknesses that would haunt the Gators the rest of the season.

Jason Anderson, Brian Thompson, and Greg Williams played an average of 25 minutes and combined for just four points. DeClercq outclassed Kansas All-American Greg Ostertag, scoring 20 points and getting 14 rebounds to the Kansas 7-footer's two points and 11 boards. Dan Cross led Florida with 25 points.

But Kansas was hot. Jay Haase had 25 and Jacque Vaughn had 11 points and seven assists. Kansas made eight of 17 three-point shots. Florida's only lead of the game came at the 2:39 mark in the first half on a free throw by John Griffiths. The Big Eight power had Florida down by 15 points before the Gators made a late-game run to cut the final 69-63 margin to six.

"Anyone who expects to have an easy time with Florida doesn't know a thing about basketball," said Kansas Coach Roy Williams. "They are a fantastic defensive team. They challenged our team to play as well on the defensive end as they did."

The Gators' boss, who had a disappointing homecoming, said, "Their big guys had a huge impact on the game. They made our big guys change a lot of shots. We just got outplayed tonight and we got beat by a better basketball team."

Florida's two starting seniors were the team's co-captains, and both on and off the floor they enjoyed an especially strong partnership. Dan Cross was a black kid from Carbondale, Illinois. Andrew DeClercq was a white kid from Clearwater, Florida. From almost the moment they arrived as freshmen in the fall of 1991, they bonded, and their friendship was another of the intangible aspects of the program's success.

A year earlier, every time Cross sneezed, Craig Brown said "excuse me." This year it would be necessary for Cross to bring his own handkerchief. Cross played in the back-court shadow of Florida's brightest light, and now he had the challenge to shed some light of his own.

Cross had already delivered more than his share of knockout punches. He provided Gator fans a taste of things to come when, as a freshman in 1992, he made a 10-foot jumper to beat the Rebels of Ole Miss 86-84. As a sophomore, he led the team in field goal percentage at 56.8 percent. Cross then made four game-winning shots during his junior season (the Final Four year) that deserve their own book. With 18 seconds left, his driving layup beat LSU 74-73. He slid into the lane and dropped a one-hander to beat Auburn 68-67. With two seconds on the shot clock and one minute to play, he hit a leaning, top of the key three-pointer to hold off Mississippi State. His one-hander off the glass with 7.2 seconds to play beat James Madison in the NCAA first round. How do you describe Dan Cross? Dan "Clutch" Cross says it all.

DeClercq was the hardest-working big man ever to wear the Florida colors. He personified the term "running the floor." Connecticut Coach Jim Calhoun said DeClercq "plays every possession like it's the end of the game." If you want to define emotion, you say DeClercq. If you want to illustrate enthusiasm, you show DeClercq's hard-nosed, intense, hustling style of play.

When Andrew DeClercq blocked Howard Eisley's breakaway layup in the Gators' East Regional win over Boston College, it was *the* defining moment of his career. In much the same way that Joe Lawrence nailed a last-second jump shot to beat TCU so Florida could advance in the NIT, DeClercq's effort on that play to make a successful block of what seemed like a game-changing layup will forever make fans proud to be Gators.

The Kansas loss was tough to digest because the players realized they had a chance to win. But it didn't stop their early-season momentum. Florida easily beat Texas 91-73 in the O'Connell Center three nights after losing to Kansas and nipped Florida State in the Orlando Arena Milk Challenge. That game had required two

Dametri Hill free throws in double overtime for the 71-65 victory. Florida was 5-1 and continued to hold on to its No. 8 national ranking, but the Gators had one more game before the Christmas break.

If there is one game during a season that coaches dread, it's a home game just before Christmas. At most schools, semester exams are finished. The campus is quiet. The players have more time than usual on their hands, and for the most part, sugar plums are dancing in their heads. Their brains are heading for Christmas break and their thoughts are on family and friends. The spirit of the season competes with team spirit in the mainstream of their thoughts. Their line of reasoning begins to go something like this, "It sure would be a great week if we didn't have to play this next game. Let's just get it over with so we can all go home."

To make matters worse, the team on the schedule wasn't the "sugarplum fairies." It was in-state rival Jacksonville University. The Dolphins had always felt they received little respect, and for the most part, they were right. But on this occasion, the lack of respect really worked to Jacksonville's advantage. Kip Stone scored 24 points and eight of JU's last 10 as the Dolphins upset eighth-ranked Florida.

"Jacksonville basketball has been knocking on the door," said Stone. "We finally got let in. We're in the spotlight."

Jacksonville had a one-point edge at the half and played with the upset-minded determination that would propel them to a 68-67 victory. Mick Hubert's "Oh My" that night wasn't the kind he had in mind when the game began. Florida shot just 39 percent. DeClercq had 28 points and 15 rebounds. Cross had 26 points. Their combined 54 points represented 81 percent of the scoring. With the team distracted by a jolly old man and eight tiny reindeer, the outcome was a real lump of coal in the Christmas stocking.

"This is a very bad time for Christmas break," a disappointed Cross said. "Very bad. We have too long to think about this." Kruger, although disappointed, was perhaps not surprised and had seen some chinks in Florida's armor in recent games. "We've been close to disaster on a few occasions," Kruger said. "Tonight we went over the edge."

Perhaps the expectations were just too high. LSU started the conference schedule by handing the Gators a 70-66 loss in Baton Rouge. Kentucky roughed up Florida in the O'Connell Center 83-67, and then Villanova's Jonathan Hayes surprised Florida with a buzzer-beating 18-footer from the right wing of the O'Connell Center's south end. It gave the CBS national television audience a dramatic 72-70 upset of the 15th-ranked Gators.

Florida finished the first half of the conference schedule 5-4. The Gator team was in second place in the league's Eastern Division but no longer held any ground in the nation's top 20. In the second half of the schedule, Florida won three of its first four, including a second win over FSU 75-62 in Tallahassee.

But three consecutive losses to Georgia, Alabama, and Arkansas gave the regular season a sour finish. The Georgia and Alabama defeats were in the O'Connell Center where 11,000 fans came to help, but Florida couldn't deliver. A year earlier the Gators were 9-3 in games decided by six points or less. This year they were 1-6.

"This loss might be the toughest," said Dametri Hill following the 69-66 defeat by Alabama. "Everything was set up for us ... we were all having fun, the crowd was into the game, and we fought our butts off. But it always seems to go the other way, and I don't know why."

The Gators had more on the line than they knew. That night, UF's No. 1 recruiting priority, Vince Carter, was in the stands. Despite the encouragement of a vocal crowd that shouted "We want Vince!" the Daytona Beach native may have concluded that he needed to head in another direction.

Florida salvaged a .500 conference season by beating Vanderbilt in Nashville 69-58 and got by Ole Miss in the SEC Tournament's first round in Atlanta's Georgia Dome 63-59. The Gators beat Mississippi State in the quarterfinals 80-64 and for the third time matched their season-best three wins in a row. It was Florida's 17th win of the season, and although the team was sitting on the NCAA Tournament bubble, that victory plus the strength of one of the nation's most difficult schedules earned Florida a second straight trip to the Big Dance.

Florida lost the semifinal tournament game to Kentucky and then came back to Gainesville and watched the Sunday afternoon NCAA pairings in the O'Connell Center locker room. Kruger and his assistants were meticulously reviewing the power ratings of all the teams likely to get in the tournament field and those on the bubble. There was plenty of uncertainty.

Florida's 17-12 record and its strength of schedule made it a 10th seed in the Southeast Region. The Gators were matched with seventh-seeded Iowa State in a first-round game to be played in Tallahassee-Leon County Civic Center.

"I was just praying," Cross said. "For a split second, I didn't think we were going to get in. I didn't want to be remembered for going to the Final Four as a junior and then going to the NIT as a senior. That's no way to go out."

Kruger was also relieved that the Gators received a bid. "It's so fitting that the seniors have the opportunity to go out like this," Kruger said. "I'm just delighted for them. Everyone talks about all the things they've done since they've been here. But I'm not sure everyone recalls the conditions that existed here when they made the decision to come to Florida. I was in Dan's home the day the NCAA sanctions were announced, but he still came to Florida, determined to establish a foundation here."

Florida got balanced scoring and placed four players in double figures, with Greg Williams playing one of his career-best games and scoring a team-high 16 points. Iowa State, however, overcame a 36-33 halftime deficit and outscored Florida 9-0 in the final four minutes to end the Gators' season 64-61. The first-round loss to Iowa State put a damper on what were perhaps unrealistic expectations for a better year.

DeClercq was an All-SEC selection for the fourth time, and this season he was named to the first team. He started a school-record 128 straight games and was Florida's third all-time leading rebounder and second all-time shot blocker. One of only five Florida players to score 1,200 points and grab 900 rebounds, DeClercq was a second-round NBA pick of the Golden State Warriors.

Cross became a first-team All-SEC selection for the second straight year and led the team in scoring with an average of 18 points a game. He also led the team in steals with 52 and holds the career mark with 198 steals. Twice named an Associated Press Honorable Mention All-American, Cross made a school-record 31 straight free throws his senior year.

"When you have seniors like these two, it's difficult to replace them," said Kruger. "These two have given so much more than just points and rebounds. What they brought to the University of Florida cannot be overstated. They helped set the standard that all future players will strive for."

The "Norwegian Collegian," Svein Dyrkolbotn, finished his four years after playing in 102 games and making every one of his front-line minutes count. And he graduated with a degree in engineering. The fourth senior was Tony Mickens, a junior college transfer who played in 53 games and started nine times. His career high of 10 points helped Florida get a big win on the road against Jacksonville in the 1994 season.

"These four players gave our program an important reference point every day," said Kruger. "Both in the classroom and on the practice court their effort was characteristic of what we strive for at Florida. They leave behind great memories for the program's future."

A Family at Last

The basketball program's success on the court had raised the interest level among more people than just diehard basketball fans. The Final Four year, two back-to-back trips to the NCAA Tournament, and the unprecedented national exposure had cast the program into a much more prominent state of Florida spotlight. Now that Florida's fans had been to the top of the basketball mountain, they wanted to know who was being recruited to make the next climb up the slippery slope.

Florida basketball's success had brought the program a lot of new fans. But they weren't necessarily knowledgeable basketball fans and for the most part had a shallow perspective on the challenges facing basketball at this football school. Sports fans in the Sunshine State have an absolute obsession with what has become practically its own sport – football recruiting. People whose perspective was football recruiting wanted to know why the coaches weren't landing some of the state's and nation's more prominent basketball names.

Kruger told Jerry Izenberg of the *Newark Star-Ledger*, "It starts with identifying the kind of people you want to recruit. There is no shortage of players. There are lots of prospects out there. You study them all, knowing that you are going to recruit the ones who will fit into the environment you want to create."

But building a winning basketball program is a dramatically different process than building a football program. The similarity is that both sports must recruit talent. But in many other ways, the differences are striking.

A football team has 100 players or more with a coaching staff of 10 to 15 people. Managing the program is like managing a medium-sized company. While most of the members know each other, there is no real premium on their interpersonal relationships.

In contrast, a basketball team is comprised of just 13 to 15 players and four or five coaches. The critical factor here is relationships. Everyone is closely associated every day. The players do almost everything together, and the portrayal of a close family really does describe a basketball experience. But there are factors that can fracture even the closest family. Some coaches are influenced by the clamor of alumni drums which beat for winning records. And more than one solid team has seen its chemistry unbalanced and its success spoiled by the ego of a superstar. Recruiting was about restoring balance.

Florida was signing some heavily recruited players, and those close to the program realized this staff had broken new recruiting ground. Florida was head to head with America's best basketball schools for the nation's finest student-athletes.

When Florida wanted to sign Greg Williams, the Gator program had to compete with and beat Bob Knight's Indiana Hoosiers. Williams visited Florida the same weekend as Jeff McGinnis, who eventually signed at North Carolina.

The signing of Ben Davis was a huge success, considering that the Big Eight all-freshman selection could have chosen to take his career anywhere. After transferring from Kansas to Florida, Davis eventually landed on his feet at Arizona.

The Gators had Jeff Sheppard all but inked when Kentucky said he was needed in Lexington. Chris Collins was on a plane to Gainesville when that other Coach K in Durham called Collins' dad and said, "I understand Chris' dream is to be a Blue Devil." Do you remember watching Collins line up against Florida in the Final Four?

Assistant Coaches Ron Stewart and Robert McCullum worked hard chasing down future Gators. Both scoured the country to sell the program's virtues, and for the first time they had some positive stuff to sell. But fans sometimes fell into the common trap of expecting more than anyone could deliver in recruiting Gator basketball players.

On a national stage, Florida football is one of the premier programs in the nation. But basketball at Florida was just beginning to get a respectable toehold on the recruiting front. This Florida coaching staff had the Gators in the hunt for the top five percent of the nation's high school prospects. They were the players that Duke, Kansas, Kentucky, and UCLA wanted. Many asked why Florida didn't sign these players. Perhaps they should have asked how Florida managed even to be in the running.

Vince Carter was the most-coveted prospect in the Kruger era. Carter chose North Carolina. People couldn't understand why. Perhaps it's because many Florida fans don't see what a basketball prospect sees.

A high school basketball prospect walking through the Raleigh-Durham Airport feels the presence of a college basketball environment. Carolina Tar Heel, Duke Blue Devil, and N.C. State Wolfpack basketball memorabilia are everywhere. Signs proclaim, "Home of the NCAA National Champions." To a recruit, the effect is intoxicating.

Dean Smith's office on the Chapel Hill campus – the Dean Dome – is modern and high tech. When Dean Smith pushes a button on his office desk, the window shades close, a screen drops down, a projector comes on, and a video tape shows Carolina beating Georgetown for the national championship on a Michael Jordan jumper. What great high school basketball prospect wouldn't be impressed?

Imagine being a young athlete on just such a visit. You walk down a corridor into the Carolina Blue memorabilia room. More videos. Life-size Jordan. Pictures of all the Carolina greats, etc. etc. You walk into the locker room, and it's like the lounge in one of America's best country clubs.

Then you walk into the arena – 22,000 Carolina Blue chairback seats in a quiet,

LON KRUGER: 1991-1996

empty building that comes to life just for *basketball practice and games*. Maybe an occasional concert. Not many. Perhaps now you can appreciate the picture in a great college basketball player's mind. That, folks, is a slam dunk.

The University of Florida is every bit as fine a personal basketball experience if you have a Lon Kruger-type staff. It's just as nice a campus to enjoy the fun of being a college student. Gainesville is certainly a community that is more progressive than Chapel Hill. In an objective comparison, the University of Florida may be the best college campus in America. But to the Vince Carters of the world, it's like comparing Breyer's ice cream with the store brand. If they're going to offer you Breyer's, that's the one you grab.

Some believe Florida's failure to recruit more effectively was an Achilles' heel to Kruger's overall accomplishments – particularly with the Final Four appearance in 1994. Kruger felt if you kept your P's and Q's straight, you would achieve the results everyone wanted in the end. This staff recruited the type of Person who could be successful as a Player in the type of Program which would make everyone Proud. These were the Priorities.

A close look with 20-20 hindsight at Florida's recruiting might reveal that the program invested too much in trying to influence the marquee players who were also being actively courted by the nation's premier schools. There are a lot of great second-line (red chip) players who have proven to be athletically and academically gifted in the right program's environment who were overlooked by Florida.

With all due respect to Kruger, McCullum, and Stewart, it may have been somewhat premature to believe then that Florida was ready to land the nation's best talent. That time is getting closer, though, in large part because of their efforts.

The history of Florida basketball proves that Kruger's coaching staff had its P's straight. Perhaps others will need to keep the "Q"uestions straight. If people want a basketball program that reflects what is best about the University of Florida, they may have to more patiently grind out the question and answer process of building their basketball reputation.

Despite the loss of Vince Carter, Kruger's final team, one of the youngest squads ever, was nationally recognized for its recruiting accomplishments. Greg Cristell, a 6-foot-10, 235-pound center, chose the Gators over Duke, North Carolina, Pittsburgh, and Vanderbilt. Eddie Shannon, an explosive point guard from Palm Beach, Florida, selected the Gators over Arizona. Kendrick Spruel, a 6-foot-8 forward, chose the Gators over Alabama and UCLA. Greg Stolt, a 6-foot-8, 230-pound forward, picked Florida over Wake Forest. Antrone Lee and Mike McFarland also were talented high school players who chose from among the nation's upper level Division I schools. It's quite a change from the sixties when a player like Skip Higley came from Ohio sight unseen because his high school coach knew something about the Gators.

It was Kruger's sixth team, and nine of the 15 players were freshmen and sophomores. Only Dametri Hill, Brian Thompson, and Greg Williams had substantial game experience. Everyone – the coaches, the players, the fans – had hoped that this season would produce more. But everyone was also aware that this would be a building experience. Big holes were left in the Florida lineup with the departure of Jason Anderson, who took time off to refocus his personal priorities, and by Ben Davis' brush two years earlier with substance abuse.

Florida had its most demanding schedule ever. Nine opponents were ranked at game time, of which three had been named the nation's No. 1 team at some point during the season. Twenty games were played against teams that made it to the post-season, and 12 of these teams were in the NCAA Tournament. Florida played three of the four teams that made it to the 1995 Final Four.

"It was a very demanding schedule," Kruger later said. "But that's okay. It was probably not a schedule that fit this young group real well, but it was exciting to face quality opponents. As coaches and players, you always like to line up against the best competition. I think our kids will be better in the long run for it. Our schedule forced some of our kids to grow up faster."

With two freshmen in the opening-day starting lineup for the first time in over ten years, the Gators looked to their senior leaders Dametri Hill and Brian Thompson to carry the load. Hill's buzzer-beater at Knoxville capped a career-high 30-point effort and gave Florida a 73-71 win over Tennessee. It was Florida's 11th straight win over the Volunteers.

Hill averaged a league-best 18.8 points per game in SEC action and an overall 17.6 points per game, which was seventh best in the conference. The St. Petersburg native scored in double figures in 26 of 28 games and had nine 20-plus point outings. The space-eating post man played his final season at 275 pounds after entering school four years earlier at 350 pounds. Hill finished his career ranked 14th on Florida's all-time scoring list. *Basketball Weekly* named him first-team All-SEC, and he was a second-team selection by the SEC coaches.

Brian Thompson was also a four-year player who was not only instrumental in Florida's run to the Final Four but also gave his final season's team great leadership with his effort and intensity. Thompson stepped forward and demonstrated to the younger players the importance of senior leadership. He was one of the program's best offensive rebounding small forwards and took on the assignment of guarding the opposing team's best offensive player. His nine rebounds and 10 points in Florida's 1993 win against Villanova were one of his best career efforts.

Florida's third senior was hometown product Clayton Bates, a four-year fan favorite who began his career as a walk-on. He was named Florida's most inspirational player following the 1992-93 season and earned the Lt. Fred Koss Award following his final year. Bates received his diploma on December 16 and later that day played for the Gators against FSU in Orlando. Bates was three times named to the SEC Academic Honor Roll.

"I can't say enough about what Dametri, Brian, and Clayton have meant to the Florida program over the past four years," Kruger said. "They have done a tremendous job of setting an example for our younger players and have represented the University of Florida in a great way both on and off the floor."

The 12-16 '96 season was a disappointment although most realized the team's record was the result of inexperience. The staff, however, was evaluating not just the team's performance but also their overall concerns about the prospects for Florida's basketball future. Florida fans loved winning, but the coaches wondered if they really loved basketball. The enthusiasm for the Final Four accomplishments was exciting but was there a genuine appreciation for the program's challenges.

"The first disappointment came in December of 1994," said Assistant Coach Robert McCullum. "We had just beaten Boston College and Wake Forest, and fourth-ranked Kansas beat us by six. All three games were on the road, and we came home to play Texas. We thought there'd be 12,000 in the O'Dome but only 9,000 showed up. It was a quality opponent. It was a week after the SEC football championship. We began to realize that Florida fans just might not be that enamored with hoops. There was no other explanation."

Kruger was privately analyzing the situation and after six years of pouring all of his energy into University of Florida basketball, he reached a startling conclusion. It was time to move on. In April of 1996, Lon Kruger stunned the Florida faithful when he announced his decision to become the head coach at the University of Illinois.

The reasons weren't that complicated. Kruger was as passionate about basketball as Florida fans were about football. At this stage in his coaching career, he felt compelled to experience a genuine passion from others for his professional objectives.

"It was a number of things," Kruger said. "You can't put too much weight on any one of them. We will really miss Florida but are excited about the opportunity to run our program at Illinois."

The university lost the leadership of a man whose inspiration reached far beyond the basketball court. When Kruger came to the University of Florida in 1990, Florida desperately sought forgiveness from society's judgment of its athletic indiscretions. By 1996, Florida had experienced a reincarnation of campus pride. The entire athletic program was genuinely united, and the university had achieved an athletic moment that surpassed its wildest dreams.

The players will miss Kruger's reassuring winks of confidence and his deeply genuine emotions. The community will miss the unselfish volunteerism that made him a local hero. His Find a Way youth program, the city's recreation initiative, the city youth basketball program, the Red Ribbon Campaign Against Drugs, and the parent-child basketball weekends were some of the many contributions of Kruger and his family toward making Gainesville a better place to live.

In Kruger's six years, he also opened the doors to Florida basketball's extended

A FAMILY AT LAST

family, and for the first time in many years, former players were made welcome and encouraged to participate in the program. For years, the pride Florida football players felt for their program's heritage was fostered through university initiatives that would forever link the past to the present.

But Florida basketball players had never experienced that association. To be a Gator had always meant to be a football Gator, and with coaching changes through the years, basketball players hadn't experienced the connection to the past that created a common bond of historical perspective.

There is no doubt that the University of Florida is a great football school. And many of Florida's basketball players are football's greatest fans. The enthusiasm which so many feel for the football program also has the potential to inspire a big-time college basketball mentality. Nationally, the two sports are comparably recognized, and University of Florida fans are the best in America. Indeed, today, Florida may be as committed as any school in the nation to helping each of its athletic programs succeed at the highest level.

In the lifeline of Florida basketball, Lon Kruger is forever indelibly etched as the man who helped Gator basketball finally turn the corner. When the 1994 Final Four team went back into the locker room after cutting down the net on one end of the floor after defeating Boston College, Kruger said to team captain Craig Brown, "Craig, you're supposed to cut down both nets." Brown replied, "Coach, we're new at this stuff."

For the first time in this program's 81-year history, a new coach is transitioning Florida basketball with a positive note. Most are sad to see Kruger leave but respect the professional challenge he perceives with the basketball-rich traditions in the state of Illinois. There are no broken promises. There are no fractured spirits. No one is questioning any misplaced motives. The university is not defending its honor. The basketball program at the University of Florida is a reflection of the institution's best potential. But perhaps most important, and with deep gratitude to Lon Kruger, the basketball program is now a family and all of us are "new at this stuff."

From Augie Greiner in 1950 to Brian Thompson. From Cliff Luyk in 1960 to Dametri Hill. From Gary Keller to Andrew DeClercq. From Tony Miller to Dan Cross. Lon Kruger's special gift is left behind for everyone to share.

So it's only fitting that the Gator basketball family says so long to Lon and puts out the welcome mat for Billy Donovan's "Billyball."

Epilogue

In October of 1989, Dr. Robert Bryan asked me for candid thoughts with regard to Florida basketball. We discussed the many issues the basketball program had prompted that disturbed the core integrity of the University of Florida. In the conversation, I asked Dr. Bryan if he thought this university truly wanted to have a great basketball program. He replied that he wanted a basketball program that reflected the greatness of the university.

I smiled and said, "Dr. Bryan, you have just said the most beautiful words I have heard in the 29 years I have been in Gainesville. Believe me, Dr. Bryan, there is one thing about which I am certain. Florida basketball can reflect the greatness of this wonderful institution."

We talked for more than an hour, and I shared with him my feelings and my convictions. I said there was a bottom-line solution. You must offer the head basketball coach the same compensation package that you pay the head football coach.

"Piece of cake," Dr. Bryan responded. "When they gave me this job, they put me in charge of the bank account."

"Dr. Bryan, if you can assure me you have the money," I said, "you will get the right man to do the job."

I asked Bob Bryan if I could help in the most confidential manner and he consented. I suggested that he employ a coaching headhunter and proposed Richard Giannini.

In my mind, Giannini was the best person for the task because he knew this school intimately and had an excellent understanding of what was required. In addition, I told Dr. Bryan that there was a coach I thought might be interested, and I asked for permission to pursue him personally. He agreed to support the courtship of Kansas Coach Roy Williams.

Years ago, I knew Williams when he was a University of North Carolina assistant. Williams was the type of individual who would bring instant credibility to Florida's basketball program. But he was considered by most to be unapproachably locked in at Kansas. Things like that never had stopped me in anything else, so why should it matter now?

"Roy, what do you think? Florida will pay you Steve Spurrier's salary, etc., etc. Roy, this school is a sleeping giant in basketball. It's a great university, but it's just lacking quality basketball leadership. What do you say, Roy?"

He listened. We talked. He listened some more. We corresponded through the winter months. He asked questions. I was pumped!

"Dr. Bryan, he's interested," I said.

EPILOGUE

"Keep me posted," Dr. Bryan responded.

January came and went with Don DeVoe bailing water and Norm Sloan burning bridges.

"Dr. Bryan," I said, "I talked with Bill Arnsparger the other night and offered to help him in his search. He was as cold as a Shaquille O'Neal free throw."

"Koss, dammit, don't worry. I hired Giannini."

"All right!"

By early February, things were cooking and Arnsparger was "scouting basketball coaches." Do you know what can happen when a defensive football coach scouts a prospective basketball coach? Football Coach Gene Ellenson actually said to Tony Miller, "Christ sakes, Miller, you're awfully small to be a guard."

And Arnsparger, who probably watched a game and wondered why a field goal wasn't always three points, was "scouting" for Florida.

A Florida man was trying to capture Florida's next basketball coach, but the Florida man's name wasn't Arnsparger, it was Giannini.

By late February, things were getting exciting. Williams still hadn't said no, and as the Big Eight Conference Tournament got underway in Kansas City, Giannini was there to fulfill a dual role. First, he was assisting the orchestration of the telecast for Raycom Sports. Second, he was a 007 undercover agent for Florida.

At 8:30 one night, Williams called me at home. "Bill, I can't do it. This is just my second year at Kansas. The people gave me a great opportunity and I can't leave them now. Everyone with Florida has been super, but the timing is bad. I'm sorry."

That was the bad news. The good news came the next morning when Giannini was having breakfast and saw Lon Kruger.

He thought to himself, "Now there's a guy who would do the job for Florida. But if Williams said no, there probably isn't any way to get Lon Kruger out of Kansas State either." Out loud he said, "Hey Lon! Can I talk with you about something?"

That's how it happened. For the record. There is no way a football man could possibly know how to hire the best basketball coaching prospect in America. In fact the football-minded Arnsparger almost messed the whole thing up. But that's another story for another book some day.

Lon Kruger reflected the greatness of the University of Florida. Bob Bryan made the commitment to hire Lon Kruger. All of us loved Bob Bryan because he had the wisdom to see what was needed and the courage to be decisive. He also genuinely loves basketball.

Well, for those of you who had the interest to stay with me to the end, I hope

EPILOGUE

Well, for those of you who had the interest to stay with me to the end, I hope you enjoyed the book. It's been a labor of love.

After book sales cover expenses, I'm going to use revenue from this project to support basketball-related objectives. My goal is to have some money to send underprivileged youngsters to basketball camps or basketball schools, and to help high school basketball programs. I hope to channel a little money into places where kids who demonstrate a work ethic in the classroom and responsible ideals in their personal lives can gain some ground through athletics.

It's been a lot of fun to reminisce on the subject that takes a back seat only to my wife Mary, my daughter Mary Beth, and my son Bill. At times they probably don't think that's true. You have my word that everything else you have read in these pages is.

Clockwise from the top right to left: Augie Greiner, Andrew Moten, Dick Tomlinson, Ric Clarson, Ronnie Williams, Mark Thompson, Paul Morton, Dwayne Davis - Craig Brown - Livingston Chatman, Dametri Hill, Dwayne Schintzius

Center Left: Dr. Stephen O'Connell and Tony Miller

Center Right: Gene Shy

Center: Dick Vitale is razzed by Gator players Scott Stewart, Dwayne Davis, and Brian Hogan after Florida's upset win over LSU in 1990.

Coach Mac

Jim McCachren – A Player's Coach

Florida Coach Jim McCachren was born September 16, 1911 in Charlotte, North Carolina, and genuinely enjoyed working with young people. From the moment he met players, McCachren conveyed a sincerity that separated him from others both inside and outside the world of sports. He was a hero to people in Chapel Hill, N.C., where he established winning records for basketball and football teams at the University of North Carolina in 1934, 1935, and 1936. But it was his personality, his sense of humor, and his affection for sharing his view of the simplest experience as a profound event that earned him so many admirers.

As a professor in the College of Physical Education, McCachren's devotion to teaching and learning inspired students to become proficient in their knowledge of sports. At a time when education rewarded research and graduate education, Coach Mac spent his time and talent mentoring undergraduate students in physical education.

Along with his lifelong friend, P.A. Lee, McCachren challenged students to three-wall handball games on the outdoor courts on University Avenue. Every afternoon for over 40 years, he could be found slapping away at a little black ball and entertaining young people with humorous anecdotes. Everyone was welcome in Coach Mac's spaces, and he had a great talent for putting people at ease.

McCachren joined the physical education department at the University of Florida in 1946, and three years later the former Tar Heel All-American became the freshman basketball coach, a responsibility he savored intermittently for over 25 years. Coach Mac always found some aspect of a young man's life that he could influence positively—every Florida freshman basketball player who was coached by McCachren came away from the experience a better person.

Most of the time McCachren was just fun to be around. His corny phrases and quick wit brimmed with self-confidence. His lack of pretense permitted others to share themselves in an open and unguarded manner. Young people knew he could be trusted, and Coach Mac

Jim McCachren – A Player's Coach

Coach Mac provides some instruction for the 1963 Baby Gators. From left to right: Frank Wicker (44), Norman Riggle (33), Edd Poore (32) and Coach Jim McCachren.

valued the role of physical education instructor as a high calling. No man ever ministered to others more compassionately or with more dignity for his profession.

Everyday Jim McCachren could be spotted pedaling around campus on a bicycle that could have easily been acquired at the local junk yard. Few were better qualified to temper the expanded ego of a freshman who had arrived on campus with an unrealistic self-image as the result of the college recruiting process. McCachren brought players back down to earth gently while challenging them to develop their potential at an accelerated rate. His freshman teams won consistently.

Wearing the two hats of an intercollegiate head coach and a physical education instructor meant he was continually walking a tightrope to balance the demands on his time and energy. He continues to give of himself unselfishly, and in so doing, still impacts young men and women profoundly. Florida basketball will forever be indebted to the kindness and the generosity of service that defines the life of Coach Jim McCachren.

Unsung Heroes

Managers & Trainers

Their names never appear in the box scores. The media seldom ask them for an opinion. The fans rarely know any of their names. But the team can't take the floor without them. The coaching staff consults them when they want to know the mood of a particular player. They can make, and sometimes break, a team's morale. It's the managers who keep everyone humble, and it's the managers who are the real unsung heroes of the roundball sport at Florida.

They are responsible for almost every material detail. Did you bring the white uniforms? Do we have an extra size 14 shoe? Where are the warmups? Do you have a piece of gum? How many minutes have we run this drill? Where are the towels? Why are we out of Gatorade?

The managers do most of the real work and all of the truly dirty work. They handle the laundry and make sure there is soap in the showers. They arrive hours before practice or a game and go home hours after everyone else has left. They are the first ones to be blamed if something isn't right, and they receive the Rodney Dangerfield award for getting little respect.

With the managers there is never a dull moment, and through the years they have concocted a lot of fun. There was the time in Knoxville, Tennessee, when the king of pranks, Eric "Ice" Poms, had Assistant Coach Phil Weber's underwear hanging from the rafters above center court as Florida prepared to play Tennessee in the 24,000-seat Thompson-Boling Arena. Or the early morning road trip to Alabama when Assistant Coach Towe got back in bed and found a mattress full of ice under the covers. Legends abound from tales of *Bengay* in a player's jockstrap to mismatched socks with one too large and another too small; from the

Top Five

Small Forward
Owen Weber
Thickest glasses & biggest heart.

Strong Forward
Rick Ahlberg
He spit-shined bars of soap and operated with the precision of a Swiss watch.

Center
Tim Klein
Will receive a state pension for years of service (1988-1995).

Shooting Guard
Eric Poms
Could sell ice boxes to Eskimos and maintained tight control of his responsibilities.

Point Guard
John Visscher
Kept his eyes open, his mouth shut and was dumb like a fox.

Unsung Heroes

road trip when the managers forgot Tommy Bartlett's tennis rackets to the road trip when Chuck Cooperstein forgot the rings.

There were also plenty of screwups that weren't quite so benign. In 1969 the managers took the wrong jerseys for a home game in Jacksonville and the team had to wear white practice jerseys.

Perhaps the biggest faux pas occurred in 1989 when Florida's basketball team acquired some backup services from football team linebacker Michael

Tim Klein, a Florida manager from 1988 to 1995, is seen here helping Patrick Aaron (L) and Pat Lawrence (R).

Managers

Year	Name	Year	Name	Year	Name
1916	J.F. Sikes	1937	Peyton Yon	1962	Butch Davis
1917	No team	1938	Joe Wittenstein	1963	Neil Cody
1918	No team	1939	Ed Mitchell	1964-67	Owen Weber
1919	No team	1940-43	None listed	1968-70	Les Loggins
1920-21	Bill Madison	1944	No team	1971	Rick McGinnis
1922-23	C.Y. "Check" Byrd	1945	None listed	1972-73	Wayne Galloway
1924-25	Edgar Jones	1946-47	Erwin Fleet	1974-76	Rick Ahlberg
1926-27	Tom Fuller	1948	None listed	1977-78	Bob Crayne
1928	Jack Thompson	1949	Steve Weisman	1979-80	Bob Grubar
1929	Marcus Owens	1950	John McLain	1980-82	Mike Cook
1930	Bob Boley	1951	Sidney Richards	1983-85	John Visscher
1931	Bo McClellan	1952	David Jensen	1986	Garth Adams
1932	Bill Yarnall	1953	Bruce Johnson	1987-90	Eric Poms
1933	Dan McCarty	1954	Jennings Argo	1991-92	Tim Klein
1934	Byron Herlong	1955	William Argo, Jr.	1993	Todd Zehner
1935	Earl Harby	1956-57	Lavern Jamenson	1994-95	Tim Klein
1936	Byrd Fryer	1958-59	Chuck Brendler	1996	Jeff Guin
		1960-61	Vennie Pent		

Unsung Heroes

Kerr. The Gators were short-handed, and Kerr literally went from the football practice field to the O'Connell Center to suit up for the Gators' first exhibition game of the year. Manager Eric Poms grabbed a uniform number and slapped it on a jersey for Kerr to wear. The next day the sports information office got a call asking if Florida had unretired Neal Walk's number. Poms had given Kerr number 41 by mistake. Needless to say, the next game Kerr was wearing his new number—34.

From Sam Lankford to Chris Koenig, trainers have patched up and shaped up Florida basketball players through the years. Trainers have a talent that combines the hands of a craftsman with the wisdom of a healer. In the training room, broken spirits are mended as often as torn ligaments. The trainer knows what's inside a player's heart and how to get things straight inside a player's head. Florida basketball players are indebted to the tireless commitment of these men who have been the backbone of Gator teams.

Without trainers and managers there is no basketball. We salute them.

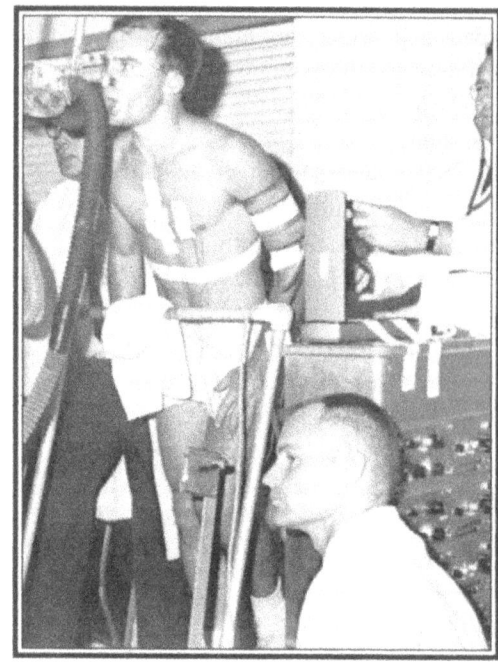

The Gators' Tom Baxley is the laboratory gym rat running the treadmill in September of 1964. The motorized device was a training experiment to measure personal stamina.

Trainers

1950-62	Sam Lankford	1974-80	Tony Griffith
1963-65	Jim Cunningham	1981-82	Keith Webster
1966-67	Brady Greathouse	1983-88	Jim Mackie
1968-69	Ken Lynn	1989-92	Tony Sutton
1970	Brady Greathouse	1993-96	Chris Koenig
1971-73	Bobby Barton		

Coaching Records

COACHING RECORDS 1915-1960

Year	Coach	Seasons	Overall Won	Overall Lost	Pct.	SEC Won	SEC Lost	Pct.
1916*	C.J. McCoy	1	5	1	.833			
1920	No Coach	1	2	5	.286			
1921 and 1922	W. G. Kline	2	10	11	.476			
1923	C.Y. Byrd	1	2	5	.286			
1924 and 1925	J.L. White	2	7	17	.292			
1926 to 1933	Brady Cowell	8	62	86	.419	4	4	.500
1934 to 1936	Ben Clemmons	3	24	24	.500	10	13	.435
1937	Josh Cody	1	5	13	.278	1	9	.100
1938 to 1942, 1947 to 1951	Sam McAllister	10	119	96	.554	45	62	.420
1943,* 1945, and 1946	Spurgeon Cherry	3	22	33	.400	6	14	.300
1952 to 1960	John Mauer	9	98	102	.490	43	82	.344
TOTALS		41	356	393	.475	109	184	.372

*No teams in 1917, 1918, 1919 and 1944.

COACHING RECORDS 1961-1996

Year	Coach	Seasons	Overall Won	Overall Lost	Pct.	SEC Won	SEC Lost	Pct.
1961 to 1966	Norm Sloan	*6	85	63	.574	48	40	.546
1967 to 1973	Tommy Bartlett	7	95	85	.528	62	64	.492
1974 to 1980	John Lotz	*7	83	88	.485	46	66	.411
1980	Ed Visscher	*1	3	14	.177	1	13	.071
1981 to 1989	Norm Sloan	9	150	131	.534	78	84	.482
1990	Don DeVoe	*1	7	21	.250	3	15	.167
1991 to 1996	Lon Kruger	6	104	80	.565	51	47	.520
Totals		37	527	482	.522	289	329	.467

*Sloan's combined coaching record is 235-194 for an overall 54.8 percent. SEC record is 126-124 for 50.4 percent.
*Lotz coached 11 games in 1979-80.
*Visscher was interim coach for remainder of 1979-80 season.
*DeVoe was interim coach for complete 1989-90 season (took over for Norm Sloan on Oct. 13, 1989).

Florida / Georgia

The Rivalry
1924-1996

The two teams' first meeting was in the 1924 season, and Georgia won in Athens 45-24. Florida lost 15 of the first 17 meetings with the Bulldogs. On January 11, 1933, the two schools made their SEC debut in Athens where Georgia prevailed 37-34. The next night, Florida once again played the Bulldogs and got its first SEC win 33-32.

Overall, the two programs have faced each other 172 times with Georgia winning 89 and Florida the victor 83 times. Since the 1961 season, Florida has won 42 and lost 35. To date, the longest winning streak was seven—from March, 1965 to January, 1968. Florida's 105-78 win in 1962 was the most points scored against Georgia and one of three 100-point wins over Georgia in Florida history (1977, 1994).

From 1952 to 1968 the Georgia game was always the last game of the regular season, and through the years, the rivalry has produced some of Florida basketball's most memorable moments.

David Dunn (Georgia) challenges Florida's Kenny McClary (21) as Gators' Vernon Maxwell looks on. All three had a major role in the 1986 fight in Athens.

Florida / Georgia

1963   The last game ever played in Woodruff Hall – Billy Rado, All-SEC, scored 31 points and made the winning basket to give the Gators a losing season (11-12). Sloan punished the returning players for the 79-77 defeat.

1964   Florida handed Georgia its first SEC loss in the new Georgia Coliseum, 69-64.

1965   Florida won 90-66 and finished the year 18-7 for the best season in the school's history to that date (4th best today).

1967   Florida beat Georgia 96-63 in Florida Gym for the third time in one season to finish 21-4, and recorded the school's best year ever. Three technical fouls almost forfeited the game to the Bulldogs.

1971   Florida won at Georgia 88-79 – just one of four SEC road wins in four seasons. Tony Miller stopped Ronnie Hogue with positive molecules.

1978   Georgia's Lucius Foster punched out Florida's season and Malcolm Cesare's mouth as Georgia won 57-54.

1980   Florida upset Georgia at home 57-52 for John Lotz' final victory. He had been fired earlier in the week, but kept the whole matter under wraps.

1986   Horace McMillan and Vernon Maxwell began a fight which ended with a heavyweight confrontation between David Dunn and Ken McClary. Georgia won the game 89-69.

1988   Sloan was hassled by University of Georgia fans. The situation escalated into a confrontation with a university police officer who tried to handcuff Sloan and lock him up. The final score – Georgia 71, Florida 65.

1988   Florida's Ronnie Montgomery and Georgia's Alec Kessler were ejected for fighting in the first three minutes of this SEC 2nd-round tournament game. Dwayne Schintzius refused to re-enter the game in the closing seconds as Florida lost 72-70.

1989   Clifford Lett started his first game as a senior after Jose Ramos was kicked off the team, and Florida started the SEC championship run, upsetting Georgia 80-66.

1994   Florida beat Georgia in Athens, scoring 100 points for the first time in Lon Kruger's tenure. The 100-78 victory tied a Florida overall best season start at 15-3.

Recognition

All-America

Recognition for a basketball All-America has its roots in the Helms Athletic Foundation. With similarities to the New York Athletic Club's recognition of a Heisman Trophy winner, the Helms organization beginning in 1929 was the official NCAA source for college All-America designations. In 1949 the NCAA stopped officially recognizing Helms and adopted the Associated Press (AP) selections. Helms continued to make selections but did not have the same stature of an AP or UPI (United Press International) award.

Joe Hobbs was named a third-team Helms Athletic Foundation All-American in 1958. Brooks Henderson was one of a 36-member selection in 1965. Andy Owens was one of a 36-member selection in 1970.

Florida's most notable AP and UPI selection was Neal Walk who was a member of the five-man second team for both wire services in 1968. Walk was a five-man third team AP and UPI selection in 1969. Vernon Maxwell (1988), Dwayne Schintzius (1989), Stacey Poole (1993) and Dan Cross (1994 and 1995) have earned honorable mention AP All-America honors.

Neal Walk, Florida's only bona fide All-American, led the nation in rebounding in 1968. He scored 1600 career points and was the number 2 pick by the Phoenix Suns in the 1969 NBA draft. His jersey, number 41, is UF's only retired number.

Recognition

First-Team All-SEC

Jimmie Hughes
1934

Curt Cunkle
1953

Joe Hobbs
1958

Gary Keller
1967

Neal Walk
1968, 1969

Andy Owens
1970

Tony Miller
1972

Chip Williams
1974

Eugene McDowell
1985

Vernon Maxwell
1987, 1988

Dwayne Schintzius
1989

Stacey Poole
1993

Dan Cross
1994, 1995

Andrew DeClercq
1995

Florida All-Time Numerical Roster From 1938 to 1996

Players by the Numbers

00
Ronnie Montgomery
Nino Lyons
Richard Glasper

3
Brian Thompson
Pat Lawrence
Travis Benton
Marty Perry
Frank Guthrie
Ed Benjamin
George Fogle
Vinny Zdanzokas
Ray Boozer

4
Antrone Lee
Craig Brown
Damon Dragotis
Joe Lawrence
Andre Corbeau
Thomas Mitchell
Bill Talbot
Hugh McClure
Bill Godwin
Ray Carroll Williams

5
Jason Anderson
Andrew Moten
Ted Sizemore
Stan Friedman
Dick Weller
Al Raybun

6
Scotty Henderson
Bill Welch

7
Harry Platt
Jack Maynard

8
Ralph Licker
Eddie Hausenbauer
Bud Walton

9
Dennis Fillingim
Ken Hartsaw
Dick Woolery
Frank Yinshannis

10
Greg Williams
Tony Davis
B.J. Carter
Jose Ramos
Patrick Aaron
Mike Moses
Quan Roseboro
Bruno Caldwell
Bob Nims
Elam Stokes

Jack Hagar
Dean (Sonny) Miller

11
Dan Williams
Scott Stewart
Vernon Maxwell
Dave King
Melvin Roseboro
Tony Miller
Willie Ratliffe
Roy Roberts
Gordon Atkinson
Bill Stobbs
Doyle Carlton
Norris Thompson
Harold Hughes

12
Dan Cross
Francisco Leon
Vernon Delancy
Tim Fletcher

Richard Glasper led the Gators in assists and steals in 1977 - 1978. He is interviewed here by former play-by-play man Otis Boggs (L) and his assistant Bob Leach (R).

Florida All-Time Numerical Roster From 1938 to 1996

John Fernandez
Pat Reen
Henry Chalker
Dewitt Dawkins
Ike Gordon

13
Willie Jackson
Wyndell Jenkins
Jimmy Cotton
Don Bostic
Darryl Ceravolo
Richard Vasquez
Joe Hobbs
Bob Davis
Theo Hampton
Julian Miller
Steve Ellish
Charles Krejcier

14
Eddie Shannon
Mike Ramirez
Darryl Gresham
John Jones
Jay Hoffman
Ted Jaycox
Eugene Lee
Bud Manchester
Hub Chason

15
Martti Kuisma
Ken McCraney
Chuck Fritz
Greg Armstrong
Jerry Hoover
Mike Leatherwood
Walter Rabhan
Harry Coe
Pete Peterson
Bob Peterson

17
W.C. Savage

20
Mike McFarland
Terry Edwards
Renaldo Garcia
Stephen Edelson
Reed Crafton

Danny Sheldon
Jeff Kelley
Bob Van Noy
Len Sanders
Bruce Moore
Taylor Stokes
Bobby Shiver
Rick Wheeler
Bob Emrick
Don Shaffer
Lamar Bridges

21
Joel Reinhart
Louis Rowe
Tim Turner
Kenny McClary
Mike Aldridge
John Coy
Bob Lindsay
Ed Mahoney
Brad Baraks
Joe Meigs
Dick Hoban
Bill Leach
Hans Tanzler

22
Stacey Poole
Todd Zehner
Chris Capers
David Visscher
Mike Milligan
Steve Porter
Chip Williams
Troy Walker
Jeff Miller
Kurt Feazel
Tom Baxley
Jim Jarrett
Ronnie Poh
Newell Fox
Ted Copeland
Hubert Morrow
George Hitchins

Harold Bert
Bill Atkinson

23
Hosie Grimsley
Clifford Lett
Charles Griffin
Rob Harden
Mark Giombetti
Ed Barnes
Gene Shy
Hal Kelley
Harry Dunn
Paul Morton
Neil Cody
Tommy Simpson
Don Boone
John Burgess
Red Wetherington
Henry Cornell
Dick Pace

Renaldo Garcia was a starting guard for the 1988-89 SEC Championship team and scored a career-high 20 points in Florida's 104-95 win against LSU.

Florida All-Time Numerical Roster From 1938 to 1996

24
George Jackson
John Adamson
Hal Kelley
Todd Lalich
Lanny Sommese
Gene Sadler
Paul Mosny
George Telepas
Charlie Smith
Harold Haskins
Chonnie Myers

25
Kendrick Spruel
Brian Hogan
Ronnie Williams
Ric Clarson
Joe Repass
Skip Lewis
Mike Rollyson
Brooks Henderson
Eddie Clark
George Jung
Chuck Brendler

Tom Puschak
Andy Stevenson
Edgar Johnson
Ed Johnston

30
Clayton Bates
Travis Schintzius
Rodney Williams
Tyrone Young
Bill Moody
Ernest Lorenz
Nick Fotiou
Edd Poore
Carlos Morrison

31
Jeremy Ulmer
Scooter Houston
Mike McGinnis
Gary Keller
Richard Leibowitz
Lou Merchant
Larry Scott
Howie Tesher
Harry Mance

32
LeRon Williams
Nick Sanchez
Livingston Chatman
Cornelius Brodus
Tony Rogers
John Corso
Al Bonner
Tom Purvis
Vernon Chewning
David Miller
Dick Tomlinson
Joe Metzger
John Tringas
Nelson Vinal
Gil Farley
Lou Garcia

33
Greg Cristell
Tony Mickens
Darryl Findley
Dwayne Schintzius
Jon Currington
Nabe Palmer
Tony Matthews
Jerry Moore
Steve Williams
Ed Lukco
Harry Winkler
Tom Barbee
Frank Etheridge
Charlie Pike
Ron Stokley
Harold Schulman
Larry Gangi

34
John Griffiths
Michael Kerr
Johnny Walker
Tony Williams
Melven Jones
Roger Rome
Mark Thompson
Cliff Cox
Boyd Welsch
Bill Koss
Cliff Luyk

Tom Barbee made 83% of his free throws in 1962 and had a career average of 79%.

Florida All-Time Numerical Roster From 1938 to 1996

35
Dametri Hill
Mike Lederman
Malcom Meeks
Bill Nagle
Tony Duva
Skip Higley
Jerry Gates
Buddy Bales
Lew Doss
Harry Hamilton
Bill Edward

40
Svein Dyrkolbotn
Eugene McDowell
Jerry Bellamy
Bob Smyth
Dan Boe
Jeff Ramsey
Mont Highly
Jerry Henderson
Curt Cunkle
Bob Nichols

41
Neal Walk*
Bob Hoffmann
Wayne Williams
Frank Dryden
John Eggleston
Burt Touchberry
Frank Harry

42
Cesar Portillo
Mark Saso
Malcolm Cesare
Don Close
Ken Van Ness
Earl Findley
Gary McElroy
Dick Roher
Roger Benefiel
Les Johnson
Matty Nestler

43
Randall Leath
Jerry Billings

44
Damen Maddox
Jermaine Carlton
Gary Willoughby
Kelly McKinnon
Rollie Castineyra
Reggie Hannah
Aaron Bryant
Curt Shellabarger
Gary Waddell
Robert Agee
Richard Peek
Bob Sherwood
Russell Briggs

45
Maurice McDaniel
Doug Brown

Bob Smyth was a Gator center from 1973-1977. He was the nation's 9th best rebounder in 1976 and a difficult post man to defend.

Andy Owens
Rick Casares

50
Dwayne Davis
Tim Strawbridge
Mike Brown
Larry Brewster
Billy Graham
Jim Zinn
Henry Hodges

51
Augie Greiner

52
Bill Gurley
Chip Watts
Sonny Powell

54
Robert Agee

55
Greg Stolt
Andrew DeClercq
Wade Harris
Jim Grandholm

Neal Walk (#41) – Florida's only retired jersey

With apologies for any errors or omissions

LT. FRED KOSS MEMORIAL AWARD

On July 7, 1972, my 26-year-old brother Fred's F-4 Phantom jet was shot down over Vietnam. It was his third mission of that day and 107th mission during his 97 days of combat in the Vietnam War. Our family established this award in Fred's memory. It has been given annually since 1974 to the Gator senior who during a four-year career has displayed the most leadership, sacrifice, integrity and sportsmanship.

Koss' Best

DOCTOR OF DUNKS
Dwayne Davis
Andrew DeClercq
Vernon Delancy
Earl Findley
Eugene McDowell ➤

SHOOTERS OF THE "J" (BEST JUMP SHOT)
Tom Baxley
Al Bonner
Brian Hogan
◄ *Tony Miller*
Andrew Moten

Koss' Best

GUARD TANDEMS

Baxley-Henderson
Bostic-Lederman
◄ *Brown-Cross*
Higley-Miller
Maxwell-Moten

GREAT FINISHES

Craig Brown - Boston College 1994
Ric Clarson - Fairfield 1979
Brooks Henderson - Tennessee 1965
Joe Lawrence - TCU 1986 ➤
Clifford Lett - Vanderbilt 1989

THE GLASS EATERS (BEST REBOUNDERS)

Dwayne Davis ➤
Bob Emrick
Eugene McDowell
Neal Walk
Ronnie Williams

PERSONAL TOUGHNESS

Rick Casares
Cliff Luyk
Vernon Maxwell
Paul Morton
◀ *Andy Owens*

ICE IN THEIR VEINS (BEST FREE THROW SHOOTERS)

Brooks Henderson
Joe Hobbs
Andy Owens
Sonny Powell
◄ *Scott Stewart*

LEADERSHIP PERSONIFIED

Craig Brown
Rick Casares
Skip Higley
Jerry Hoover
Clifford Lett ►

TOUGHEST PLAYERS TO DEFEND

Richard Glasper
Vernon Maxwell ➤
Andy Owens
Neal Walk
Ronnie Williams

MOST COURAGEOUS

◄ *Livingston Chatman*
Mike McGinnis
Lou Merchant
Stacey Poole
Bob Smyth

Tournament Play

TOP – Halftime score of Gators' Final Four meeting with Duke.
CENTER – Gator guard Ronnie Montgomery celebrates the victory over S.W. Missouri State which sent the Gators to the NIT Final Four in the 1986 season.
BOTTOM – Seniors Len Sanders (L), Don Bostic (C) and Bob Smyth (R) receive the Big Sun Championship trophy in St. Petersburg. It was December of 1976 and Florida beat South Florida and Memphis State to win the program's first championship outside the city of Jacksonville.

Post-Season Play

First NIT Game, March 13, 1969
Madison Square Garden, New York, N.Y.

FLORIDA	FG-FGA	FT-FTA	REB	A	PF	PTS
Owens	5-15	0-1	5	1	2	10
Lukco	3-6	0-0	1	1	1	6
Walk	10-16	6-12	17	1	5	26
Welsch	6-18	3-3	7	5	2	15
Leatherwood	2-7	1-1	1	8	2	5
McGinnis	1-4	0-0	2	3	1	2
Vasquez	0-1	0-0	0	1	3	0
Feazel	1-2	0-0	0	0	0	2
Agee	0-0	0-0	0	0	0	0
Fotiou	0-0	0-0	0	0	0	0
Team			3			
TOTALS	28-69	10-17	17	20	16	66

TEMPLE	FG-FGA	FT-FTA	REB	A	PF	PTS
Baum	5-11	3-4	10	0	4	13
Cromer	7-15	5-7	7	6	1	19
Mast	8-13	4-4	9	1	2	20
Strunk	6-8	3-4	7	3	2	15
Brocchi	6-11	1-2	4	6	4	13
Snook	0-0	0-0	0	0	0	0
Wieczerek	0-0	0-0	0	0	0	0
Cassidy	0-0	0-0	0	0	0	0
Brooks	0-0	0-0	0	0	0	0
Richardson	1-1	0-0	1	0	0	2
Team			5			
TOTALS	33-59	16-21	38	16	13	82

	1st	2nd	Final
FLORIDA	37	29	66
TEMPLE	35	47	82

Post-Season Play

**First NCAA Game, March 13, 1987
Carrier Dome, Syracuse, N.Y.**

FLORIDA	Total FG-FGA	3-Points FG-FGA	FT-FTA	REB	A	PTS
Lawrence, Joe	3-5	2-4	0-0	1	2	8
Lawrence, Pat	2-3	1-2	0-0	4	1	5
Schintzius	4-12	0-0	1-1	4	4	9
Maxwell	6-16	2-4	14-21	7	1	28
Moten	5-8	2-3	7-7	7	3	19
Montgomery	0-2	0-1	0-0	1	0	0
Lett	0-1	0-0	1-2	4	1	1
Capers	1-2	0-0	2-2	3	1	4
McClary	4-5	0-0	0-1	3	1	8
Team				3		
TOTALS	25-54	7-14	25-34	37	12	82

N.C. STATE	Total FG-FGA	3-Points FG-FGA	FT-FTA	REB	A	PTS
Brown	3-5	0-0	3-4	5	0	9
Bolton	7-14	4-7	2-3	4	2	20
Shackleford	6-10	0-0	0-2	8	3	12
Jackson	3-6	1-3	2-2	5	5	9
Del Negro	6-14	0-3	0-0	4	4	12
Giomi	0-3	0-0	0-0	5	1	0
Lester	0-0	0-0	0-0	0	0	0
Weems	1-2	0-0	0-0	1	0	2
Lambiotte	1-2	0-1	0-0	0	0	2
Howard	1-2	0-0	0-0	0	0	2
Team				2		
TOTALS	29-59	5-14	7-11	34	15	70

	1st	2nd	Final
FLORIDA	33	49	82
N.C. STATE	30	40	70

Post-Season Play

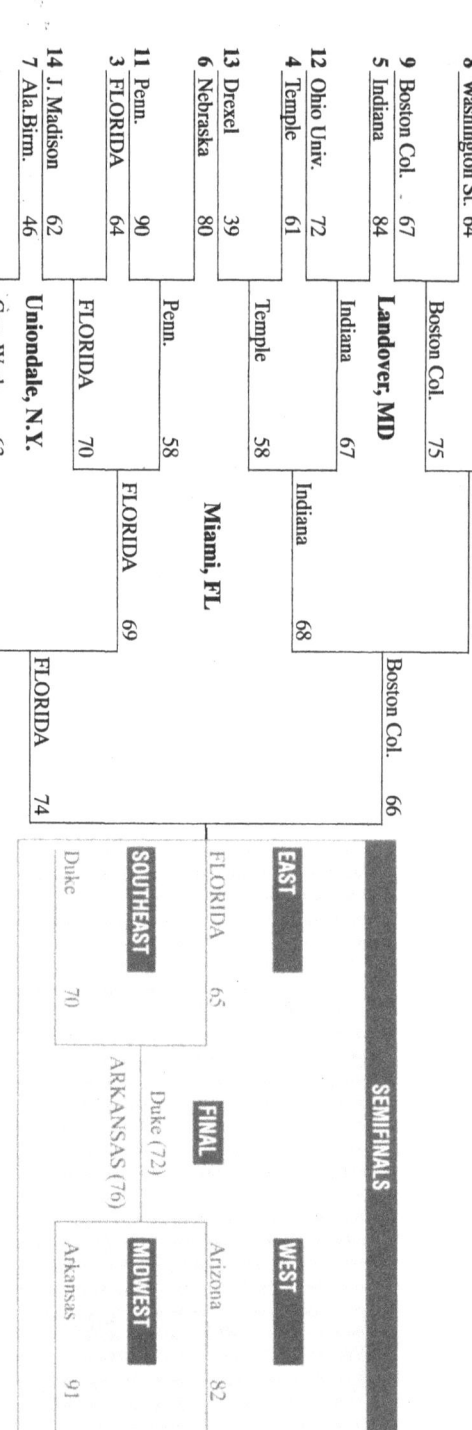

Road to the Final Four
1994 NCAA Tournament

First Round – March 17-18
Second Round – March 19-20

Regionals – March 25
Quarterfinals – March 27
Semifinals – April 2

EAST REGION

- 1 No. Carolina 71
- 16 Liberty 51
- 8 Washington St. 64
- 9 Boston Col. 67
- 5 Indiana 84
- 12 Ohio Univ. 72
- 4 Temple 61
- 13 Drexel 39
- 6 Nebraska 80
- 11 Penn. 90
- 3 FLORIDA 64
- 14 J. Madison 62
- 7 Ala. Birm. 46
- 10 Geo. Wash. 51
- 2 Connecticut 64
- 15 Rider 46

No. Carolina 72
Boston Col. 75
Indiana 67
Temple 58
Penn. 58
FLORIDA 70
Geo. Wash. 63
Connecticut 75

Boston Col. 77
Indiana 68
FLORIDA 69
Connecticut 60

Landover, MD

Boston Col. 66
FLORIDA 74

Miami, FL

SEMIFINALS

EAST — FLORIDA 65
SOUTHEAST — Duke 70

FINAL — Duke (72)

WEST — Arizona 82
MIDWEST — Arkansas 91

ARKANSAS (76)

Uniondale, N.Y.

250

Post-Season Play

Lon Kruger cutting down the net after 1994 Sweet 16 victory over Boston College.

Post-Season Play

On the Road to the Final Four

Above: East Regional final (round of eight) against Boston College.

Left: Andrew DeClercq cuts down the net after Boston College game.

Below: Charlotte Coliseum, site of the 1994 Final Four.

Final Four
April 2, 1994
Charlotte Coliseum, Charlotte, N.C.

FLORIDA	Total FG-FGA	3-Points FG-FGA	FT-FTA	P-R-A
Thompson	1-3	0-0	2-4	4-3-0
DeClercq	7-11	0-1	0-2	14-7-1
Hill	6-17	0-0	4-6	16-9-3
Brown	3-9	2-3	0-0	8-6-5
Cross	3-14	2-5	2-4	10-6-8
Kuisma	0-2	0-0	2-2	2-1-0
Anderson	4-6	0-0	1-2	9-4-0
Dyrkolbotn	0-0	0-0	0-0	0-1-0
Williams	1-1	0-0	0-0	2-0-0
TOTALS	25-63 (40%)	4-9 (44%)	11-20 (55%)	65-41-17

DUKE	FG-FGA	FG-FGA	FT-FTA	P-R-A
Lang	3-6	0-0	6-6	12-5-0
Hill	8-13	3-4	6-8	25-6-5
Parks	4-11	0-0	3-4	11-11-2
Capel	3-10	2-4	1-1	9-3-0
Collins	1-4	0-3	0-0	2-1-1
Clark	3-6	2-3	0-0	8-3-3
Meek	0-1	0-0	3-4	3-2-0
Newton	0-0	0-0	0-0	0-0-0
TOTALS	22-51 (43%)	7-14 (50%)	19-23 (83%)	70-33-11

	1st	2nd	Final
FLORIDA	39	26	65
DUKE	32	38	70

Gator Teams That Set High Standards

66/67 GATORS

Front Row:
21, Boyd Welsch; 23, Kurt Peazel; 35, Skip Higley; 14, Harry Dunn; 33, Harry Winkler; 30, Edd Poore.

Back Row:
25, Mike Rollyson; 32, David Miller; 31, Gary Keller; 11, Neal Walk; 40, Jeff Ramsey; 42, Gary McElroy; 24, Andy Owens.

COACH: Tommy Bartlett

The 1966-67 Gator squad has Florida basketball's best win-loss percentage, 84%. The team's 21-4 record was Florida's first 20-win season and this was the first Florida team ranked in the nation's Top 10, rising to the #8 position in the Associated Press poll that year. It was also the Gators' tallest starting five with an average height of 6'6." This team missed tying for the SEC championship when Tennessee beat Mississippi State on the final night of the regular season in triple overtime. With a second-place conference finish, Florida was denied a post-season opportunity because a conference rule permitted only the champion to represent the league in tournament play.

The 1986-87 Gators ranked as one of the best teams in Florida history. Not only did they become the first Gator team to reach the NCAA Tournament, but they earned a berth in the NCAA's Sweet 16. They also established 11 all-time single-season highs, including 23 wins (tying the school record for victories in a season. FRONT ROW (L-R): Reed Crafton, Ronnie Montgomery, Joe Lawrence, Andrew Moten, Vernon Maxwell, Clifford Lett. BACK ROW (L-R): Rollie Castineyra, Melven Jones, Kenny McClary, Dwayne Schintzius, Pat Lawrence, Chris Capers, Patrick Aaron.

Gator Teams That Set High Standards

The 1988-89 Gator squad captured Florida's first-ever Southeastern Conference regular-season basketball title in 55 years of competition in the SEC. The team also advanced to the NCAA Tournament, notched 21 victories and won an all-time school-record 11 consecutive SEC games during the year. FRONT ROW (L-R): Clifford Lett, Dwayne Davis, Dwayne Schintzius, Livingston Chatman, Renaldo Garcia. BACK ROW (L-R): Mike Ramirez, Kelly McKinnon, Tim Turner, Michael Kerr, Todd Zehner, Brian Hogan.

The 1993-94 Gator squad was the winningest team (29-8) in the 75-year history of the Florida basketball program, while advancing to the NCAA Tournament's Final Four for the first time in school history. The squad was ranked an all-time school-high No. 4 in the final USA Today-CNN Poll, while becoming the first team in school annals to finish the regular season ranked by the Associated Press (no. 14). In Southeastern Conference action, the team won 12-4, good for a share of the SEC Eastern Division Championship. UF also advanced to the finals of the SEC Tournament for just the third time in history and become the first UF team to go undefeated in the O'Connell Center (13-0). BACK ROW (L-R): Ron Stewart (asst. coach), Lon Kruger (head coach), R.C. Buford (asst. coach), Svein Dyrkolbotn, Andrew DeClercq, John Griffiths, Martti Kuisma, Dametri Hill, Robert McCullum (asst. coach), Mike Shepherd (admin. asst.), Chris Koenig (trainer). MIDDLE ROW: Greg Williams, Jason Anderson, Dan Williams, Clayton Bates, Brian Thompson, Joel Reinhart, Tony Mickens, Craig Brown, Dan Cross. FRONT ROW: Mike Stein (mgr), Ryan Hardin (mgr.) Steven Grimberg (mgr), Tim Klein (head mgr), Josh Waddell (mgr), Jeff Guin (mgr).

The Place to Play – Florida's Gyms

The Gyms of Florida

Completed in 1919, Florida's first official gym was located just east of the stadium in the Murphree Hall area and later served as a women's gym.

Georgia beat Florida 37-35 on January 5, 1928, to inaugurate the "New Gym." The wood-frame building was an eyesore on campus and a fire hazard. Later the building housed the school of music.

The Place to Play – Florida's Gyms

Florida Gym (Alligator Alley) was constructed in 1949 at a cost of $1.65 million. It was the best facility in the SEC when constructed and housed the College of Physical Education and Health.

The O'Connell Center was named for former UF President Stephen C. O'Connell. It is a multi-purpose building and was long overdue when it was completed in 1980. Its seating capacity for basketball is 12,000.

Ready To Run

They Call It Billyball...

Billy Donovan was named Florida's 16th head basketball coach on March 27, 1996, and from the moment he was introduced, it was clear that Florida's returning players would need to get *ready to run*. "We're going to get up and down the floor," said the Gators' personable 31-year-old new head coach. "It's going to be a 94-foot game. It's going to be constant pressure both offensively and defensively. I believe it's a style that you can win with because I've coached it and I've played in it."

Donovan played for Rick Pitino at Providence where he led the Pitino-coached Friars to the Final Four. He later played for Pitino with the NBA's New York Knicks and followed him to Kentucky as an assistant coach on the Wildcat staff. "Billy has as good a grasp on our offense as anyone I've seen," said Pitino. "Billy is the hardest worker I've ever coached and the hardest working person in the office I ever had."

From all appearances, Florida basketball will be running hard into the 21st century. It seems the best is yet to come and indications are that everyone is *ready to run*.

Coach Donovan is introduced to the media and holds his first Gator basketball press conference. As the head coach at Marshall University, Donovan had a two-year recore of 35-20. His teams averaged 88.8 points a game.

Over the past 64 years, Bill Koss has perspired both on the basketball court and in court-side broadcast settings as a player and color analyst for college basketball. Koss earned the respect of Florida fans for his inspirational competitiveness as a center for the Florida Gators from 1963 to 1965 and then became the eyes and voice for thousands of the Florida Faithful as a radio and television commentator for various outlets, including Sun Sports, Fox Sports, and ESPN.

Growing up in Bridgeport, Ohio, he played high school basketball with Hall of Fame great John Havlicek and brought a midwestern basketball influence to the Sunshine State. Living most of his life in Gainesville, Florida, no other individual has been more closely linked to the Gators' basketball program, and his perspective provides historical literary significance.

A 2008 inductee to the UF Athletic Hall of Fame, he was also named an SEC Basketball Legend in 2013.